MADNESS, RELIGION, AND
THE LIMITS OF REASON

SÖDERTÖRN
PHILOSOPHICAL STUDIES 16
2015

Madness, Religion, and the Limits of Reason

Edited by
Jonna Bornemark &
Sven-Olov Wallenstein

Södertörn University
The Library
SE-141 89 Huddinge

www.sh.se/publications

With the generous support of
Axel and Margaret Ax:son Johnson Foundation

Cover image: *Extas – Den Heliga Teresa / Ecstasy – The Holy
Theresa*, 1988, 75x183 cm, photography and lacquer on
board, Maya Eizin Öijer
Graphic Form: Per Lindblom & Jonathan Robson

Printed by Elanders, Stockholm 2015

Södertörn Philosophical Studies 16
ISSN 1651-6834

Södertörn Academic Studies 62
ISSN 1650-433X

ISBN 978-91-87843-24-2 (print)
ISBN 978-91-87843-25-9 (digital)

Contents

Introduction: Madness, Religion, and the Limits of Reason

Jonna Bornemark and Sven-Olov Wallenstein

I

Madness and religion have traditionally signaled that from which philosophy must take a distance, either by simply rejecting them as foreign to reason, or by dominating them in a discourse that fixes them as objects and inscribes them in the conceptual grid of understanding. While the philosopher *as philosopher* cannot be mad, and not religious, as least not in the sense of listening to some other voice than the one of reason *while thinking*, his or her power lies in reason's capacity to hold its other at bay, situating it at, and as, a limit. Religion, and *a fortiori* madness, may appear "within the limits of reason alone," as Kant would say, or perhaps within the limits of "mere reason," depending on how we translate the title of his treatise *Die Religion innerhalb der Grenzen der blossen Vernunft*, published in 1793 as a kind of afterthought to his three Critiques. Does the "bloss" here indicate a limit to reason, beyond which we need to give room for something else, or does it signal that reason alone is capable of drawing a magic circle around itself and decide what may be allowed to enter into our experience, lest we are to succumb to something like—madness? What is this limit, and to what extent does it condition the very sense of reason as constituted by a process not just of exclusion, but also holding the other at a distance, allowing it to speak within *certain limits*?

The idea of the limit has been inherent in philosophy since its very inception in many and conflicting ways. At least three such interpretations of the idea of the limit may be discerned. It can be a mark of the finitude of understanding and a warning of what may befall us—metaphysically, ethically, theologically, politically—if we overstep our boundaries. But it can also, and just as much, be understood as that which we must grasp in order to locate our own position: to acknowledge the limit ensures us of our possession of a defined territory. Finally, it signals a permanent temptation that must not simply be repressed if thought is to remain on the way to what it could one day become. In the first case, the limit is what we neither should nor can go beyond, since passing beyond it means to venture into a space where we no longer know or perceive what makes sense; it is the limit of discourse, of what can be said and thought. In the second, it is precisely this understanding of the limit, our *grasp* of it, that in a reverse movement pulls thought back onto its own ground, where it may be exercised according to established protocols. As for the third, it is what gives thinking a particular momentum, unleashing a fundamental inquietude and agitation that we must not too soon appease in the name of false safeties, if thinking is to remain an activity that does not simply settle for a series of achieved results.

Thus, if philosophy in a certain way begins as a quest for the infinite—for that which surpasses the here and now of the singular case, and the vicissitudes of time, as in the introductory moves that organize the Poem of Parmenides—this just as soon reverts to a fear of its abyssal and vertiginous structure, which necessitates that we not too quickly take leave of our finite abode if we are to remain in possession of ourselves. Possession of what thinking desires may become a dispossession of ourselves, just as self-possession entails a certain asceticism in relation to the lure of the absolute, all of which institutes the game of philosophical truth as a wager that must be won and lost, acknowledged and repressed.

In another register, this would amount to something like a double desire, or more precisely, desire in what has often been understood as its constitutive double structure: conditioned by its own limit, it is what ceaselessly approaches this limit, working to displace and negotiate that which would be its fulfillment as well as its own death. From the Platonic understanding of *eros* as that which pushes thinking ahead, to the various modern analyses of desire, either as lack and negativity, or as production and proliferation, limits are there to be pushed and overcome, but in this also displaced and redrawn.

The Kantian moment was a decisive shift in this tradition, in locating the limit inside, or even *as*, consciousness. After the Transcendental Dialectic of the first Critique, any excessive transcendence, any movement that threatens to dislocate reason's self-possession, will be derived from its immanent structure, as a temptation that emerges from within the depths of consciousness itself. The preceding formulas may even seem to be a retroactive projection of problems of Kantian and post-Kantian thought, as is indicated by the obvious Kantian resonances of the very idea of a "limit of reason," which already in the *Critique of Pure Reason* engages all of three above interpretations: the limit as prohibition, as a source of stability, and as promise. While the last is perhaps the least emphasized by Kant, it is pivotal in the aftermath of Criticism: beginning in the idealist and romantic attempts to move beyond the strictures of Kantian finitude, both in terms of aesthetic and religious experiences, as well as in the more strictly epistemological claims successively advanced by Fichte and Hegel, the claim is constantly made that the Kantian limitation necessarily, albeit unknowingly, implies a knowledge of the limit's other side, and thus already entails its own overcoming.

In twentieth-century thought, this problem of boundaries is staged in many ways, particularly in the phenomenological tradition. Husserl's project to establish an expanding sense of reason on the one hand opens toward an infinite horizon that sometimes seems to makes him into an heir of pre-Kantian rationalism; on the other hand, it constantly runs up against a series of interior limits that yet are not simply negative boundaries, but always call for a return to more profound constitutive layers of consciousness in which the limits will be shown to belong to the order of the constituted. For Heidegger, thinking of the ontological difference and, in turn, the withdrawal of being appears like a fundamental limit to what consciousness and subjectivity may achieve; however, in keeping with the remarks made both in *Being and Time* and in later work that the possibility of phenomenology stands higher than its actuality, it also signals an experience of thought as openness and a clearing beyond the subject, perhaps an "asubjective" phenomenology as it was developed in different ways by Eugen Fink and Jan Patočka (discussed below by Marcia Sá Cavalcante Schuback and Gustav Strandberg). For someone like Derrida, the problem of limits is pushed further in a way that both negates and pursues Heidegger's openness. The deconstruction of metaphysics as presence inclines towards moving away from what in Heidegger still may have appeared as an appeal to the originary and to foundations, while still preserving the sense of the transcendental as the freedom of thought, as in Derrida's early debate with Foucault on the status of madness as outside of reason (discussed below by Sven-Olov Wallenstein) or, in his later work, as a relation to an otherness that remains to come, with both ethical and religious connotations (brought forth in John D. Caputo's essay below) even though Derrida always wanted to retain a distance from all such traditional categories.

But while this question on the limit of thought as an interior divide that we can neither simply respect nor transgress may be considered to be one of the fundamental features of modern thought, it has profound roots in the past. As the references to the Poem of Parmenides and the Platonic *eros* indicate, the motif of a limit which at the same time constrains, protects, and seduces is by no means absent from the beginnings of philosophical thought. Madness, ecstasy, excess, and desire are indeed features that from the outset appear as that Other of philosophy known as myth and religion, from which philosophy has constantly attempted to disentangle itself with a force that suggests that the rival is not merely an external enemy but comes from within thought as such, to the point of often being virtually indistinguishable from it.

Already before the emergence of philosophy in its Platonic guise—that is, contemporaneous with the open and yet non-institutionalized form of thought that we, through a projection backwards of Plato's and Aristotle's ideas, have come to know as "pre-Socratic"—Greek tragedy was one of the primordial places where this conflict was staged. The fear of *hubris*, the injunction to stay within one's limits as defined by the gods and the cosmic order, is a theme that traverses the great dramatic texts from Aeschylus onward, precisely because the overstepping of boundaries defines the human being; this is perhaps most dramatically encapsulated in the great Sophoclean stasimon in *Antigone*, which speaks of man as the most placeless and uncanny of all beings, inspiring awe but also a profound anxiety for whatever strays beyond the limits set by the order of the *polis* (the "orgiastic," as it is called by Patočka, which is discussed by Gustav Strandberg below).

Even though Plato's response to the challenge of tragedy is at first sight largely negative, he too has a need for the dimension of excess, as can be seen in his many and shifting accounts of the kind of divine frenzy that accompanies philosophy's itinerary toward the eidetic light. The ascension that takes us out of the world naively given to the senses may seem like madness to those that remain chained in the cave, and to some extent it is, which is why it must be contained and transformed into an ally of the logos. The mad excess cannot be eradicated, but rather needs to be applied in measured doses, and precisely like rhetoric, mimesis, the body and its passions, it forms a strategic resource and not something to be simply repressed. The strategic use of madness and excess follows the logic of the *pharmakon* as analyzed by Derrida (and discussed in Anders Lindström's contribution), negotiating the risk of a loss of self-possession, while still acknowledging that this risk is required for the self to achieve a superior philosophical status. This is why Plato's account of tragedy, on the surface a discourse against a straightforward enemy, is more like a complex exposition dealing with one of philosophy's most insidious rivals: if tragedy does not lead to the right mix of passions, but produces an imbalance in the soul, then philosophy can handle the problem better, by incorporating what seems like the mad unreason of art and religion in an economized structure that extracts the power and impetus they contain, but does not fall prey to disorder.

In Aristotle, this dramatic tension has diminished although not disappeared, and philosophy now seems to approach the question of limits as an internal one, relating the divisions and lines of demarcation proper to its own subject matters: physics, metaphysics, logic, ethic, politics, art theory. The idea of a madness or frenzy inherent in philosophy itself has become somewhat distant, and the "wonder" or "amazement" that we feel before the world is what initiates the movement of thought as a process of conceptual grasping, rather than threatening to throw it into an abyssal vertigo. But even if the wonder fades, a second-order wonder may emerge over this loss (discussed in Marcia Sá Cavalcante Schuback's essay) which reaches all the way into the present. How to preserve the first wonder instead of settling down in the safe haven of a *theoria* sure of itself is a task bequeathed to us by antiquity, perhaps even a task that stands opposed to what the Greek thinkers themselves thought it to be, as Heidegger has reminded us.

II

In Christianity, the problems of madness, unreason, and of what it means to be "rational" acquire a new dimension, and are transformed into a conflict between the inheritance of Greek thought and the new demands of a religious discourse that claims not only the power of prophecy, but also that the event of incarnation has already occurred. On the basis of this event, it needs to be conceptually encoded and transmitted in a way that challenges the very foundation of the logos as it had been handed down from Greek philosophy through its various Roman translations and adaptations. Key documents of the early encounter between Judaic wisdom and Greek philosophy are the letters of Paul, where (Greek) wisdom and learning is actively refuted in favor of faith and passion, which will appear as "madness to the wise."

The problems that beset the early Church Fathers generated a spectrum of answers, from the emphatic denial of the relevance of classical learning for the Christian teaching, as in Tertullian, to the affirmation of their full compatibility on the basis of a hermeneutical reading of the textual sources, as in Origen. These conflicts were eventually settled, above all in Augustine, to the effect that a Greek philosophical vocabulary was needed to system- atize the revelation into theology, a word whose very etymology signals the kind of compromise that was reached. Human and pagan reason had its place, and even though it is surpassed by revelation and faith, and can never contradict it, reason must be strategically used for a body of transmissible learning to be created.

In this way, we can see how concepts like the Trinity and the incarnation transpose both Platonic and Aristotelian concepts into a Christian context. Already the logos that commands the beginning of the Gospel of John bears witness to such a debate, the "Word" here being the relation between the model, the copy, and their mediating bond, later systematized by Augustine as the "persons" of the Trinity. Similarly, the debates around the incar- nation may be read as new takes on what it means for the Form to take part in a finite, embodied entity, and in their successive versions they rehearse all the options in the quarrel between Plato and Aristotle over where the Forms are located. A third case would be the Pelagian fights over the will, which also continue Greek thought, although perhaps more obscurely, by asking whether the individual's choices and decisions in fact stem from a nature that would have a separate existence outside of particular individuals, an essence that precedes its singular embodiment, and which may have been corrupted by a sin understood as "original."

Generally, the transposition of philosophy into the emerging theological discourse followed a movement that somewhat anachronistically could be called an "existentialization." Ontology—more or less consciously modeled upon the third-person, thing-like entity, or the verb "to be" in the third person present indicative (all other derivations, Plato says in the *Timaeus*, ultimately stem from the "is," *esti*)—became reorganized along the lines of an I that seeks salvation and a You as the Other that holds the truth, a para- digmatical case of which would be Augustine's *Confessions*. Even though this shift should not be made into a clear break (as has been demonstrated in great length in Foucault's later work, the "care of the self" and the demand for introspective reflection was a key issue already in Plato and his successors) we may still speak of a general displacement, so that to attain truth no longer means to identify with cosmic order beyond the singular perspective, but more and more becomes a question of identifying what lies within oneself, all of which transforms the coordinates within which "subjectivation" occurs. The ancient idea of philosophy as "wisdom" (dealt with in John Caputo's essay below) survived in a transformed fashion, now inserted into a Christian metaphysics, which would treat it in terms of faith vs. secular knowledge, through the many and shifting medieval solutions up to the great synthesis in Aquinas. The limit of reason becomes the boundary that separates philosophy from religion; for the medieval thinker, madness would be the refusal to respect this limit, often precisely the madness of a reason that goes too far and claims to subject revealed truth to its own procedures.

Renaissance philosophy twists the figure of the limit of reason into a more sinuous and meandering line. At stake is both a new infinitization of reason (discussed in Jonna Bornemark's essay in relation to Giordano Bruno) that draws both on the legacy of Neo-Platonism, and, somewhat later, on breakthroughs in astronomy and mathematics. Seen in the light of Cartesian rationalism, this shift is still caught up in a reading of nature as symbolic—or simply caught up in the idea of reason as the *reading*, an attempt to extract meaning from a withdrawn text, as has been analyzed by Hans Blumenberg and Foucault—and it is first with the advent of universal mathematics that the more ancient wisdom is displaced by a reason that is self-sufficient and autonomous with respect to all given orders. Whether this amounts to an expulsion of madness and excess to the outer limits of thought, and the beginning of a modern monologue on madness, or to a welcoming of madness as a moment in a reason whose hyperbolic transcendence points to the very freedom of thought, as was argued respectively by Michel Foucault and Jacques Derrida remains an open question (a debate further discussed in Sven-Olov Wallenstein's contribution).

Regardless of how we see this, the Cartesian move was in a certain way intensified in the Kantian moment (interpreted differently in the essays by Caputo and Monique David-Ménard) in which the Enlightenment culture reaches a state of self-reflection and self-questioning. For Kant, the Enlightenment was a task that needed a clarification, which he sketches first in the essay "Response to the Question: What is Enlightenment?" (1784), and then in the preface to the second edition of *Critique of Pure Reason* (1787), and with respect to religion in *Religion within the Boundaries of Mere Reason* (1793). For Kant's immediate successors, Enlightenment was more like a problem, whose own limits, shortcomings, and eventually dark underside had to be investigated (Patočka, discussed in Gustav Strandberg's contribution, would be a sequel to this movement beyond Kant), and particularly so in relation to its rationalist and fundamentally moral interpretation of religion.

After Kant, modern philosophy has never ceased to ask the question what it means to limit reason. Identified as the legacy of the Enlightenment, as the belief in the self-mastery of the subject, or as the idea of language that would be fully able to account for its own rules and thus once and for all limit shifts of aspect (dealt with in Espen Dahl's essay on Wittgenstein and Cavell), or in an almost infinite number of other versions, the problem of reason haunts all of modern thought.

III

In the first chapter of this volume, John D. Caputo takes his point of departure in the particularly modern divide between rationality and irrationality, which has often been linked to the divide between religion and philosophy. This idea of modern and largely procedural rationality stands in contrast to the more substantive conceptions of wisdom, logos, and truth that were prevalent from antiquity through medieval Christianity. The break-up of this larger unity signified the eclipse of truth and the emergence of a rationality that from Descartes to Kant became identified with mathematical and categorization-oriented reasoning, in the process relegating "religion"—another modern invention itself—to the sphere of irrationality. For Caputo, Kant is the main protagonist in this drama where philosophy is gradually separated from the true, the good, and the beautiful in the name of Enlightenment, even though Caputo also discerns other facets of Kant's thought, particularly in the sublime and the analysis of enthusiasm.

Against Enlightenment formalism, Caputo marshals the more expansive and substantial understanding of reason that we find in Hegel, for whom religion could not simply be confined "within the limits of reason alone," as Kant suggests, but has to be understood as pointing toward the absolute, although grasping and explicating this will in the end be the task of philosophy. In this sense Hegel too was a successor to the Enlightenment, which is why Caputo finally must part ways with him, in this case citing Kierkegaard as his ally. If there is a truth to religion that goes beyond particular content as well as beyond all traditional and dogmatic claims about there being one true religion, for Caputo this is ultimately located in the dimension of the "event." Following Derrida's reading of prayer in St Augustine, Caputo understands this as a paradoxical notion in relation to the impossible, or rather the possibility of the impossible: the prayer relates to an unknown "x" that cannot be confined to any particular religion, and yet preserves a dimension of futurity, of the "to come" (*à venir*).

Marcia Sá Cavalcante Schuback returns us to the origin of Greek thinking and the way it narrates its inception in terms of wonder and amazement, the *thaumazein* that we find already in Plato but perhaps most famously in the first book of Aristotle's *Metaphysics*, where it is placed at the beginning of philosophy. This wonder, however, forgets its origin in the encounter with being, which becomes reinterpreted as the ground of beings, initiating a long sequel of metaphysical determinations. Today, Cavalcante Schuback argues, the initial wonder—the "pathos of distance" that opened the ontological difference—may have been lost, but this gives rise to a different wonder, relating to the distance from this first distance, and which comes to us in the form of a particular sensation, which she develops as "enthusiasm." Drawing on Eugen Fink's analysis of Greek enthusiasm as an encounter with the divine that branches out into philosophy, art, and religion, but also (similarly to Caputo) on Kant—more precisely on his historico-political concept of enthusiasm—she suggests that what is at stake is an experience of touching and being touched. This is an experience that cuts through the division between the active and the passive, an intense intimacy that is also outside of itself, as the poet Hölderlin once attempted to grasp with the term *Innigkeit*. Neither inside nor outside, neither transporting to a supersensible beyond nor drawing us back to the merely factual, this "transcendental sensation" can be taken as indicating a particular nearness to oneself as well as to others that also has political implications, and permits a new understanding of the sacred as the "strange and mysterious identity of life and death in their abyssal difference."

Anders Lindström interrogates the place of madness in Greek philosophy, and he too takes his cues from the concept of enthusiasm, as it is delineated in Plato's *Ion*. Enthusiasm becomes a way of deciphering the messages of the gods, but as such it is always threatened by a loss of the original sense, which is why Plato deems it necessary to contain the influence of the poet's inspiration within strict limits in order to safeguard the status of philosophy itself. The "ancient quarrel" between poetry and philosophy, referred to at the end of *The Republic* (607b), can in this sense be taken as part of a complex of operations that Platonism must perform for the philosophical logos to emerge, and which bear on a series of dangerous rivals: myth, rhetoric, and the arts.

If Greek philosophy in one sense can be taken as the general movement from *mythos* to *logos*, the two nevertheless remain intimately connected, and Lindström points to their mutual entanglement in both Pre-Socratic thought and tragedy, from which Plato also needs to draw his own resources. The quarrel is in this sense never completely settled, but instead is displaced onto the terrain of philosophy itself; it forms a historical foil that must be acknowledged, as well as a present concern to be addressed, and philosophy must at once accommodate and alleviate both manifestations in order for its own logos to emerge as a mastery over its rivals rather than a violent expulsion of them. Platonism marshals myth against myth, rhetoric against rhetoric, and most forcefully, a perspectival art of writing against the perspectivism of writing, in a game over which the thinker can never ascertain mastery once and for all.

Thus, madness and excess are never far away, as is indicated by Plato's various strategies for incorporating them into his own discourse, most notably perhaps in *Phaedrus*, where divine *mania* is even cherished as a "divine release from customary habits" (265a). Tragedy would in a certain way constitute the most powerful counter-statement to this, and Lindström points to Euripides' *Bacchae* as the irruption of a divine dispensation and frenzy inside the *polis*, showing the persistence of a profound otherness inside the emerging Platonic dialectic; the *Bacchae* was in fact contemporary with the Socratic call to order that someone like Nietzsche perceived to be equivalent to the neutralization of the Dionysian power of madness.

With the advent of Christianity, the conflict between (Greek) reason and the various forms of thought deemed outside it takes on a new form, although here too the division soon becomes an internal one, as the need to systematize revelation and faith increasingly means relying on the language and vocabulary of the philosophers. Hans Ruin's article addresses this entanglement through the lens of *spirit*, a notion that, by drawing on a Greek conceptuality while still infusing it with a sense of what goes beyond our comprehension—of "foolishness" as the Pauline letters have it—seeks to straddle the divide between religion and reason. In Ruin's reading, such foolishness of spirit should first and foremost be understood in terms of history, tradition and the ancestral: the *pneuma*, which simultaneously has a complex meaning in Greek philosophical and medical writings from Anaximenes to the Stoics and echoes the Hebrew *ruach*, is what gives life. In opposition to the "letter," as in the famous formula of the second epistle to the Corinthians, spirit is that which ensures that there is something beyond the individual's death and the finitude of communities. As Ruin notes, it is also in this sense that the idea of spirit re-emerges in Hegel, and then in Husserl, not as something otherworldly and irrational, but as a figure of that which binds history together beyond all particular sciences and rationalities.

In Paul, the spirit mediates between human beings and God as a principle of life, but it is also a life that unfolds as the nearness of the old, and as that lives on from one generation to another. Drawing on Heidegger's 1921 course on the phenomenology of religious life, which attempts to understand religion in terms of a particular form of meaning-fulfillment rather than a determined theological or confessional content—that is, to circumvent the too facile division between the "rational" and "irrational"—Ruin suggests that we should emphasize the temporal dimension of the Pauline *pneuma*. It is an experience of waiting and openness toward the horizon of the unexpected, which however also invites us to address the particular features of the Jewish tradition that appear to be repressed in Heidegger's interpretation. For Ruin, the Pauline spirit contains the promise of a transformed life, which also achieves a more authentic access to the scriptural tradition, i.e. to the "letter" in the sense that does not kill but gives life in the movement of transmission and the reception of tradition, which in the end is what forms the bridge between the *pneuma* and the claims about *Geist* from Hegel to Husserl.

During the renaissance period, the first embryo of modern science appears, although without any fixed limits between science and magic, philosophy and religion. Jonna Bornemark's article looks at one of the most striking cases of such a fusion of Christian mysticism, heliocentric science and hermetic magic, in Giordano Bruno's philosophy. She argues that modern, predominantly phenomenological, philosophy of religion, occupied with the Kantian discussion of the limits of experience and of reason, of radical alterity, and of the impossible, might be less well equipped to deal with pre-modern expressions such as Bruno's. What we find there instead is an overflowing creativity that knows no limits, with no fixed center or periphery. In this metaphysics, there is no dualistic separation between matter and spirit (or form), and matter instead becomes exactly the capacity to take on form from within. On this point, just as on many others, Bruno argues for a mutual dependency of oppositions, to the point where opposites coincide. Instead of a world ordered through dualistic oppositions, he investigates the manifold with its intrinsic infinity.

The human being nevertheless has a specific place within such a world, as the one who not only understands in a passive way but also creates understanding. Bruno opposes what he calls "pedants," who aim for an understanding based on fixed formalizations and categories, and instead opts for philosophical concepts that are fluid and changing, as they in their movement attempt to include the universe as such. Understanding is not a passive contemplation but a continuation of the creativity of life, which is why the problem is not its limit but the possibility of its limitless expansion, its elevation to the infinite (a theme that later permeates the rationalist tradition): in other words, a continually changing understanding that creates and understands the world in infinitely new ways and attempts to include everything. In this, too, an unavoidable hubris arises within the human being, a desire to comprehend all things from within, which is also the task of the magician. This insatiable hubris, which traverses Bruno's philosophy as a whole, can thus be characterized precisely as a madness *of* reason, but not as a madness *outside* of reason.

It is in relation to this conception of thought that Kant's Critical philosophy marks a decisive caesura. But while his philosophy of the limit, which gives the concept its transcendental twist by reinterpreting it as a constitutive boundary *inside* thought, nevertheless takes place against the background of rationalism as a whole, and more precisely the Cartesian turn to the subject as the new foundation. That Descartes's move is linked to madness in a particular way was for a long time rarely acknowledged; the sheer insanity of the world according to the divine Evil Genius, depriving me not only of my body and the things around me but also of the truth of simple arithmetical statements, was generally reduced to a more or less technical feature in the process of doubt that ushers in the cogito. The reappraisal of the status of madness in Descartes undertaken by Michel Foucault in his 1961 *History of Madness*, and the exchange with Jacques Derrida that it provoked, form the object of Sven-Olov Wallenstein's contribution.

For Foucault, Descartes's essential gesture is the rejection of madness before the Evil Genius appears, when Descartes, in doubting the veracity of his immediate surrounding, asks if this does not make him mad, and then proceeds to the argument about dreaming. Descartes, according to Foucault, does not really dwell upon madness as a possibility in thought, but rejects it without further ado. On the one hand, this severs the traditional connection between reason and folly that was still visible in a writer like Montaigne, who in this sense is the last link in the long chain that was broken by Classical Reason; on the other hand, this makes Cartesian reason into a kind of metaphysical accomplice of the "Great Internment" that in the mid-seventeenth century was at the origin of the long and meandering development of the modern discourse on madness that remains deaf to the Murmurings of its own other. Against this, Derrida claims that Descartes by no means excludes madness, but in fact, in the guise of the Evil Genius, welcomes it into philosophy as its own most radical possibility of a transcendence that cannot be enclosed in any finite worldview. When Foucault finally answers, it is by changing terrain: at stake is no longer the promise of an Outside of Reason as a singular and absolute limit, but rather a reading of how Descartes's *Meditations* produce a new subject position for which the ability to be the legally responsible author of one's thought is at stake, i.e. a kind of modulation inside the genealogical history of subjectivity as a *multiplicity* of limits. In this way, the exchange between Foucault and Derrida not only addresses the particular status of Cartesian philosophy, but the status of philosophy itself, what it means to locate a limit of reason in general, and whether such a limit must remain internal to philosophy, or if it can find resources in other types of discourse.

The birth of modern philosophy is further investigated in Monique David-Ménard's contribution, now with reference to Kant and his early attack on Emmanuel Swedenborg, famously put forth in his *The Dreams of a Ghost-Seer* (1766). Kant's rejection of Swedenborg's ghosts and demons is normally seen as belonging to his pre-critical phase, and while the metaphysics that the later *Critique of Pure Reason* wants to delimit indeed also has its fair share of spiritual and otherworldly entities, the positive contribution of the later work tends to be read as unrelated to his previous attack on the Swedish ghost-seer. Against this, David-Ménard argues that important traces of Swedenborg can also be found in Kant's mature critical thought, in fact as one of the main sources of the difference between the Analytic and the Dialectic. If we read the first Critique in inverse order, from the Dialectic backwards, the problem of transcendental illusion as a necessary and integral part of reason that cannot simply be made to vanish but is something that we must learn to see through becomes central. For David-Ménard, what connects the dialectic and the earlier polemic against Swedenborg is Kant's discovery, particularly in the antinomies, that a mere logical contradiction does not suffice to decide in favor of any of the two parties. In the end, the antinomy is a fight over "nothing" as Kant says, and for the seemingly metaphysical conflict to be settled we need to introduce a real conflict, a "something" that lies within the scope of possible experience as bound by the rules of understanding.

And yet, as David-Ménard concludes, this by no means exhausts the implications of this debate. For if Swedenborg's logic lies elsewhere than within the strictures of Kant's Analytic, and from the point of view of the latter must appear as pure delusion, the question remains what its positive features are. In a certain sense, Freud would pick up precisely this thread, in attempting to analyze the dreamwork as a particular kind of logic at work beneath the discursive regularities of waking reason, thereby also pushing the transcendental question into a more obscure domain that has exerted a lasting fascination on post-Freudian philosophies of consciousness and its limits.

One of the problems posed by Kant, which was identified already in Hegel, and in recent times was reopened especially in the debates initiated more than thirty years ago around the "postmodern" where the role of Kant once more was at the center, is the extent to which we are still within something called the Enlightenment. Taking his cues from Jan Patočka's historico-philosophical reflections, Gustav Strandberg's contribution deals with the Czech philosopher's ambivalent assessment of this legacy, and the extent to which the limit of reason can still be understood in terms of a historically situated self-critique.

For Patočka, history is not simply a phenomenon that would be rooted in a general structure of historicity, but what interrupts our captivity in everyday life and opens us to the world as a problem; it emerges from a crisis of sense that still produces new sense, rather than senselessness. As such it belongs to the order of the event, ultimately to what he calls the domain of the "orgiastic," which has a paradoxical status. It is what shatters our security, an ecstatic experience of limits, but also a call to responsibility; it is the dual structure of finitude, which both draws us out of ourselves towards that which cannot be possessed and mastered, and at the same time pushes us back to our own condition.

Rather than locating this as a timeless conflict, Patočka understands it as profoundly historically articulated, even as the hidden source of the historical, in a way that connects a reading of the origin of philosophy to a critical appreciation of our present. If Greek philosophy was able to attain a balance between the orgiastic and the rational, for instance in terms of the Platonic "care of the soul" (*epimeleia tes psyches*—a term that interestingly enough was also picked up by Foucault in a related sense, in his far-reaching analysis of a "care of the self," the *epimeleia heautou*) this was partly lost in Christianity, for which the dark underside became something to be repressed; subsequently, the relationship became even more obscured in the modern mathematization of nature and its Enlightenment sequel. The repressed returned however, as becomes evident in the violent disasters of modernity, and for Patočka this signals the need for a critical rethinking of renewal of the Enlightenment that does justice to the finite and somber dimension of reason: a critique of reason through reason that it many respects pursues a Kantian legacy, although infused with the tragic experiences that separate us from the self-assuredness of Enlightenment thought.

Carl Cederberg's essay looks at the problem of the limit of reason from the perspective of a position that often appears as philosophy's bankruptcy: that of a skepticism that declares the claims of philosophy to be impossible since no reliable truth can ever be attained. As the traditional refutation of skepticism immediately retorts, this is a self-contradiction, since at least this statement must be taken as true if the skeptic is to be right. Taking his point of departure in Emmanuel Levinas's late work *Otherwise than Being*, Cederberg argues that skepticism needs to be understood as an opponent of philosophy as such, but forms a resource for the thinking of the other beyond knowledge and ignorance, and a new foundation of reason in being-for-the-other.

In Levinas, this is connected to the idea that any beginning in the subject has a prehistory, an absence of ground, or an anarchy that is more ancient than the first and primordial, and instead must be understood as a proximity which is a diachrony refractory to thematization. This claim, as understood by Cederberg, bears on the status of the language of philosophy as such, and the possibility of its constitutive failure to express what it wants to say. The "said" in such a language might obscure what for Levinas is the essential part, the "saying" the precedes it and can only be reached through an "unsaying," which is how he understands skepticism's ability to escape the merely logical contradiction of which it is traditionally accused. There is, Levinas suggests, a "secret diachrony that commands this ambiguous or enigmatic way of speaking," which is why the "at the same time" of the logical contradiction is unable to account for it. The responsibility that demands to be said is lost as soon as it becomes a theme placed in front of a subject, which is why the unsaying is needed to bring us back to saying as a movement and opening, which always remains a past in relation to what has become thematic and mastered as subject or object. Skepticism then, for Levinas, would be the possibility of breaking with such mastery; it is a limit of reason, itself neither simply rational nor irrational. This is lost in the classical refutation of skepticism, which remains at the level of the said.

As we noted at he outset, the idea of a limit of reason—whether it is understood as prohibition, as source of stability, or as promise—as it is traced in most of the contributions in this volume, seems largely to be a problem that has occupied the tradition which has become known as Continental philosophy, to the extent that one can put one's trust in such labels. Regardless of such (perhaps ultimately misleading) classifications, the theme has however also been treated in productive fashion in the line of analytic philosophy that draws on the early as well as the later Wittgenstein. Espen Dahl's concluding essay looks at one such development in the thought of Stanley Cavell, where the limit of reason is drawn inside our everyday life, and eventually points to a sense of sharing and community through language.

Dahl focuses his discussion on a problem that touches directly on the topic of the limits of reason: wonder and miracles, all of that which for classical metaphysics, as for instance Leibniz, belonged to the principles of grace rather than those of nature, although both of these were for him ultimately founded in reason. In the tradition of Wittgenstein and Cavell, nature is however inflected toward our shared world of language, and Dahl argues that the miraculous and wondrous, the wonder that once set Aristotle on the path toward philosophy, today is most fruitfully seen in terms of what Wittgenstein called "aspect-seeing." The question is no longer one of ontology or metaphysics, and no longer one that pits the rational towards the irrational, but one of how we can meaningfully shift perspectives inside a shared language, displacing its empirically given limits, though still continuing to make sense, as for instance in art and poetry. "Reality," following Cora Diamond, is a "difficult" concept, and calls for a linguistic elasticity that however can only exist against the backdrop of a set of implicit agreements—not because these agreements would be somehow unshakeable, but simply because we are finite, embodied beings. Religious language would then amount to a certain type of break with the ordinary, presenting us with an "inordinate knowledge" (Cavell) that surely from another perspective would be taken as containing a certain madness; but religious language also points to the constant possibility of perspective shifts inside the language that we already share, which is why it should not enclose us in multiple and solipsistic universes—which, as already Kant had argued, would be madness in the negative and unproductive sense—but rather portrays the common world as always in the making.

Forget Rationality: Is There Religious Truth?

John D. Caputo

The fact that we are discussing religion in terms of rationality and irrationality means that we are already sailing in modernist waters and have agreed to the terms set for the discussion by modernity. Before modernity we would have distinguished those who love and serve God (modernity's "theists") from the fool who says in his heart, there is no God (modernity's "atheists"). Such a denial was deemed unwise in the extreme, because it cuts us off from God, who is love and truth, and it is excessively foolish to deprive oneself of love and truth. The love of truth is the mark of wisdom, which means, Augustine said, the only true philosopher is one who loves God. Before modernity we would have distinguished wisdom and foolishness, *sophia* or *sapientia* and its lack, not rationality and irrationality. To be sure, before modernity, there was a robust idea of "reason" (*logos*, *ratio*). Indeed Aristotle had defined humans as rational animals, but reason was integrated into a fuller, richer, deeper conception of human life which bore the name of wisdom, whose ends reason served.

That is why charging "scholasticism" with excessive "rationalism" is a bad rap. That is the mark of early modernist scholasticism, but it has nothing to do with Augustine or Bonaventure or Aquinas. They put *ratio* in the service of explaining their deepest and most profound orientation as human beings, their Christian faith, in order to make their life intelligible to themselves (*fides quaerens intellectum*). Their theological works, like those of medieval Jewish and Islamic theologians, were not "systems" because they made no pretense to being comprehensive. Their works were orderly but reverent reflections on God, whose first, last and constant mark was incomprehensibility. If you comprehend it, Augustine said, it is not God, who is love itself and truth itself and far beyond our grasp. Their work as theologians was a part of their life of prayer and did not fit what Heidegger, using a term found in Kant, called "onto-theologic." Aquinas called his five proofs "ways" (*viae*) out of respect for the incomprehensibility of God, which did not fit inside what modernity meant by a "rational" argument. *Ratio* itself for Aquinas was the lowest rung in the analogical order of intelligence, the weakest form of intellectual life (*debilitas intellectus*), greatly surpassed by angelic *intellectus*, both of which are themselves participations in the subsistent *intellectus* of God. Reason does not stand in judgment over God. Reason is a finite participation in the life of God. Even the notorious "ontological argument" of St. Anselm was neither "ontological"—the word was coined only in modernity—nor an "argument" in the modern sense, as Barth, von Balthasar and Marion have all shown. The argument belongs to a prayer that Anselm directs to God, much like Augustine's *Confessions*, whose literary genre, as we will have occasion to note below, is not an "autobiography" but a prayer.

The eclipse of truth in modernity

But in modernity "reason" broke loose from its place in life as a whole and in the order of being and took on a life of its own, an ultimately purely formal and lifeless life, independent of wisdom, truth, love and God, over all of which it purported to stand in judgment. From the medieval point of view, that was excessively unwise. What the moderns call "reason" is from a medieval point of view foolishness—although it was not in medieval terms "mad" because, as Foucault has reminded us, the medievals respected the mad as friends of God. They thought that the mad were "touched" by God, that the voices they heard were not subjective noises inside their head but the words of angels whispering in their ears, which is why they did not segregate or institutionalize them. Modernity may well be defined by the eclipse of truth and the invention of the category of "Rationality"—now it is best to capitalize it, because it has grown into a hegemonic force of its own—which famously defined itself against what it excluded as "irrational," among which it included both the mad and "religion." "Religion" was another category invented by modernity—previously there were Christians, Jews and Muslims, or believers and infidels, but not "religions," which is a category on the maps drawn up by rationalism and colonialism. Indeed modernity is perhaps best defined not by the invention of any one of these categories, not even of Reason itself, but by its invention of the category of the "category," the various chambers within which modernity immured science, ethics, politics, art and religion.

That makes Kant the preeminent philosopher of the light of the Enlightenment. Philosophy does not do first-order creative work in Kant. It does critical work. It stakes out the borders of the various creative work others do—in science, ethics, and art—and then polices them. It is not first-order scientific knowledge but a science of science, knowledge of knowledge. Kant's reason is purely formal, purely universalistic. Reason does not have content; it is a system of formal universality. What makes science rational is not its insight into the truth but its power of a priori synthesis; what make ethics ethical is not the good it does or the good it seeks, but its formal universalizability; what makes art artistic is not the beauty of our life but our ability to appreciate its formal perfection. What the medievals called the true, the good and the beautiful, the very stuff of being, its transcendental properties, is hollowed out by what Kant called Reason. Pure reason is pure form, pure formalism, pure lifelessness, the dissipation of being, the dehydration of the good, the desiccation of the beautiful, and the eclipse of truth.

One of the most remarkable things about Kant is how much focused he is upon the formality of knowledge and how little focused he is on truth as a content. He does not define Reason as a faculty of being or truth but as a faculty of principles, of a priori synthesis. If anything, his interest lay in making sure that 'knowledge' is denied access to the true world—a move that would have left everyone from Plato to his own modernist predecessors dumbfounded—in order to make room for ethics. That might suggest that ethics has access to the true world. Not quite. Ethics is blind; it answers a command it hears but cannot see. Ethics knows nothing at all. It does not do or make contact with the good. The only thing we can call good, he says, is a good will, a will whose maxims are formally universalizable. Were a will to be moved by what is substantively good, well, that would not be a good will. We do not tell the truth because it is good or God-like, but because it is a formally universalizable duty. Then perhaps art makes contact with the beauty of being? Not so: the paradigm work of art for him is an Arabesque, in whose formal properties we take a properly formal subjective delight but in whose content we remain disinterested. Knowledge does not know the true world; ethics does not do the good; art does not make contact with being's glow.

But have we rushed to judgment? We have not mentioned religion. It is even worse with religion, which is nothing more than a chapel built on land owned by ethics. We are free to regard the categorical imperative as the voice of God, but no matter whose voice we might believe it to be, our duty is our duty. That reduces religion to ethics, which is itself reduced to formally universalizable maxims, and excises everything else in religion as superstition. To call this a ham-fisted and parsimonious analysis would be too generous.

In ancient Greece or the Middle Ages that would have been regarded as foolishness. Not irrational, but unwise, foolish. The ancients might have admitted the dexterity of Kant's reasoning, the cleverness of the architectonic, but they would have been appalled by the foolishness and lack of wisdom in the outcome: a philosopher whose intent is to deny us access to the true, the good, and the beautiful, and whose formal function is to police the borders lest anyone seek in the cover of night to sneak across the lines and make contact with their loved ones on the other side. The fool says in his heart, there is only Pure Reason. Or as Shakespeare's Puck says, Lord, what fools these modern rationalists be! Nowadays we would recommend a good psychiatrist, someone who would listen very patiently to the man. He reports the following symptoms. He is convinced he lives in a world of appearances; he marches to a drum beat by an unknown drummer, and he takes every precaution lest he actually love the things he does for fear it would distract him from his duties. The doctor would surely start by asking Kant about his childhood. You were attached to your mother, you say, but your father was very strict. Very interesting; please go on.

To be sure, by the very terms of deconstruction, systems are incapable of closing up entirely. They are always marked by crevices, openings, ruptures which allow for escape and for futures that the systems do not foresee or desire. In the case of Kant, such an opening is found in the analysis of the sublime, the representation of the unrepresentable, toward which we experience the ambiguous feeling of a sympathetic antipathy. This famously provided Lyotard with an opening to postmodernism. Lyotard theorized the postmodern as a repetition of the modern, which in Lyotard's account even makes the modern possible, since the "modern" (from the adverb *modo*, meaning what exists now, the latest thing) is both the subject and the constant effect of the suspicion incurred by what is currently present (*modo*). Far be it from me to renounce this opening or to denounce the sublime.

I would only say that Kant's sublime, like the third *Critique* as a whole, is the resolution of a problem of Kant's own devising, an attempt to recover from a self-inflicted wound. His sublime proceeds from multiple presuppositions—his representationalism, his preoccupation with the interplay of "faculties," and the metaphysical dualism between sensible appearances and supersensible things in themselves: all obstacles that Kant has put in his own way in the first place, from which the sublime offers relief. Furthermore, Kant's analysis of the sublime is aimed at assuring the superiority of the supersensible faculty of reason to the imagination and to sensible nature. Human subjectivity is only temporarily and provisionally displaced (as sensibility) by the sublime, but soon recovers its equilibrium (as reason)—whereas for Lyotard the sublime signals the irremediable displacement of the "language games," which is how he has redescribed (repeated) Kant's "faculties."[1] Kant's sublime issues in Romantic longing for the infinite; Lyotard's sublime issues in the infinite affirmation of the new without nostalgia. Kant's analysis is ultimately the issue of what Heidegger called Kant's reduction of the "thing," the human experience of the world in which we live, to the perceptual experience of spatio-temporal-causal objects, the model of which is the scientific object.[2] This analysis collapses when contrasted with far more adequate accounts found in the phenomenological tradition, like being-in-the-world (Heidegger) and incarnation (Merleau-Ponty), and in particular, from my point of view, with the experience of the event. I have not the slightest intention to deny the phenomenon of the sublime, but I do deny the terms in which it is cast by Kant, and I would propose it be recast in terms of the experience of *the* impossible, the possibility of *the* impossible, which has been paradigmatically set forth by Derrida.

Descartes is another good example of what happens to wisdom, God, and truth in modernity. Descartes raises the question of truth and even invokes the ancient link between God and truth, but he does so in terms of the "criterion" of truth. He does not exactly say that God is truth but something less than that, that God is veracious, a truth-teller, and that as the author of our nature, the veracity of God supplies a warranty for a good product, which we can count on in sorting out statements about ideas that are clear to us from dubious ideas. It would not take long for God to become the subject of one of those statements whose truth value would be on the line. God would have to make an appearance before the court of Reason which would determine whether belief in God is "warranted," or whether it has "sufficient reason," which meant it would not be long until it

[1] Jean-François Lyotard, "What is Postmodernism?" in *The Postmodern Condition,* trans. Geoff Bennington and Brian Massumi (Minneapolis: University of Minnesota Press, 1984), 77–81. For a felicitous postmodern deployment of the sublime in religion which moves in a psychoanalytic direction, see Clayton Crockett, *Interstices of the Sublime: Theology and Psychoanalytic Theory* (New York: Fordham University Press, 2007).
[2] Martin Heidegger, *What Is a Thing?,* trans. Vera Deutsch and W. B. Barton (Chicago: Gateway Editions, 1968).

was concluded that it was not. The Church's attitude toward Copernicus, Galileo and Descartes was reactionary and repressive, but the Church was not stupid. It always had a good nose for trouble when it came to its own authority.

From Modern to Postmodern

Among the categories invented in modernity the distinction between public and private enjoys a certain pride of place. This distinction was created above all to solve the problem that religion has always brought with it since the invention of Biblical monotheism—strife within religion (the persecution of heretics, the suppression of inquiry) and the strife between religions (religious wars). The solution modernity came up with was to segregate religion from the public order. The public order is a formal, neutral rational matrix within which various forms of private life can be freely practiced. In so doing, modernity reached a political solution to a political problem—religious strife—but not a philosophical one, unless you think philosophy is the love of buckets. It had decided to suspend the philosophical question, which is the question of religious truth. In pre-modern times, we said God is truth. In modernity we separate religion from truth and redescribe it as a protected right. It is the right of private individuals to believe anything that can nest inside their heads provided they do not try to force others to believe it or otherwise do violence to people who do not share their beliefs. In modernity, religion is a matter of private conscience; it is formally a protected right even if it is materially a bit mad.

To be sure, modernity had very "good reasons" (as opposed to "Pure Reason") for embarking on such a course. We are all in the debt of the Enlightenment for freeing us from the hegemony of Church, King, and superstition, and for putting in their place the rule of civil rights, freedom of religion, and free scientific inquiry. It would a really foolish thing to go back on that. The separation of church and state is the continuing legacy of the Enlightenment that very few people in the NATO world would disavow. We can only be grateful to the Enlightenment for trying to contain the damage done by the idea of the "one true religion," which is the legacy of mono-theism and long antedates modernity. But in separating church and state, the Enlightenment was also separating religion and truth and therein lies the problem that interests me. It behaves like a court that refuses to hear a case. It declines to rule on whether a given religious belief is true or not (the philosophical question) and is content with the political resolution. When the philosophers themselves turn to religion they duck the question of truth and take up instead the question of "rationality." That is, they debate the formal question, not the material one. They do not debate religious truth, the truth of religion, what I will shortly call the "event" that takes place in religion, but religious "beliefs" or propositions and whether they are "justified." They ask whether there is some frame of reference within which one would be (privately) "warranted" in holding such views even if one does not expect others to share them.

That explains the simmering conflict that shows no line of easing off between religious and non-religious people. Privately, religious people in the monotheistic traditions think that their religion is *true*, even that it is *the* one true religion, that it is the eternal truth revealed to them by God which authorizes them, when push comes to shove, to follow the authority of God not the state, whose powers are finite, temporal and fallible. That is not unambiguously good or bad. It could lead either to people who bomb abortion clinics or to Martin Luther King, both of whom refused to concede that the state is God or has the last word. Privately, non-religious people view religious people with disdain; religious heads, they think, are filled with primitive superstition and nonsense and they represent a menace to science and the civic freedoms we are meant to enjoy in a democracy. It does not take much for the lid modernity has put on this pressure cooker to explode. There are, of course, cooler heads in all these camps who promote dialogue between the religious and the secular, and dialogue among the different religions, but, after pointing out various things on which they can all agree, they have finally to agree to disagree and let the political solution stand. The problem lies not in separating church and state, which I endorse, but in separating religion and truth. But the problem with uniting religion and truth is even greater. The whole idea of *the* true religion is the source of all the conflict within and among religions and getting the state involved in deciding which religion is true, in the "establishment" of religion, makes a bad situation incomparably worse.

That is the state of the question of religion in modernity and it is as far as modernity can get us. The resources of modernity in this regard are exhausted. It has said everything it has to say, has done all the good it is going to do. My own view is that the time has come to thank the Enlightenment for its services and move on. We need a new Enlightenment, by which I mean not a jettisoning but a continuation of the old one and its work of emancipation but by another means, one that is more critical of what the

Enlightenment called critique, and more enlightened about what the Enlightenment calls the light of reason. We need a more reasonable idea of reason, a less ham-fisted idea of religion and a more ambient notion of truth, one that allows the nose of "truth" under the tent of religion. We need to defend the idea of religious truth or the truth of religion but without, in the spirit of the old Enlightenment, implicating ourselves in the mistaken idea of *the* true religion or undoing the separation of church and state which protects us from that mistake. The concept of *the* true religion is a fundamental conceptual mistake about religion and truth.

So my idea is not simply to do again what the Enlightenment already has done effectively enough, which is to find a way to protect the rest of us from people who think that they are the privileged recipients of an Absolute Truth delivered from on high. The old Enlightenment can handle that. I want to argue against an underlying mistaken view of what true religion or religious truth is, which implies a fundamental mistake about both religion and truth. In other words we need to take up the question of religion and truth in more postmodern terms, where the powerful categorical walls erected in modernity are broken down, where "Reason" is taken down a peg or two and reinserted within a larger framework. In a general way, postmodernity must always find ways to "communicate" with premodernity, because they both elude the over-growth of "categorial" thinking that marks modernity, but it must do so without becoming anti-modern. Postmodernity must, on the one hand, pass through modernity but come out on the other end, while not, on the other hand, suffering a relapse into the premodern. It must be willing to learn something from premodernity without falling into nostalgia and from modernity without embracing rationalism.

I hasten to add that the depiction I provide in terms of premodern, modern, and postmodern is a strictly heuristic device. It is a fiction that as a philosopher I reject but as an author I embrace, a ladder meant to be discarded later. If my critique of modernity lies in the critique of erecting strict and rigorous borders, then I certainly know better than to defend a rigid periodization such as this. That is why every significant "postmodern" philosopher refuses the term and even Lyotard, who employed the term and provided the standard theory of it, tried to scramble the distinction and to say that the postmodern (as the production of the new) precedes the modern (the *modo*, the latest, the newest) and makes it possible. My use of it here is strictly for expository and economic purposes.

Hegel's critique of the Enlightenment

In the view I strike here, modernity is marked by displacing truth as a focal concern and replacing it with Rationality. Truth is a substantive issue while rationality is a formal one. The truth of a work of art is not its formal perfection but the insight it gives us about our life. The truth of an ethical counsel is not its formal universalizability but its advice about living the good life. The truth of religious beliefs and practices is not reducible to ethics, much less to a formal right to practice religion, but in the insight it provides about the weals and woes of being human, about birth and death, joy and sorrow, faith and despair. It is to Hegel's everlasting credit that he rejected the categorial thinking of modernity and made a profound critique of it from which modernity never recovered. It was Hegel who saw that in modernity "truth" is displaced by what the moderns were calling "reason" and who launched a critique of Enlightenment Reason that finally issues in postmodernity (which was hardly his intention!). Hegel is the first great philosopher of truth after premodernity who returned truth to a place of honor. Hegel criticized the Enlightenment for privileging a one-sided, lifeless, purely formal, ahistorical and abstract *Verstand* which he proposed needed to be integrated into a more full-bodied, concrete, historical and substantial life of the Spirit (*Geist*) and what he was calling reason (*Vernunft*). If in the view I take we have a great deal more to learn about religion from Hegel than from Kant, and from premodernity than from modernity, that is because religion is treated by both as a substantive truth not merely a formal right. In short, premodernity and postmodernity communicate with each other on the question of religion because for both religion is an event of truth, not merely a protected right or a mask worn by ethics.

Hegel thought that the part of religion in which the rationalist philosophers were interested was its least interesting part while they treated the most interesting part of all as off limits, lying across the borders of pure reason on the side of "revelation." They restricted their interest to formal proofs for the existence of God, the immortality of the soul, and the problem of evil. They were interested in proofs, propositions and entities, resulting in a misconception of "God" as a "definite" and therefore finite entity, which contradicted the infinity of God. This resulted in a misconception of religious discourse as a series of representational assertions that pick out such an entity, which is accessible to "reason." These were matters over which reason has competency, whereas the rest of the Christian religion lay off limits, dealing with matters that the unaided light of natural reason could never access. But for Hegel, the latter is precisely the genuinely interesting part of religion. The philosophers left out the substance of Christianity, its *Sache*, its substantial truth. It is precisely in these doctrines, in the content of Revelation, that the truth is revealed, where the truth means the life of the Absolute, which is both substance and subject. In religion the Absolute bears the name of God and in Christianity God is revealed in the fullness of the divine life enunciated by the doctrine of the Trinity, in the tripartite moments of God's life: God's life in itself (the religion of the Father) and God's life as it abandons its transcendence and enters into space and time (the religion of the Son), in the Incarnation (the birth of God), the Crucifixion (the death of God), the Resurrection (the rebirth of God) and finally God's afterlife, the Ascension and sending of the Spirit in and as the people of God. Hegel shocked the theologians with what they mistook as his "pantheism" and he shocked the philosophers by openly defying the categorial boundaries laid down by the Enlightenment between reason and revelation.

Hegel's breakthrough cuts both ways. On the one hand, Hegel was saying that philosophy had everything to learn from religion, which has something to tell us about the truth, because religion embodies the truth and truth assumes the form of religion. Religion incarnates and substantializes the truth of the absolute Spirit for us in a concrete and imaginative mode. He said that religion is the truth, the way the truth achieves *Vorstellung*, which means that it is both the way the absolute embodies itself, setting itself forth (*vor-stellen*) in reality (which is its substance side) and also the way we image and imagine, visualize and envisage, narrate and tell ourselves stories about the absolute (which is its subjective side).[3] Religion is the truth, the absolute truth, in the form of a *Vorstellung*. But of course, on the other hand, Hegel was also saying that there is something in religion to which religion itself has no access, that religion does not quite understand itself, that it requires philosophy to explain religion to itself. Christianity has realized in a religious mode what philosophy alone can see and understand. The Absolute does not belong to another world but becomes the Absolute only by unfolding its life in space and time, by embracing the dialectical movements of history, by passing the test of negativity and becoming what it is in truth in and through its embodiment in the world and its incarnation in humankind. Christianity spells the end of metaphysical dualism.

---

[3] For an outstanding account of *"Vorstellung"* in Hegel, see Catherine Malabou, *The Future of Hegel: Plasticity, Temporality and Dialectic,* trans. Lisabeth During (New York: Routledge, 2005).

This was the Hegel who drove Kierkegaard to an outburst of irony and scorn, of parody and outrage, leading him to quip that it was as if God came into the world in order to arrange a consultation with German metaphysics. This was the Hegel who did not break with the Enlightenment in the sense that he agreed with the Enlightenment that Reason is a system and it encompasses everything, which is what Lyotard called "terror." On this point, I am at best an eccentric Hegelian who has no *Begriff*, no Absolute Spirit. That is, I take the Hegelian point that religion is an irreducible embodiment of the truth and such truth is realized only in the world. But I am in part a Kierkegaardian because I reject the notion that the *Vorstellung* can be monitored from above by absolute knowledge, and that religion is a *Vorstellung* of something to which philosophy holds the key. So I am a heretical Hegelian who lacks absolute knowledge or the absolute Spirit, and a heretical Kierkegaardian without a transcendent eternal God.

But if the *Vorstellung* is not a presentation of the Absolute Spirit, then what is it? To simplify to an extreme I would say it is the presentation of an "event," which means the embodiment of a desire beyond desire, of a hope against hope, of a faith in the impossible. This it does in a multiplicity of ways in a multiplicity of cultural forms of life—it includes but is not confined to what we call "religion"—which differ from each other rather as does one language or culture from another. That means it makes no more sense to ask which religion is the true religion than it does to ask which is the true language, the true form of art, or the one true culture. Consequently, the argument to be made against a modernist view of religion is not to defend its rationality against those who charge it with irrationality. We do not meet the charge of irrationality with the counter-claim that it is rational (a "warranted belief"). It is to argue that it is neither rational nor irrational in the modern sense, that there is a truth in religion—quite analogous to the truth in the work of art, which is its closest ally in this regard—to which Enlightenment rationality has closed itself off.

That means we reject the terms in which Enlightenment has framed religion. Any religion that would emerge as rational in the terms set by Enlightenment reason would be a good deal less than religion. It might be ethics but it would be a lifeless ethics. It would be exactly what Hegel said it is, abstract, formal, and lifeless, because what the Enlightenment calls the light of reason is in the dark when it comes to the substantive or substantial truth of religion (as well as art and ethics), what in German we call its *Sache*. Religious truth is not reducible to a set of propositional assertions which are to be scrutinized in terms of their capacity to pick out facts of the matter to which they refer—no more than is a work of art. Religious truth is not found in having certain information or beliefs that will gain one insight into a supersensible world or a ticket of admission to an afterlife. Religious truth is not a matter of information—as if it reveals certain facts of the matter otherwise unavailable to empirical inquiry or speculative "reason"—but a matter of transformation, with the result that religious truth takes place in and as the truth of a form of life.[4] Religious truth is more a matter of doing than of knowing, as when Kierkegaard said that the name of God is the name of a deed. That means that religious truth flies beneath the radar of both the theism and the atheism of the Enlightenment. Its truth has to do with a more elemental experience that precedes this distinction, one that cannot be held captive either by confessional religion or reductionistic critiques of religion. The debate between "theism" and "atheism" is a futile propositional debate that does not touch upon the events that take place in religion before propositions arrive on the scene. Religious truth is made accessible only by a "repetition" of religion in the garden variety or confessional sense. But Hegel proposed a philosophical repetition of religion in terms of the Spirit which claimed to be omniscient about what is going on in religion. I propose a repetition that confesses its unknowing, a more confessional repetition of religion.

Derrida's repetition of St Augustine

To both make this point and illustrate it, I turn here to the repetition of St Augustine, a paradigmatic premodern figure, made by Jacques Derrida, a paradigmatic postmodern one (even though he would have properly rejected this description) in a text he called "Circumfession." Derrida neither scrutinizes *The Confessions* in search of rationally warranted true beliefs nor mocks Augustine for clinging to irrational superstitions. Instead, he undertakes a "repetition" of the text, a repeat performance, in which he goes very far in reconstructing the scene of the *Confessions*, beginning with

---

[4] Bruno Latour has been saying a number of very sensible things about the distortion of religion by Enlightenment Rationality in "'Thou Shalt Not Take the Lord's Name in Vain'—Being a Sort of Sermon on the Hesitations of Religious Speech," *RES: Anthropology and Aesthetics*, No. 39 (Spring, 2001): 215-234; *On the Modern Cult of Factish Gods*, trans. Catherine Porter and Heather MacLean (Durham: Duke University Press, 2010).

the crucial and elementary point that in this text Augustine is praying.[5] In reading the *Confessions,* it is as if we the readers have come upon a man at prayer whose back is turned to us, who addresses his words—*in litteris,* in writing—to "you" (*te*), "my God." Derrida shows a special interest in Augustine's account of the death of Monica, as his journal is written while monitoring the condition of his own mother, Georgette, who lay dying on the southern coast of France (Nice), even as Monica lay dying in the coastal town of Ostia. Both mothers, worried over their sons (the sons of their tears), had followed the emigration of their sons from the same region of North Africa (ancient Numidia, modern Algeria) to the metropolitan capital of continental Europe (Rome, Paris) in search of a career in the "big Apple." So the analogy is quite nicely rounded out: Augustine/Derrida, Monica/Georgette, Ostia/Nice, and "you" (God/x).

The "x" marks the problem. Augustine is praying to the God revealed in the Jewish and Christian Scriptures, and he can do so in community with his "brothers" in faith, in a book of common prayers handed down by the tradition, and he has some expectation that God is there to hear his prayers and act upon them, albeit in ways too mysterious for him to comprehend. But to whom is Derrida praying since, as he says, he "quite rightly passes for an atheist?"[6] Surely then what Augustine is doing makes sense, even if you do not share his faith, while with Derrida, the whole thing is just a parody, an irreverent bit of impudence from an avant-garde writer who always has one trick or another up his sleeve and a devilish look in his eye. (The best his Enlightenment critics can do with Derrida is to solemnly conclude that his works are irrational, perhaps even "mad," certainly undeserving of an honorary degree at Cambridge). It would appear that Augustine's religion is a true religion, even if you think religion itself is an illusion, but Derrida's is just a ruse.

But why does Derrida say he "quite rightly passes for" an atheist? Why not just come right out with it and admit that he *is* (*je suis, c'est moi*) an atheist? Because he says he does not *know* any such thing and cannot identify himself so thoroughly, so completely.[7] He has an "identity," of

---

[5] Jacques Derrida, "Circumfession: Fifty-nine Periods and Periphrases," in Geoffrey Bennington and Jacques Derrida, *Jacques Derrida*, trans. Geoffrey Bennington (Chicago: University of Chicago Press, 1993).

[6] Ibid, 155.

[7] "Epoche and Faith: An Interview with Jacques Derrida," in *Derrida and Religion: Other Testaments*, ed. Yvonne Sherwood and Kevin Hart (New York: Routledge, 2005), 46–47.

course, which he had repeatedly established before customs officials around the world, but he is not "identical with himself," not a single self-same thing all the way through. There are many voices within him, some believing who contest his unbelief, and some unbelieving who contest his belief, and they give him no rest. His whole life long, he has been asking himself Augustine's question, "What do I love when I love my God?" Notice the compound question, which assumes he loves God, that he loves something under the name of God, something he calls his God, the God of a certain faith and love. He confesses a faith and love in a certain God, albeit not the God of Augustine's faith—still a faith in something, but he knows not what, some *je ne sais quoi*. Notice too the name of this journal, "Circumfession," which repeats both "confession" and "circumcision," the Christian Latin word for *bris* used by the assimilated Algerian Jews. The word emphasizes the cut, including the literal cuts, the bedsores on his mother's body, but it also evokes an opening image of blood running like wine (*cru*), the blood of faith (*croire*), which is meant to signal a kind of ontological cut.[8] He is cut off from any knowledge of God or of what he believes. He is cut off, as he says at the end of the journal, from the truth in the sense of knowing the truth of his love and desire and his God, which is crucial to the form truth takes for him.

Truth for him is found not in the domain of actuality, presence, essence, and identity, but in the open space between what is present and what is coming, a place where the present is exposed to what is 'to come', to what he desires with a desire beyond desire, which is something unforeseeable. Truth thus is not primarily a propositional matter, a property of a proposition, but an experiential one, prepropositional, as Husserl and Heidegger would say, having to do with the in-breaking (*invention*) of the new and unexpected (*tout autre*) upon the settled horizons of the present. Derrida's view of the true as the in-breaking of the wholly other is analogous to Heidegger's notion of the true as an emergence from concealment, of which it is a kind of Jewish and messianic variation or counterpart.[9]

---

[8] "Circumfession," 3–6.
[9] In a general way, my own presentation here of the movement from the experience of truth in Greek and medieval thought, through the rationalism of modernity which reduces truth to a property of propositions, into the experience of the truth of the event, is influenced by the history of truth and the critique of "principle of reason" in modernity found in Heidegger's *The Principle of Reason*, trans. Reginald Lilly (Bloomington: Indiana University Press, 1991). But I have insisted throughout on

Truth takes place—it is an event—not (primarily) in warranted beliefs but in the distance between the present and what is coming (always already concealed) which disrupts the stable body of accumulated belief, which Derrida formulates in terms of the distinction between the possible and the impossible.

"Circumfession" is itself a staging or performance of such an event. It is, for example, quite unforeseen by us, his readers, when we are told that we know nothing of his religion, that he is a man of prayers and tears and that he has been praying all his life. But to whom is he praying? If I knew that, he responds, I would know everything. The name of God is for him the name of the impossible, just as the Scriptures say ("With God, nothing is impossible"), which means that for him to pray is to pry open the possible in search of the possibility of *the* impossible. Prayer takes place in the distance between the possible and the impossible. His is a faith which is all the more faith inasmuch as it confronts the incredible, a hope in which he hopes with a hope against hope, even as he says we are asked to forgive the unforgiveable. Faith and hope and love, forgiveness and hospitality—notice the highly Biblical character of this list—are truly what they are, and are possible at all, only if they are impossible, only if they are directed at what shatters the horizon of possibility and transforms us. That unforeseeable incoming (*invention*) of the unexpected (*tout autre*) is the event. His faith and hope and love are lodged in the event, in events in the plural, which bear many names and have to do with many forms of desire. This is what he calls, in another context and speaking of others than himself, a "religion without religion," a religion that repeats religion without sharing the dogmatic faith or rituals or communities of faith in the confessional religions.[10] It is, I would say, the truth of religion, religious truth, but not in the sense of a true creedal assertion in a confessional religion, and hence not in the sense of *the* true religion. Derrida here touches upon the sort of truth religion is or has, in just the way we would speak of the truth a work of art is or has, the truth that is lived in a form of life, the experience of truth, the truth of experience. Most pointedly of all, this is the truth of the experience of *the* impossible, the in-breaking of something unforeseen.

Derrida's more messianic version of this history, where the focus is not on a blinding manifestation of being but on the hope of the coming of something unforeseeable.

[10] Jacques Derrida, *The Gift of Death*, trans. David Wills (Chicago: University of Chicago Press, 1995), 49.

That is why, at a crucial point, Derrida cites an expression Augustine uses when Augustine speaks of his confessions in terms of "*facere veritatem*,"[11] doing or making (*poiesis*) the truth, as when he makes something by writing his confessions and does something by making a confession.[12] Just so, truth is something to make or do for Derrida, it is a matter of a faith and hope and love of something that cannot be contracted to a "belief" (*croyance*) in something finite, determinate and present. Beliefs have to do with entities and propositions, but faith has always to do with the infinite and pre-propositional, not a transcendent being but the in-finitival, the "to come" which attaches as a coefficient to any name we have for any determinate thing, like "democracy." The work done by the infinity of God in Augustine is done by the in-finitival *à venir* in Derrida. The *true* democracy is something to come, something promised by what we nominate at present with the word democracy—or justice or love or God, etc. As such its truth is steeped in un-truth, in not yet coming, in hovering before us as a risky chance, maybe even a monster. Such truth does not dissolve into Romantic longing for an impossible ideal or hover over us as distant possibility that never arrives, which is a caricature of it. On the contrary, nothing is more demanding than the "to come," which presses with infinite urgency upon the present, burning like a white light that mercilessly exposes the blemishes of the present and makes its transformation in the here and now imperative. Any such "faith" (*foi*) in the "to come" cuts deeper than a particular belief in this or that, even as it cuts deeper than any reason we give for this or this. Such faith is the reason for the reasons we give, the deeper root of both giving reasons (*rationem reddere*) and faith in the narrower sense of belief, the deeper root of the secular and the religious order, the deeper root of calculation, science and ethics, of art and politics. Such faith is the truth of a religion without religion where religion is the stuff of what Augustine called the confessions of our restless heart (*cor inquietum*).[13]

The difference between Augustine and Derrida, then, is not that Augustine practices a true religion while Derrida is trying to pull off a ruse. The difference is that Augustine has a set of proper names to give word to his desire and Derrida's religion sustains a more profound unnameability. Derrida's religion springs from a negative capability, an affirmative capacity

[11] *The Confessions of St. Augustine*, trans. Rex Warner (New York: Penguin Books, 1963) Bk. 10, c. 1, 210. Augustine is glossing John 3:23: "*poion ten aletheian.*"
[12] "Circumfession," 48.
[13] *The Confessions of St. Augustine*, Bk. I, c. 1, 17.

to sustain uncertainty, which make his religion more truly prayerful and confessional, more truly religious and not less, more true to the restlessness of his quasi-Augustinian somewhat atheistic ever restless heart.

Conclusion

Rushing then to a conclusion, let me say this much. (1) Compared to the subtleties of Derrida's reenactment of Augustine's *Confessions*, the project of the Enlightenment—which is to put "religion" on trial by testing whether its faith is made up of "warranted beliefs," failing which it is judged "irrational"—is profoundly misguided and wrong-headed. It asks the wrong question, so that whatever answer it comes up with is irrelevant. It confuses faith with beliefs and pure Reason with good reasons; it is blind to the deeper restlessness which precedes all reasons, and to the deeper experiential deposit of the event which precedes and follows every proposition. (2) The "postmodern" religion of Derrida is a repetition of premodern "wisdom," constituting a more eccentric or decentered or chaosmic wisdom, one that strangely is not immune to a certain moment of madness, to a certain foolishness of *the* impossible.[14] It was a source of some consternation to Augustine that while everyone admits we desire happiness (*beata vita*), we cannot agree on what happiness is. For Derrida, such non-knowing is not a lack but constitutive of happiness. For Derrida, wisdom begins and ends with a confession of our non-knowing which repeats religion not by reproducing the classical beliefs of confessional religion, but by repeating the events that take place in religion, which I am calling here the truth of religion or religious truth.[15]

---

[14] In saying this I am thinking of the foolishness of the logos of the cross in I Cor. 1, where the wisdom of the world, the pride of being, is displaced by the foolishness of *ta me onta*, those whom Derrida calls "rogues," the outsiders, but also the cut in "Circumfession." I would pursue this point by linking the logic of the cut in Derrida's "Circumcision" with the logic of the cross in Paul. The latter has been suggestively analyzed by Stanislas Breton, *A Radical Philosophy of Saint Paul*, trans. Joseph N. Ballan (New York: Columbia University Press, 2011).

[15] My thanks to Marcia Sa Cavalcante Schuback for her insightful comments on the first version of this paper from which I have greatly benefited.

On Enthusiasm

Marcia Sá Cavalcante Schuback

Philosophy not only has a history, it also tells a lot of stories. To tell a story can be said in ancient Greek with the expression *muthon diégesthai*. This expression reminds us, despite all mythology around the meaning of myth, that myth means first of all "story" and hence that philosophy has a lot of myths. One of its myths concerns how philosophy begins. As a way of existing in the knowing of existence, philosophy keeps telling the myth—the story—of its beginning out of admiration and wonder.[1] What kind of admiration and wonder gives birth to philosophy? It is the wonder that *there is being*, that *being is being*, that being is in everything that appears as being something, as being this or that. Out of this admiration and wonder, philosophy begins to ask a kind of question, the question *"ti to on?"* or "what is being?", recalling the famous passage from Aristotle's *Metaphysics*.[2] From out of admiration and wonder, philosophy begins as the question about the meaning of being, searching for grounds, reasons, and principles of all that is, looking for the essence of all beings and of the All of being. This myth about the beginning of philosophical inquiry in wonder tells

[1] "SOCRATES: Surely you're following, Theaetetus; it's my impression at any rate that you're not inexperienced in things of this sort.
THEAETETUS: Yes indeed, by the gods, Socrates, I wonder exceedingly as to why (what) in the world these things are, and sometimes in looking at them I truly get dizzy.
SOCRATES: The reason is, my dear, that, apparently, Theodorus' guess about your nature is not a bad one, for this experience is very much a philosopher's, that of wondering. For nothing else is the beginning (principle) of philosophy than this, and, seemingly, whoever's genealogy it was, that Iris was the offspring of Thaumas (wonder), it's not a bad one." Plato, *Theaetetus*, trans. Seth Bernardette (Chicago: The University of Chicago Press, 1986), 155c–d.
[2] "For men were first led to study philosophy, as indeed they are today, by wonder. Now, he who is perplexed and wonders believes himself to be ignorant.... they took to philosophy to escape ignorance..." Aristotle, *Metaphysics*, trans. A. E. Taylor (Chicago: Open Court, 1907), 982b.

about the ingress of human beings into the realm of the essential and of essences as an admirable and astonishing way of dealing with what is given to human existence and with the human condition.

Heidegger developed a strong interpretation of the origin of philosophy in the wonder about the "fact" that there is being and that being is, claiming that philosophical wonder should be understood as the wonder about the difference between Being and beings. Being is not beings. Being is nothing and no-thing, but is being. The central point of Heidegger's interpretation of philosophical wonder is that wonder about the "ontological difference" between being and beings was forgotten at the very moment of its discovery, and hence that philosophical wonder was at the same time and at once the oblivion of philosophical wonder by means of its trivialization.[3] This view on philosophical wonder as the wonder that forgets its wonder is the point of departure in Heidegger's *Being and Time*. If Plato and Aristotle can be considered the founders of philosophical inquiry, it is because they have seen the ontological difference between being and beings but have nonetheless forgotten it when grounding the meaning of Being as the being of beings, as essence and ground of all beings. With Plato and Aristotle, it became impossible to say that being is being, for the only philosophical phrase became that being is the ground, the reason, or the essence of all beings. Being received the meaning of substance and thinghood, that is, of *what* is. Dislocating the question about the difference between Being and beings to the one about the being of beings, Plato and Aristotle placed philosophy in this very dangerous place of *theoria*, a place without places, where vision detached from beings is required but in which the danger of losing oneself in theories and concepts, in ideas, ideals, and ideologies, in a phantasmagoric *beyond*, is always present. Out of admiration or wonder, philosophy emerges as a "pathos of distance," as Nietzsche phrased it, "the nostalgia for being at home everywhere," to recall Novalis. This nostalgic distance from the world that has defined philosophy is dangerous: by detaching from beings, things and their determinations in order to apprehend and comprehend them under the light of their ground and from

---

[3] Heidegger, *Sein und Zeit*, GA 2 (Frankfurt am Main: Vittorio Klostermann, 1977), § 1. "What these two thinkers (Plato and Aristotle) achieved has been preserved in various distorted and 'camouflaged' forms down to Hegel's *Logic*. And what then was wrested from phenomena by the highest exertion of thought, albeit in fragments and first beginnings, has long since been trivialized." Martin Heidegger, *Being and Time*, trans. Joan Stambaugh (Albany: State University of New York Press, 1996), 1.

where things appear *as* things, beings *as* beings, etcetera, philosophy is thrown into the danger zone of losing itself in formalisms and formalizations, remaining beyond the world and life. The danger of philosophical vision—called *theoria* by the Greeks—is the danger of losing oneself either in a place beyond beings and things or in the reduction of Being to beings and things. Considering how the Greeks were able to wonder and admire the fact that Being is, only because they had "seen" the difference between Being and beings while losing this vision in a determination of the Being of beings, Heidegger suggested that the condition for envisioning this difference is losing it. In other words, it is in losing Being in beings—that is, understanding Being as the Being of beings, as essence, ground and truth— that the difference between Being and beings appears. The difficulty in understanding these expressions, such as the giving itself withdrawing itself, the appearing while dis-appearing of Being and of all this obscure Heideggerian jargon lies not so much in its paradoxical and oxymoronic formulation but in the tacit but nonetheless eloquent admission that philosophy begins in a wonder that loses and forgets itself, and hence in an fundamental experience of loss, oblivion and self-distancing that seems very close to that which this same philosophical tradition has defined as its most extreme opposite, namely, madness.

The strange distance between Being and beings that oscillates between a distant beyond and a beyond-the-beyond appears today more than ever as a haunting question pervading our multiple questions. Thus today, we experience globally the excess of the oblivion of the meaning of being, what in Heidegger's terms means the oblivion of the difference between being and beings, in our world of omni-reification and "uni-dimensionalization"[4] of the meaning of being as pure resource. Today the oblivion of the difference between being and being has been itself forgotten. If there is no place and time for wonder and admiration today and above all in today's philosophy, the impossibility to wonder and admire that *Being is*, is itself, however, full of wonder. And further, insofar as philosophical wonder is wonder of and from within the vision of a distance between being and beings, at stake today is the strange distance of philosophical distance. The question about wonder and admiration as the *pathos* in which philosophy can emerge should therefore be discussed as a question about the distance of phil-

---

[4] I am using this term under the inspiration of Herbert Marcuse's influential book from 1964, *One-Dimensional Man* (London and New York: Routledge, 1991).

osophical distance, as the question about what Nietzsche called the *"pathos of distance,"*[5] of this strange distance that separates and unites "at once" Being and beings, man and world, the human and the human. I would like to suggest that at stake here is not only the "pathos of distance," but distance as pathos, as *sensation*. And further, the question about the meaning or *sense* of Being should be slightly rephrased as a question about the *sensation* of being. This sensation has nothing to do with sensitiveness, thus here still there is *nothing* that is an object of sensation, insofar as Being is not a being, but is simply being. Being is being and a being. This sensation is neither referring to anything beyond here and now nor to any here or there, neither to transcendence nor to immanence, being from where these differences and their differends can differentiate and expose themselves as such. The question is, moreover, if wonder is the pathos in which distance as pathos, as sensation, can be sensed?

This same Greek philosophy that seems to have met the distance or difference between Being and beings while misunderstanding it as the Being of beings has described something close to this sensation of distance, of distance as sensation of being, when using the term *enthusiasm*. "Enthusiasm" was said in the Greek language to mean the sensation of a distance that both unites and separates at once. Considering that philosophical wonder, since its first enunciations in Greek philosophy, is related to the philosophical "pathos of distance," enthusiasm can be viewed as more related to distance as pathos. The tension between these two terms can be found already in Plato. This difference can be investigated through the uses he makes of the words *thaumazein*, for instance in the dialogue *Theaetetus*, and *enthousiázo* or *enthousiasmós*, for example in the dialogue *Ion*. To a certain extent, "to wonder"—*thaumazein*—appears in Plato as something more proper to philosophers, those who deal with ideas, whereas enthusiasm, *enthousiasmós* as something more due to poets, those who deal with sensations. There are still other words in the Platonic lexicon that express this realm of "out of mind," as for instance the terms *manteia, mantis* and *thauma* which evoke prophets and oracles, building a vocabulary closest to

---

[5] Friedrich Nietzsche, *Zur Genealogie der Moral. Kritische Studienausgabe*, vol. 5 (Berlin: de Gruyter, 1988), 259.

magic or practices of consecration.[6] As in an impressionist painting, it appears here to be a sketch of different sensibilities to deal with the gaze which detaches from the house of beings and oscillates at the edge of the world. In the *Ion*, the experience of enthusiasm is the one of coming into (*en*) radical otherness (*theos*, the divine). The main question is what it means to come into radical otherness, and which kind of distance is at stake in this coming into divine otherness and into the otherness of the divine. In order to deepen this question proposed by Plato, I would like to discuss briefly some thoughts of the German phenomenologist Eugen Fink, presented in a text called *Vom Wesen des Enthusiasmus*,[7] read as lecture in February 1940 and repeated during summer 1946.

According to Fink, enthusiasm terms a sensibility in which a distance of the world and being brings human existence to a closer intimacy to being and the world. In this sense, enthusiasm is conserved by Fink as the source for different forms of what he called "enthusiastic existence." These different forms of "enthusiastic existences" correspond to philosophy, art and religion. These three forms of enthusiastic existence derive from one and the same source, the source of the divine or, to say it better, they have the divine as source, named by the Greeks with the term *to theion*. *To theion*, the divine, such as is evoked in the Eleusinian Mysteries, exposes itself in the triple way of *the true, the beautiful,* and *the sacred.* The point of departure for Fink's thoughts is that enthusiasm brings a revelation into the space of the mystical archaic revelation ("Der Enthusiasmus bringt eine Offenbarung im Raume der mystischen Ur-Offenbarung").[8] Philosophy, art and religion—these three ways of enthusiastic existence—correspond, in Fink's view, to the true, the beautiful and the sacred, to the three ways the divine (*to theion*) is immemorially and archaically revealed. A central aspect in Fink's discussions is that these three enthusiastic existences expose human existence as capable of and longing for detachment from beings and things, although not because something more transcendent and bigger is lacking. Fink insists that "motivations *ab inferiori* (of that kind) are impossible in the realm of the essential."[9] It is because of neither hunger nor

---

[6] For a study on this platonic vocabulary and its philosophical dimensions, see John Sallis, "A Wonder That One Could Never Aspire to Surpass," in *The Path of Archaic Thinking*, ed. Kenneth Maly (Albany: State University of New York Press, 1995).

[7] Eugen Fink, *Vom Wesen des Enthusiasmus* (Freiburg: Verlag Dr. Hans V. Chamier, 1947).

[8] Ibid, 18.

[9] Ibid, 21.

thirst, neither a need for trust nor a need for assuring oneself before the uncertain that existence becomes enthusiastic. Fink considers that in fact it is not human existence that becomes enthusiastic, but it is enthusiasm that appropriates human existence, conducting it beyond itself and not towards something else which lies beyond. Fink understands enthusiasm as a "revelation," so to speak, of what Heidegger in *Being and Time* called the "ek-static temporality"[10] of human existence, of being-in-the-world, as a movement of self-transcendence or of self-overcoming (*Selbst-Überwindung*). Enthusiasm is treated here as a kind of phenomenology of being human, a way of being in itself beyond and outside itself. For Fink, this outside and beyond itself is however inside the *theion*, inside the sacred, the beautiful and the true of the divine source of Being. Despite the metaphysical tonality of Fink's discussions, we can here follow a thought on enthusiasm as the experience of being touched by the *theion*, by the divine as source, in which human existence exposes itself as being in itself outside and beyond itself, what he formulates as "the enthusiastic being out of him/herself of the human" ("das enthusiastische Außersichsein des Menschen").[11] Enthusiasm does not mean "out of mind" but "being as an out of him/herself." In this sense, human being is neither a being in search for a transcendent realm beyond the world nor him/herself as a transcendent realm in relation to nature: human being is neither nature plus something nor God minus something. Enthusiasm shows how human being is itself a beyond, which in Latin is said with the prefix *trans*, but that should be understood rather as a "*trance*," being him/herself a lack of him/herself.

Although enthusiasm reveals, as Fink insists, the ek-static structure of human existence as a structure of disquiet and self-transcendence, where the possibility to detach from beings and things is related to the very "constitution" of human existence as being itself a lack of being, as being in itself out and beyond itself, Fink's discussions in this text remain somehow insensitive to the very *experience* of enthusiasm, to the way enthusiasm raves and enthuses, to how enthusiasm is conjugated as a verb, so to speak. A more detailed description of the way one becomes enthusiastic can be found indeed in Plato, in the dialogue *Ion*, considered by many as a minor

[10] Heidegger, *Being and Time*, § 65.
[11] Fink, *Vom Wesen des Enthusiasmus*, 27.

dialogue, and even as the "dialogue of an amateur" (Wilamowitz).[12] In this dialogue, we can find a proto-phenomenology of enthusiasm. If a difference between philosophical wonder and enthusiasm is to be found in Plato's thought, and if the great antagonist of philosophy seems to be the poet, in the *Ion* enthusiasm is not described as poetic. Enthusiasm is here barred from the poet, and appears as belonging instead to the rhapsodist. Ion received the prize for being the best one reciting the poems by Homer and not poetry in general or any other poet. He was praised for doing this because of neither technique nor science, but enthusiasm. Enthusiasm is defined from the beginning as other than technique or science. Indeed, what is in question here is the capacity neither to repeat nor to remake the other's words: at stake is how to *transmit*—not to transmit contents, but to transmit transmission, what is nothing more than the being-touched. At stake in this dialogue is the transmission of being touched. What touches is the being-touched. It is not *Ion* that touches us. Ion is himself touched by the being-touched of the poet by divine forces, *theia dynamis*. What touches is the being-touched by the being-touched of *Ion* by the being-touched of the poet in a chain of rings binding chains of rings. To describe this experience, Plato compares it, in the mouth of Socrates, to a stone from Heracleia called by Euripides "magnetic." Touching-being-touched is magnetism, the force transmitted through rings attracting rings like lovers in love. Here, it is enthusiasm that becomes enthusiastic and not something outside that provokes enthusiasm in the sense of a body that would receive external stimuli. The description proposed by Fink of a being in itself outside and beyond itself seems not enough to describe this magnetic chain of enthusiasm, insofar as it departs from the geometry of inside/outside and outside/inside. At stake is rather a touching-being touched, a passive activity and active passivity in which it is no longer possible to differentiate who touches and who is touched, although this in-differentiation never erases the difference. In the proximity of the touching the distance between who touches and the touched, the touching and the being-touched does not disappear; on the contrary, this distance appears first in its proximity. The question is not being inside the divine, in the *theion*, but the divine of enthusiasm, the divine as enthusiasm. In his commentary on Plato's *Ion*, Jean-Luc Nancy

---

[12] Cited in Joachim Ritter, *Vorlesungen zur philosophischen Ästhetik*, ed. Ulrich von Bülow and Mark Schweda (Göttingen: Wallstein-Verlag, 2012), 101. See also Ritter's discussion of Plato's *Ion* and the concept of enthusiasm in this same book.

brings to clarity how, in this Platonic dialogue, it is the divine, the *to theion*, that is enthusiasm and hence what is in itself outside and beyond itself.[13]

The Greek word *enthousiasmos* means literally inside, within the divine, to *theion*. As sensation of touching by being touched, enthusiasm says something of being-in-the-divine. In Plato, its magnetic nature wants to indicate that this inside-ness or within-ness (the divine) is not the same as interiority, and thus the *theion* is not exterior to it. Indeed, the magnetic transmission proper to this sensation of a touching-being touched indicates the strange experience of an "inside" that is neither interior nor exterior, nor inside nor outside, nor immanence nor transcendence. Hölderlin had a word for it. He said: *Innigkeit*, a word that could be translated, in a tentative way, as either intense intimacy or intimate intensity. It is neither interiority nor promiscuity. As a matter of fact, we could claim that Hölderlin was the poet that tried to say—what in poetry means to think—up to its extreme possibility this being-in-the-divine, being-in-*tô-theiô*—that is, enthusiasm. He described it as an *Empfindung*, a sensation, indeed as a "beautiful, sacred and divine sensation" and not as a sensation of beauty, of the sacred, of the divine. In Hölderlin's essay "Über die Verfahrungsweise des poetischen Geistes,"[14] he calls this "beautiful, sacred and divine sensation" *transcendental sensation*.[15] It should not be understood as a means to transport the finite into the infinite, human to god, but to expose how existence is infinitely finite within the finitely infinite, the *to theion*. Hölderlin describes "transcendental sensation" neither as consciousness nor as mere longing, and neither as mere harmony nor as intellectual intuition, and even less as mere reflection, but "all that at once."[16] The beautiful, sacred, and divine "transcendental sensation" exposes the ecstatic enthusiastic way of being all that at once, an outside inside the outside of the divine—in which human existence discovers, as Hölderlin says, its destiny. "Transcendental sensation" shows that the magnetic rings of its touching-being touched do not carry finite, human (too human) existence to any beyond but rather and precisely the contrary, to the very close, neither there nor here, of a nearness to where existence always exists, to this ugly and beautiful, profane and

---

[13] Jean-Luc Nancy, *Le Partage des voix* (Paris: Galilée, 1982).

[14] Friedrich Hölderlin, "Über die Verfahrungsweise des poetischen Geistes," *Sämtliche Werke*, vol. 4, (Stuttgart: W. Kohlhammer, 1961), 241–266.

[15] For a discussion of transcendental sensation in Hölderlin, see Jean-François Courtine, "La sensation transcendentale," in Jean-Christophe Goddard (ed.), *Le transcendental et le spéculatif dans l'Idéalisme Allemand* (Paris: Vrin, 1999), 97–114.

[16] Friedrich Hölderlin, "Über die Verfahrungsweise des poetischen Geistes."

sacred placeless place of *existing*. Enthusiasm brings existence to its *existing*, to its gerundive way, in which the here is already a little bit there—and hence neither here nor there but, nearby, "*auprès de*," to say it using a French expression.

Following this path of thought, enthusiasm can be understood anew as the "transcendental sensation" of a touching-being touched that exposes existence as existing and, as such, as a strange distant nearness or near distance to itself. This redefinition of enthusiasm has existential dimensions, politically and philosophically. We can find a contribution to the existential political dimension of an understanding of enthusiasm as transcendental sensation in Jean-François Lyotard's discussions on enthusiasm as a "strong" sense of the sublime.[17] In line with Kant's discussions on the sublime nature of enthusiasm as "idea of the Good with Affect" ("Idee des Guten mit Affekt"),[18] Lyotard claims that, much more than an aesthetic feeling, enthusiasm presents the form to political judgments "rendered not by active participants in historical events but by those who witness them from afar." Enthusiasm renders distance a sensibility and hence a privileged proximity that enables true engagement. This would displace modern discussions on the essence of enthusiasm as prefiguration of fanaticism or superstition and opposed to rationality and hence to philosophy. In sublime enthusiasm, the pathos of distance reveals how distance is itself *pathos*, a feeling for the other and others. In this sense, it could be said, in extension to Lyotard's thoughts, that magnetic transmission can provide a description of political responsibility at stake in the very *sensation* of what has happened before and is happening in front of us, in the very *sensation* (or magnetic transmission) of what has been thought and said—a sensation that is nothing but distance as sensation. In Lyotard's proposal to consider enthusiasm as a model for political judgment, the pathos of distance gains a value of intensity that allows judgment and hence politics to remain "within the boundaries of mere reason."

Enthusiasm as "transcendental sensation" of a touching-being touched can be however developed in a further political sense. A possible development of this thought can be found in Didi-Huberman's discussions about

---

[17] Jean-François Lyotard, *L'Enthousiasme: La critique kantienne de l'histoire* (Paris: Galilée, 1986).
[18] Immanuel Kant, *Kritik der Urteilskraft* (Berlin: Akademie Verlag, 2008), § 29.

representable and imaginary people.[19] His thoughts on the image and imaginary are today very influential in contemporary aesthetics and history of art. His main concern is to show how aesthetics has to do with "rendering sensible" rather than with "making sense," and hence with the necessity of a transformation of sensibility rather than of mentality. Or to put it more simply: for him, mentality or thought can only be transformed from out of a transformation of sensibility. This appears more and more clearly today, when the very notion of "people" has to include what Pierre Rosanvallon, historian of contemporary politics at the Collège de France, called *peuple-émotion*, "people-emotion," different from a people's opinion, and people as a nation.[20] Didi-Huberman develops this notion of people-emotion in relation to mass manifestations as in places like Turkey or Brazil, where "the people" is rather a common emotion that brings to words, songs, gestures, and signs a long history of the oppressed, the memory of the nameless, what Hannah Arendt called "hidden tradition," where history appears to be written not merely by human actions but by passions and emotions experienced by a people through history. At stake are the *thymic moments*, an expression that Didi-Huberman borrows from Ludwig Binswanger: the events of the sensible that render senses and non-senses sensible. For Didi-Huberman, these events of the sensible make senses and non-senses sensible insofar as they present a potential of "reading-ness"—of *Lesbarkeit*—on another basis than mere intelligibility. "*Émus*," moved by the rendering sensible—existence is caught in emotion and thoughts begin to move. We could say, in a very concise way that Didi-Huberman's thoughts on making sense and rendering sensible rephrases the question about enthusiasm in terms of emotion, which makes accessible through senses what hardly makes sense to senses.

Moreover, the existential philosophical dimension of the redefinition of enthusiasm as "transcendental sensation" urges a re-discussion about the meaning of the transcendental itself and together with it, a re-discussion about the meaning of the *theion*, the "divine." As touching-being touched, "transcendental sensation," enthusiasm reveals the "transcendental" as the place we *already* are and not as any place beyond. It reveals the distant near-

---

[19] Georges Didi-Huberman, "Rendre sensible," in Alain Badiou, Pierre Bourdieu, Judith Butler, Georges Didi-Huberman, Sadri Khiari, and Jacques Rancière, *Qu'est-ce qu'un peuple?* (Paris: La Fabrique, 2013).
[20] Pierre Rosanvallon, *Le Peuple introuvable: Histoire de la représentation démocratique en France* (Paris: Gallimard, 2002).

ness or near distance of the already-being of being, of the already-existing of existence, its gerundivity. The is-being of being, the gerundivity of being exposes being as a distance from itself that is nothing but intimate proximity, an "auprès-de," a nearby-ness. This intimate proximity (or distance that is nothing but sensation) cannot be experienced more radically than as the intimate proximity of life and death that gives itself in the abyssal difference of life and death. Enthusiasm is the transcendental sensation of touching-being touched by the being-touched as life and death touch each other being touched by each other. Because the intimate proximity of life and death is the only place in which we are—for where else could we exist if not in this trembling identity appearing in its abyssal difference?—transcendental sensation, or enthusiasm, does not move existence to any beyond, either beyond the world or any world beyond. It moves existence to existing, to the placeless place of the intimate proximity of life and death, to their approximating distance and distancing approximation. This sensation is transcendental because it is the touching-being touched by the being touched by this strange and mysterious identity of life and death in their abyssal difference. Maybe this is what the Greeks called *to theion*, and that we could translate with the sacred. Enthusiasm would be then the transcendental sensation of not being able to step beyond this mysterious place of existing and neither of stepping into it; thus *existing*, existence has no other place and time to exist than the touching-being touched by the abyssal identity and difference of life and death. Maybe here it becomes possible to think from within the sensation of being and thereby to ask about the meaning of philosophy as a rendering of the sensation of being to make sense.

Divine Frenzy and the Poetics of Madness

Anders Lindström

In Plato's *Ion* Socrates depicts a magnetic stone to describe how the force from this source not only can attract rings of iron, but also induce these rings with the power to attract other rings. In ring after ring the magnetic force runs, as they are suspended one from another, but every ring in this chain depends for this power (*dunamis*) upon the one original stone (533d-e). As an analogy Socrates displays the divine inspiration of the poets:

> In the same manner also the Muse inspires men [*entheous...poiei*] herself, and then by means of these inspired persons [*tôn entheôn toutôn*] the inspiration spreads to others [*allôn enthousiazontôn*], and holds them in a connected chain. For all the good epic poets utter all those fine poems not from art [*ek technês*], but as inspired and possessed [*entheoi ontes kai katechomenoi*] (533e).[1]

It is not by an art (*technê*) the poets compose, but by divine dispensation. The fine poems, Socrates stresses, are "the works of gods; and the poets are merely the interpreters of the gods" (*hermenês ... tôn theôn*) (534e). Enthused by the Muse the poets interpret the divine messages "as each is possessed by one of the heavenly powers" (*katechomenoi ex hotou an hekastos katechêtai*) (534e). The rhapsodes, forging the next ring in this chain, are in turn interpreters of the poets' work. They are, Socrates suggests, "interpreters of interpreters" (*hermêneôn hermênês*) (535a) and their audience—who are yet another step removed from the divine origin—will

---

[1] Plato, *Ion*, trans. W. R. M. Lamb (Cambridge: Harvard University Press, The Loeb Classical Library, 2001), 421. Through the text I will use the standard Loeb editions for the translations of Plato, but insert the Greek text in order to emphasize particular terms or to accentuate a divergence from the Greek text in the translation.

be, as Socrates resolves the analogy of the argument, an even more distant ring in this chain of divinely enthused people.[2]

What here could be depicted as a hermeneutics of negativity, a de-magnetizing (from a historical perspective) where the interpreter is con-tinuously moving further from the source, certainly raises valid questions from within a hermeneutical heritage;[3] but the critical potential of the argu-ment might be more interesting to decode in another direction: towards philosophy's own pre-history and what Socrates in the *Republic* referred to as "the ancient quarrel between poetry and philosophy" (*palaia … diaphora philosophiai te kai poiêtikêi*) (607b).[4] At a first glance this quarrel could of course be dismissed as "not as old as Plato himself would like to think"[5]—and in turn unquestionably silenced from our viewpoint on the eve of Platonism—but it is arguably more than this relatively short period of, say, 150 years (a history of philosophy starting with Thales) that the argument gravitates towards. What is actually at stake rather seems to be connected to a specific movement within philosophy itself—a movement, one could argue, from mythemes to philosophemes[6]—confirmed and arrested through the banishment of all poets from the *Republic*. Plato's insistence on cleansing the *polis* of poetic activity appears to be an attempt to finalize this old quarrel, but the origins of this struggle are not really discernable through the arguments given by Plato himself. And maybe he has good reasons.

In Plato's writings one can trace a variety of historical threads, drama-turgically and hierarchically organized, apparently in an order to rationalize the history of philosophy itself (in a direction towards Plato's own philosophical position), but the origins of these threads seem to be con-cealed. Or lost. Or maybe, if we pull those strings once more, in an attempt to undo some of the historical knots—suspiciously dramatized as they ap-pear (and possibly so by Plato as the master puppeteer)—in the effort to

---

[2] *Plato on Poetry*, ed. Penelope Murray (Cambridge: Cambridge University Press, 1996), 8.

[3] For a different take on the passage from the *Ion* (533–35), see for example Jean-Luc Nancy, "Sharing Voices," in Gayle L. Ormiston and Alan D. Schrift (eds.), *Transforming the Hermeneutic Context* (Albany: State University of New York Press, 1990), 211–259.

[4] Plato, *Republic*, trans. Paul Shorey (Cambridge: Harvard University Press, The Loeb Classical Library, 1969).

[5] *Plato on Poetry*, 18.

[6] "That is to say, of a history—or rather, of History—which has been produced in its entirety in the *philosophical* difference between *mythos* and *logos*, blindly sinking down into that difference as the natural obviousness of its own element." Jacques Derrida, "Plato's Pharmacy," in Derrida, *Dissemination*, trans. Barbara Johnson (Chicago: Con-tinuum Books, 2004), 91. Cf. 77, 82, 135 & 165.

unravel an origin, we just might stumble over a drama that could be considered the first cover-up story in the history of Western thought.[7]

To Plato "the ancient quarrel" is vital, I would argue, in philosophy's struggle to consolidate its own concepts—a demarcation between mytheme and philosopheme, resulting in a hierarchical structure of oppositions (and Plato's own myths having a core of *logos*)[8]—but that is a gesture which also polarizes the thought of philosophy within the history of philosophy itself (most prominent in Plato's take on Heraclitus and Parmenides). This division also resonates in the art of the tragedians—Euripides being a close associate of Socrates[9]—as tragedy becomes intertwined with the rise of sophistry in Athens.

At the core of "the ancient quarrel" we find the original division between *mythos* and *logos*, and keeping that in mind one could argue that early Greek thinking is articulated in a movement from mythemes to philosophemes, but as the tragedians (through a mythological past not separable from the writings of history) are reaching out to a possible origin, both *mythos* and *logos* become a prerequisite for their art. Plato, on the other hand (in his efforts against the spread of Sophistic ideas in classical Athens) discovers a play of differences, traceable to this specific division, which he tries to dominate and eventually has to arrest.[10]

Regardless whether it is possible to localize *the* origin of "the ancient quarrel," the movement generated—and the activity that has sprung from this movement—is without doubt injected with a most potent substance that, as it indefinitely exceeds its own bounds, harbors its own anti-substance. Perhaps the effort to conceal, to cover up the origins of philosophy itself, is connected to those flowing liquids of indefinite excess: to that divine dispensation of early Greek thought, fueled with fluids of divine frenzy, indefinitely repeating its other, as they run through both tragedy and philosophy.

---

[7] Cf. "Plato's Pharmacy," 89. Threads, in time, *following* Plato, dramatized into a family scene: "'Platonism' is both the general *rehearsal* of this family scene and the most powerful effort to master it, to prevent anyone's ever hearing of it, to conceal it by drawing the curtains over the dawning of the West." (165)

[8] Cf. "Plato's Pharmacy," 90.

[9] Friedrich Nietzsche reminds us: "In a certain sense Euripides, too, was merely a mask; the deity who spoke out of him was not Dionysus, nor Apollo, but an altogether newborn daemon called *Socrates*. This is the new opposition: the Dionysiac versus the Socratic, and the work of art that once was Greek tragedy was destroyed by it." *The Birth of Tragedy*, trans. Ronald Speirs (Cambridge: Cambridge University Press, 2008), 60.

[10] Cf. "Plato's Pharmacy," 130.

By the grace of madness

Returning to Plato's *Ion*, we note that Socrates renders Homer as "the best and divinest [*theiotatôi*] poet of all" (530b) and to apprehend "his thoughts and not merely his words, is a matter for envy" (530c). What is here at stake is, of course, the rhapsode's ability to understand what the poet says—"the rhapsode ought to make himself an interpreter [*hermênea*] of the poet's thought…" (530c). On the other hand, the poets—"inspired and possessed" (*entheoi ontes kai katechomenoi*) as they are (533e)—compare to bacchants (*bakchai*) under possession (*bakcheuousi kai katechomenoi*) (534a). Bacchants, maenads stirred by Dionysus into an orgiastic frenzy, will prove vital in Socrates line of argumentation.

Even if the *Ion* primarily demonstrates Plato's take on the rhapsodes, the dialogue is decisive to the treatment of the poets in the *Republic*: "For the poets tell us, I believe, that the songs they bring us are the sweets they cull from honey-dropping founts in certain gardens and glades of the Muses—like the bees, and winging the air as they do. And what they tell is true" (*Ion* 534a–b). The finest poems tell the truth, but the poet himself is unaware of, or incapable to determine, what is true or not in his poetry: "For a poet is a light and winged and sacred thing, and is unable ever to indite until he has been inspired and put out of his senses, and his mind is no longer in him" (*entheos … kai ekphrôn kai ho nous mêketi en autôi enêi*) (*Ion* 534b). The poet is put out of his senses and if he would try to compose when still in his mind, he would prove Socrates' point as "powerless to indite a verse or chant an oracle [*chrêsmôidein*]" (*Ion* 534b).

To Socrates, as we recall, this makes it evident that "it is not by art [*technêi*] that they compose and utter so many fine things" since "each is able only to compose that which the Muse has stirred him" (*Ion* 534c). The reason is that the god "takes away the mind [*ton noun*] of these men and uses them as his ministers, just as he does soothsayers and godly seers [*chrêsmôidois kai … mantesi … theiois*]" (*Ion* 534c). In other words, the poet not only compares to bacchants, but also to soothsayers and seers "in order that we who hear them may know that it is not they who utter these words of great price, when they are out of their wits [*hois nous mê parestin*], but that it is the god himself who speaks and addresses us through them" (*Ion* 534d).

Poetry and prophecy are connected, and so is poetry to flowing liquids: "as the bacchants [*bakchai*] are possessed, and not in their senses [*katechomenoi emphrones de ousai ou*], when they draw honey and milk from the rivers" (*Ion* 534a). Socrates also emphasized how the poets bring us "the sweets they cull from honey-dropping founts" (*Ion* 535a) and in the *Laws* Plato claims that there is an "old story [*palaios muthos*] ... that when a poet sits on the tripod of the Muses, he is not in his right mind [*ouk emphrôn*], but like a spring lets whatever is at hand flow forth" (719c).[11] The poet is like a spring that "lets whatever is at hand flow forth" and in this state, fueled by the flowing liquids of madness, he is not able to crystalize what is good and what is bad, what is true and what is false: "Since his skill is that of imitation he is often forced to contradict himself, when he represents contrasting characters, and he does not know whose words are true" (719c).[12]

The poet, even though he actually speaks the truth, cannot isolate the true from the false, since his mind has been taken away, and he is, just like a soothsayer and a godly seer, a minister for a particular god. If the poet cannot isolate the true from the false, then poetry becomes a key element in that play of differences Plato has to stop. This play of differences is demonstrated in a well-known passage from the *Phaedrus*—as Plato tries to dominate it through a myth of his own[13]—but it is also in the *Phaedrus* we find Plato's most celebrated discussion of madness.

In the *Phaedrus* we are confronted with two kinds of madness: "one arising from human diseases, and the other from a divine release from the customary habits" (265a). Earlier in the dialogue Socrates describes how "madness [*mania*], which comes from god, is superior to sanity [*sôphrosunê*], which is of human origin" (244d).[14] In this double bind the superior madness is connected to the divine, to the very ability to transcend a rational order, and Socrates discerns "four divisions of the divine madness, ascribing them to four gods" (265b) in "saying that prophecy [*mantikên*

---

[11] Plato, *Laws*, trans. R. G. Bury (Cambridge: Harvard University Press, The Loeb Classical Library, 1967).

[12] *Plato on Poetry*, 12.

[13] Theuth—father of written letters (*patêr ôn grammatôn*), but also god of medicine—presents the art of writing as a *pharmakon* to the Egyptian king Thamus: "Here, O King, says Theuth, is a discipline [*mathêma*] that will make the Egyptians wiser [*sophôterous*] and will improve their memories [*mnêmonikôterous*]: both memory [*mnêmê*] and instruction [*sophia*] have found their remedy [*pharmakon*]." (*Phaedrus* 274e) The King answers that it is not a remedy for memory, but for reminding (*oukoun mnêmes, alla hupomnêseôs, pharmakon hêures*) that Theuth has discovered. It only gives a semblance (*doxa*) of wisdom (*sophia*), not truth (*alêtheia*), which in the long run will fill men with the conceit of wisdom (*doxosophoi*), not true wisdom. See Derrida, "Plato's Pharmacy," for an extensive elaboration on the myth of Theuth.

[14] Plato, *Phaedrus*, trans. Harold N. Fowler (Cambridge: Harvard University Press, The Loeb Classical Library, 1925).

epipnoian] was inspired by Apollo, the mystic [*telestikên*] madness by Dionysus, the poetic [*poiêtiken*] by the Muses, and the madness of love [*erotikên manian*], inspired by Aphrodite and Eros" (265c).

Socrates points out that "the greatest of blessings come to us through madness" (*dia manias*), but it is a madness that has to be "sent as a gift of the gods" (244a). He accentuates how the prophetess at Delphi and the priestesses at Dodona as "mad [*maneisai*] have conferred many splendid benefits upon Greece [...] but few or none when they have been in their right minds [*sôphronousai*]" (244b); and he calls attention to how "those men of old who invented names thought that madness [*manian*] was neither shameful nor disgraceful" (244b), since they "connected the very word mania with the noblest of arts, that which foretells the future, by calling it the manic art" (244c).

As we recall, Socrates ascribes the mystic madness to Dionysus, but it is a kind of inspiration that also seems to magnetize the poetic madness. The "third kind of possession and madness [*katokôchê te kai mania*] comes from the Muses" (245a) and it "takes hold upon a gentle and pure soul, arouses it and inspires it [*egeirousa kai ekbakcheuousa*] to songs and other poetry" (245a). The pure soul is aroused, stirred into a bacchic frenzy and, Socrates concludes, "he who without the divine madness comes to the doors of the Muses [i.e. he who without the madness of the Muses (*aneu manias Mousôn*) comes to the doors of poetry], confident that he will be a good poet by art [*ek technês*], meets with no success [i.e. will remain uninitiated (*atelês*)], and the poetry of the sane man [*tou sôphronountos*] vanishes into nothingness before that of the inspired madmen [*tôn mainomenôn*]" (245a).

Socrates stresses that "our proof will not be believed by the merely clever, but will be accepted by the truly wise [*deinoîs men apistos, sofoîs de pistê*]" (245c). Only the philosophers, "the truly wise" (*sofoîs*), will be able to follow Socrates line of argumentation: "First, then, we must learn the truth about the soul divine and human by observing how it acts and is acted upon. And the beginning of our proof is as follows: Every soul is immortal" (245c). We have to suspend Socrates' thoughts on the immortal soul for a while, but still must keep in mind a possible connection to the mystic madness of Dionysus as now, in order to confront the divine dispensation of tragedy, we enter his revels in the city of Thebes.

In the presence of divinity

Euripides' *Bacchae*—"the great parousia in the city of Thebes"[15]—reveals Dionysus as the *present* god: "I have come, the son of Zeus, to this land of the Thebans, I, Dionysus, whom once Cadmus' daughter bore, Semele, brought to childbed by lightning-carried fire" (1–4).[16]

The return of Dionysus "to this land of the Hellenes" (20)—for the first time since his birth through "lightning-carried fire"—is, I would argue, Euripides' take on the *original* Bacchanal.[17] A dramatization of the violent origin of what later came to be a religious revelry in the honor of Dionysus—artistically fulfilled in the art of the tragedians—as Euripides displays the genealogy of the tragic.

Dionysus enters Thebes in the guise of a human—"changed to mortal appearance" (53)—to encounter Pentheus, ruler of Thebes, and to prove himself a god and the rightful son of Zeus (42, 47): "For this land must learn to the full, even against its will, that it is uninitiated in my bacchic rites [*ateleston ousan tôn emôn bakcheumatôn*]; and I must speak in defence of my mother Semele by appearing to mortals as the god she bore to Zeus" (39–42). Determined to punish the citizens for denying his divine origin and not participating in his rituals, the women—"stricken in their wits" (33)—have been stung in madness (*maniais*) from their homes (32). Carrying the signs of ritual they rejoice in Dionysus' wild dances on the slopes of Mount Cithaeron, as he himself, within the walls of the *polis*, initiates a divine warfare (*theomachei*) (45).

In both the *Ion* and the *Phaedrus*, we recall, Socrates elaborated on madness and prophecy, and the connection between the two is also made by the blind Teiresias in the *Bacchae*: "He is a prophet [*mantis*], too, this deity; since that which is bacchic and that which is manic possesses great mantic powers [*to gar bakcheusimon kai to maniôdes mantikên pollên echei*]; for whenever the god enters the body in full spate [*polus*] he makes those who are maddened [*tous memênotas*] tell the future" (298–301). Teiresias, himself a godly seer, reveals the nature of Dionysus' epiphanics in the

---

[15] Marcel Detienne, *Dionysos at Large*, trans. Arthur Goldhammer (Cambridge: Harvard University Press, 1989), 7.

[16] *The Bacchae by Euripides: A Translation with Commentary by G.S. Kirk* (New Jersey: Prentice-Hall, 1970).

[17] Cf. Richard Seaford, *Dionysos* (New York: Routledge, 2006), 33f, 117. René Girard, *Violence and the Sacred*, trans. Patrick Gregory (Baltimore: The John Hopkins University Press, 1979), 127.

ecstatic, bacchic revelry, when Dionysus enters the body of his worshippers—"in full spate"—as a visionary power. In the wake of Dionysian frenzy a prophetic effect is generated, displaying the divine powers of madness, but to the uninitiated (as in the case with Pentheus) Dionysus can unleash the most destructive powers.

Dionysus is the god of non-mediated oppositions as he collapses the sovereignty of reason to its other, but he is also the guardian of tragedy, or rather, he is tragedy himself, and consequently, just as in the art of the tragedians, he embraces both *mythos* and *logos*.[18] In the presence (*parousia*) of Dionysus hierarchical structures of rationality are dissolved, identity set in motion, all of which Euripides uses to articulate the tragic. The tragic experience, the tragic reversals of high/low, life/death, etc., dependent as they are on the strain *mythos/logos*, is displayed as an inversion of rationality, where we no longer can discern a stability in the polarization of man/woman, city/nature, etc., as these oppositions implode in a Dionysian transposal of extremes.

In this oscillation Dionysus breaks down and reconfigures the grid of rationality that guides the optics within the city's walls (947–48). Constantly referring to what is ungraspable by rational thought, indefinitely exceeding the bounds of rationality in displaying its other, Dionysus reveals how man is rooted in *physis* (893–96). Pentheus' worldview, as he stubbornly holds on to the *nomoi* of the *polis*, is based on his illusions of having conceptualized the world as a world of reason, of *logos* if you will. This worldview is set in motion by Dionysus, as he, from the divine roots of *physis*, unleashes an uncontrollable chaos, violently shaking the *nomoi* of the *polis*.

In his arrogance (*hybris*) Pentheus is still concerned with social values in his defence of the *polis*, but as his one-way reasoning tries to calculate everything within a rational structure, he denies its other. Dionysus shakes the foundations of this hierarchical structure of reason, undermining the structure of the *polis*, through a divine madness turned into an epidemic disease—a tribute that has to be paid for what has been ruled out by *logos*.

We recall Dionysus stirring the women of Thebes into orgiastic frenzy: "them I stung in madness from their homes" to "dwell on the mountain stricken in their wits" and "I compelled them to wear the apparel proper to my rites" (32–34). All of the women are "maddened from their homes" (36)

---

[18] Cf. Charles Segal, *Dyonysiac Poetics and Euripides' Bacchae* (Princeton: Princeton University Press, 1997), 295.

in the same way that he induces the divine power of madness in both his followers and those who oppose him.[19] In this case the women of Thebes are punished with a distorted picture of reality, when, at the same time, Dionysus' own followers of maenads, his sacred band (*thiasos*), live in harmony with the world to which he has exposed them in his rites.

Dionysus enters his worshippers, fusing two worlds, divine and human, *mythos* and *logos*, but since he harbors the original division, and in a sense *is* the original division, he does not necessarily fuse the two worlds in harmony. The maenads merge with the god in a bacchic frenzy—"the whole land shall dance" (113–14)—which is a blissful fusion with the elemental forces of Nature (*physis*): "The women, at the appointed hour, began to move the thyrsus into bacchic dances [*bakcheumata*], calling in unison on Bromios as Iacchus, the offspring of Zeus; and all the mountain and its wild creatures joined in bacchic worship [*pan de sunebakcheu'*], and nothing remained unmoved by their running" (723–27). A union usually manifested in the ecstatic *sparagmos*, but in the *Bacchae*—as the drama culminates in the devouring of Pentheus—the division *physis*/*nomos* is as present as Dionysus' divine apprehension of *mythos* and *logos*.

When Dionysus' own *thiasos* becomes *seeing* (as in two opposing mirrors they see themselves and the god), the Thebans do not *see* Dionysus.[20] They are punished with a distorted view, a non-harmonizing illusion of what they conceive to be real. Dionysus' illusions, his phantasmagorias, are all staged to break down a structure of rationality taken for granted in the ordering of the *polis*; and the citizens of Thebes are soon to discover what it means to be uninitiated in the bacchic rites, as Dionysus plunges them down into a spiral of chaos and disorder (1205–10). This downward spiral is a Dionysian corridor of opposing mirrors, reflecting the divine madness, but instead of achieving a symbiosis with the god, it opens up into an abyss of repetitions. The polarity of oppositions can no longer be upheld, the one side cannot be isolated from the other, life repeats death, the true is no

---

[19] Cf. Simon Bennet, *Mind and Madness in Ancient Greece: The Classical Roots of Modern Psychiatry* (Ithaca: Cornell University Press, 1978), 113–121.

[20] "It is based on the meeting of two gazes in which (as in the interplay of reflecting mirrors), by the grace of Dionysus, a total reversibility is established between the devotee who sees and the god who is seen, where each one is, in relation to the other, at once the one who sees and the one who makes himself seen" (Jean-Pierre Vernant, "The Masked Dionysus," *Myth and Tragedy in Ancient Greece* [New York; Zone Books, 1988], 393). "To see Dionysus, it is necessary to enter a different world where it is the 'other', not the 'same' that reigns." (394)

longer separable from the false, and it is within these winding corridors of repetition that Pentheus eventually meets his fate.

Pentheus and Dionysus reinforce the mirroring effects of the drama, emphasizing their differences, as two negative mirrors reflecting each other. Pentheus' own destructivity strikes back in a Dionysian mirror reflection of divine madness: "Look—I seem to myself to see two suns and a double Thebes" (918–19). Pentheus, blinded out of his senses, experiences a doubling of his vision—in a caesura between *mythos* and *logos*—when the god of delirium in full force brings him down. Dionysus exposes him to two aspects of reality, rooted in *mythos* and *logos* respectively—in the divine *physis* and the human *nomos*—when he shows himself as double, as both beast and man: "Were you a beast before? For you are certainly a bull now!" (921). The divine madness creates a double exposure, "correcting" Pentheus's sight, as Dionysus, in the same gesture, reveals another world—a world reason has divided as its other: "Now you see what you should see" (922).

Dionysus has lifted the veil from a world that has been separated by reason, a world here emerging as a double exposure to Pentheus, as Dionysus refuses him a harmonized vision: "your previous state of mind was not normal, but now you have the one you need" (947–48). Euripides, with the rise of sophistry in Athens, accentuates how man, as a being of rationality, is victim to a permanent illusion—the illusion of understanding a world only partly possible to understand or conceptualize by reason— which from a human perspective can generate catastrophic consequences when confronting the madness of the divine (1122–28).

The unparalleled status of the divine laws is not to be questioned, as they, in their archaic origin, always have been present through the ages: "Our wisdom is as nothing in the eyes of deity [*ouden sofizomestha toisi daimosin*]. The traditions of our fathers, from time immemorial our posses- sion—no argument casts them down [*oudeis auta katabalei logos*], not even by the wisest invention of the keenest mind" (200–03). When the divine unwritten laws, "the traditions of our fathers," are concerned, one does not practice sophistry (*sofizomestha*) "in the eyes of deity."

Excurse in the underworld

Dionysus is both the life giving principle, celebrated in rites of fertility, and the god of destruction, demanding death and sacrifice. This life/death pendulum is decisive for the *katharsis* displayed in the *Bacchae*, an archaic layer also resonating in one of Heraclitus' more obscure fragments: "If it were not Dionysus for whom they march in procession and chant the hymn to the phallus, their action would be most shameless. But Hades and Dionysus are the same, him for whom they rave and celebrate Lenaia" (DK15).[21]

The enigmatic ciphers of Heraclitus are important for an understanding of the tragic, as he emphasizes the reversals of life/death, light/dark, high/low, etc. We shall return to why "Hades and Dionysus are the same" but first we have to reconnect with Socrates to expound on the immortality of the soul. The *Phaedo* is set only hours before Socrates empties the cup of hemlock, and in the beginning of the dialogue Socrates suggests that "any man who has any worthy interest in philosophy" (61c) should follow him "as quickly as he can" (61b).[22] Purification (*katharsis*) consists in "separating, so far as possible, the soul from the body" (67c) but, as Socrates points out, referring to the secret doctrines of the divine mysteries: "we men are in a kind of prison and must not set ourselves free or run away" (62b).

In the *Gorgias* Socrates takes sides with Euripides citing his words: "Who knows if to live is to be dead, and to be dead, to live?" (492e).[23] Socrates continues: "I once heard sages say that we are now dead, and the body [*sôma*] is our tomb [*sêma*] [...] and the thoughtless he called uninitiate [*amuêtous*] [...] showing how of all who are in Hades [*Haidou*]—meaning of course the invisible [*aides*]—these uninitiate will be most wretched" (493a–c). In Plato's dramatization neither Socrates nor Euripides is hesitant in reversing the poles of life and death, the body as a prison for the soul, a shackle only death can release us from (cf. *Cratylus* 400c). This is also evident in Socrates' play on words in the *Phaedo*: "But the soul, the invisible [*aides*], which departs into another place which is, like itself, noble and pure and invisible [*aidê*], to the realm of the god of the other world in truth [*eis Haidou hôs alêthôs*]" (80d).[24] The invisible soul returns to Hades after we in

---

[21] Translations by Charles H. Kahn, in *The Art and Thought of Heraclitus: An edition of the fragments with translation and commentary* (Cambridge University Press, 1979). Lenaia was a religious festival in ancient Greece.

[22] Plato, *Phaedo*, trans. Harold N. Fowler (Cambridge: Harvard University Press, The Loeb Classical Library, 1966).

[23] Plato, *Gorgias*, trans. W. R. M. Lamb (Cambridge: Harvard University Press, The Loeb Classical Library, 1967).

[24] Socrates on Hades in the *Cratylus*: "And Hades—I fancy most people think that this is a name of the Invisible [*aeidês*], so they are afraid and call him Pluto" (403a). Plato, *Cratylus*, trans. Harold N. Fowler (Cambridge: Harvard University Press, The Loeb Classical Library, 1921).

death are released from our tomb, from our bodily prison. If we now recall
to what extent Dionysus is visible, or rather invisible to the uninitiated, we
can return to the Heraclitean cipher "Hades and Dionysus are the same."[25]
Dionysus embraces both life and death, but his presence (*parousia*) is only
visible to the *seeing*, to the ones initiated in his rites. To the ones not
participating in his rites he will be invisible, and as an analogy these people
will not be able to *see* the other.

In the *Phaedo* Socrates expounds on truth as a way of purification
(*katharsis*) (69b):

> And I fancy that those men who established the mysteries were not unen-
> lightened, but in reality had a hidden meaning when they said long ago that
> whoever goes uninitiated and unsanctified [*amuêtos kai atelestos*] to the other
> world [*Haidou*] will lie in the mire, but he who arrives there initiated and
> purified [*kekatharmenos te kai tetelesmenos*] will dwell with the gods. For as they
> say in the mysteries [*hôs fasin hoi peri tas teletas*], 'the thyrsus-bearers are many,
> but the mystics [*bakchoi*] few'; and these mystics are, I believe, those who have
> been true philosophers. And I in my life have, so far as I could, left nothing un-
> done, and have striven in every way to make myself one of them. (69c–d)

Socrates designates the bacchants (*bakchoi*), the initiated "thyrsus-bearers,"
as "true philosophers" and accentuates how he has "striven in every way" to
become one of them. Socrates? Mad? We will return to the bacchic revelries
of Socrates, but at least from one perspective, I would suggest, the *true*
bacchant is also the true philosopher, since the Dionysian rites will purify
the soul to an extent where it no longer has to be reborn, and as an initiated
bacchant one can forever remain invisible in the realm of Hades. In his presence, this is what Dionysus has to offer through the rites of initiation; that
other which just like Hades will remain invisible from an all-rationalistic
view of the world (469–80). The uninitiated are in turn, Socrates reminds
us, the "most wretched" in Hades due to their "unbelief and forgetfulness"
(*Gorgias* 493c); their souls will not be invisible but "will lie in mire" (*Phaedo*
69c), as they wait to be reborn.

---

[25] Cf. W. K. C. Guthrie, *History of Greek Philosophy* (Cambridge: Cambridge University
Press, 2003), vol. 1. 476. The Dionysian oscillation is discernable in other fragments of
Heraclitus: "Immortals are mortal, mortals immortal, living the others' death, dead in
others life" (DK62). Cf. "The same…: living and dead, and the waking and the sleeping,
and young and old. For these transposed are those, and those transposed again are these"
(DK88). See also fragment 5 (DK).

Dionysus' *thiasos* of maenads, as we have learned from the *Bacchae*, live in harmony with what he in his rites exposes them to. They are the "thyrsus-bearers," embracers of the Dionysian divine madness and to them Dionysus constitutes a *true* vision of the world, as he cleanses them, outside the *Polis*, from their civic illusions: "O blessed he who in happiness knowing the rituals of the gods [*teletas theôn*] makes holy his way of life and mingles his spirit with the sacred band, in the mountains serving Bacchus with reverent purifications [*katharmoisin*]" (72–77). Yet, the bacchant, rooted in an idyllic merge with *physis*—"shaking up and down the thyrsus" (80)—only reveals one aspect of *katharsis*, while the decisive tension in the *Bacchae*, crucial to the tragic experience, is generated through a pendulum of polar oppositions.

The tragic pendulum, if we follow another encryption by Heraclitus, makes *polemos* "father and king of all" (DK53), in the distribution of violence from high to low.[26] The reversals display a tragic structure, and reveal *katharsis* as operational on several levels in early Greek thinking. It is a driving force intertwined in the tension of an archaic past and what came to be the classical articulation of philosophy and tragedy; but the pendulum will come to a stop, and the experience of the tragic will be lost, as Plato conceals and obscures the *ritual* origin in his staging of the Dionysian life/death oscillation, and from a specific philosophical perspective dramatizes a possible release through the Orphic mystery cults.

From Plato's perspective there is no need to criticize the mysteries, but rather the way they were expressed in the cult, which is a critique he uses for his own *philosophical* purposes, in the attempts to consolidate philosophy in a rational, hierarchical structure. When Heraclitus, around a hundred years earlier (being a contemporary of Aeschylus), confronts the degeneration of the religious ceremonies, it is more of an attempt to salvage something on the way to being lost: "The mysteries current among men initiate them into impiety" (DK14). In the *Bacchae*, Dionysus responds to the same lack of religious respect: "The god's rites are hostile to the one who practices impiety" (476).

Dionysus, in the *Bacchae*, accentuates the higher transparency of night. The darkness harbors a holy power, conveys awe to the initiated, to the

---

[26] Cf. Martin Heidegger, "The Origin of the Work of Art," in Heidegger, *Off the Beaten Track*, trans. Julian Young and Kenneth Haynes (Cambridge: Cambridge University Press, 2002), 22 and Girard, *Violence and the Sacred*, 88. They both accentuate Heraclitus' fragment 53 as vital in their discussion of tragedy.

seeing: "Darkness possesses solemnity" (486). The critical aim of Heraclitus—"*nuktipolois, magois, bakchois, lênais, mustais*" (DK14)—is not directed toward the Dionysian, neither the ecstasy nor the holy, but against how religion was institutionalized, how the ceremonies were carried out as a release from the strict ordering within the walls of the city, and in this deterioration, with the mundane expectations of a better life after death, the tragic experience was lost.

The bottomless pharmacy

Euripides' dramatization in the *Bacchae* is a brutal exposition of divine sovereignty, a genealogy of violence and sacrifice, but the active substance still seems to be concealed in the dramatic structure, as something indecisive operating in the hidden texture, and this might be the key to why Plato wanted to ban tragedy in the *Republic*.

We recall Socrates connecting poetry to flowing liquids—"as the bacchants [*bakchai*] are possessed, and not in their senses, when they draw honey and milk from the rivers" (*Ion* 534a)—with allusions to "founts" (*Ion* 535a) and a "spring" that "lets whatever is at hand flow forth" (*Laws* 719c).[27] The poet, out of his mind, fuelled by the divine fluids of madness, "does not know whose words are true" (719c), and if poetry is not possible to assimilate and master as a poetics, if poetry is abundance, excess, a flow out of control, then poetry is a play of differences, of madness. And if so, poetry has to go. The flowing liquids of madness, infinitely exceeding its own bounds, resist the attempts by reason to expulse the ambiguity of its own element. If the fluids of madness can be called a substance (and now we have to keep all the aspects of the metaphor in mind), they are also fluids harbouring their own anti-substance, indefinitely repeating their other, as in the case of Dionysus himself.

In Dionysian dramaturgy, just as in the case of our understanding of the tragic, the indecisiveness of the Greek *pharmakon* is vital. It is a prime attribute of Dionysus, and the ambiguities of this element correspond to

---

[27] In the *Bacchae* the maenads are ascribed with the power to strike their thyrsus "into a rock from which a dewy stream of water leaps out; another struck her rod on the ground and for her the god sent up a spring of wine; and those who had a desire for the white drink scraped the ground with their fingertips and had jets of milk; and from out of the ivied thyrsi, sweet streams of honey dripped" (704–11). Cf. Seaford, *Dionysos*, 25.

Dionysus' presentation of himself as "most terrible and to men most gentle" (*deinotatos, anthrôpoisi d' êpiôtatos*) (860–61). Dionysus is himself both the poison and the antidote, both the illusory drug and its vaccine. As a wizard or enchanter (*goês epôidos*), he can distribute the ambiguity of his *pharmakon* to ease pain, but is at the same time the element that triggers confusion and divine madness.[28] In being the present god, which he is through his different guises in the drama, the *pharmakon* of Dionysus is the *only* philtre for a human to extract the false from the true: "nor is there any other cure from distress (*pharmakon ponôn*)" (282). Dionysus gives the *pharmakon* a determination that it otherwise lacks; only through his divine intervention, mastering the *pharmakon* as the *pharmakeus*—a wizard, master of phantasms—can a harmonized world emerge. On the other hand, the madness of Pentheus, in his eagerness to fight a god, is beyond any cure: "for you are most grievously mad [*mainêi*]—beyond the cure of drugs [*pharmakois*], and yet your sickness must be due to them" (326–27).

The divine madness contains a double attribute of remedy and despair, truth and falsity, a hallucinogenic poison and at the same time a beneficial medicine; and in his role as the *pharmakeus*, Dionysus (and this could arguably be the tragic "degree zero" of Greek tragedy) demands the civic heart of the Greek *polis* in a ritual sacrifice. The crisis of the *polis*, the deterioration that threatens from within, can only be mended if Pentheus becomes the *pharmakos*: "You alone take on the burden for this city, you alone" (963).

Through the incantations of Dionysus, illusions merge as the divine madness turns opposites into its other, reversals in a mad play of differences, which makes the polarity of concepts slide from one side to the other. The movement of the *pharmakon* contains a simultaneousness of falsity and truth; it is an element of both poison and remedy, the one side cannot be isolated from the other, as they in their origin cannot do anything but repeat each other. Dionysus exposes us to a bottomless pharmacy, a winding labyrinth of mirrors, without identity; but it is also here, in the indecisiveness of the *pharmakon,* in that indefinite abyss of repetitions, that we are able to discern the tragic experience. In this double bind, in a pendulum reaching from high to low, in an oscillation between the different layers of the drama, it is possible to localize the tragic structure of Dionysian tragedy

---

[28] Cf. Segal, *Dionysiac Poetics and Euripides' Bacchae*, 232f.

through the chain *pharmakon-pharmakeus-pharmakos*.[29] The delineations of this motion, or the outlines of this movement, are detectable in the *Bacchae*, but it is the ambiguity of the *pharmakon*, its indecisiveness, that embraces the tragic. No wonder Plato, with all the efforts to *stop* oppositions from turning over into each other, wanted to banish tragedy in the *Republic*.[30]

Connecting to the earlier discussion of "the ancient quarrel" (*Republic* 607b) we return to Dionysus' pharmaceutical "correction" of Pentheus' vision: "Look—I seem to myself to see two suns and a double Thebes" (918–19). I suppose it is here, in this tragic experience, accentuated as a struggle between two suns, that we can discern the rudiment to the *philosophical* conflict between *mythos* and *logos*. The hierarchical ordering of concepts, following this original division, is a struggle finalized with the consolidation of philosophy's own concepts, converging in that transformation of Plato's in the *Republic*, when an *intelligible* sun coincides with the Truth and the Good:

> It was the sun, then, that I meant when I spoke of that offspring of the Good [*ton tou agathou ekgonon*], which the Good has created in its own image [hon tagathon egennêsen analogon heautôi], and which stand in the visible world in the same relation to vision and visible things as that which the good itself bears in the intelligible world to intelligence and to intelligible objects. (508c)[31]

With the consolidation of philosophy's concepts, in Plato's demarcation between *mythos* and *logos*, in his efforts to isolate the one side from the other in a movement of pharmaceutical violence, he tries to separate "the medicine from the poison, the good from the evil, the true from the false."[32] Conforming to the separation of *nomos* from *physis*, analogous to the walls of the *polis* delineating nature from culture (cf. *Bacchae*, 653–55), it is a violent attempt to articulate a philosophical division by structural force. In the center of the solar optics we find the dissection *mythos/logos*—traditionally accentuated as constitutive to Western thought—but if the solar caesura is the original division, it is an internal *dissension*, a rupture *internal* to *logos* itself. This caesura, in turn, has generated a heritage of reason struc-

---

[29] I have elaborated further on this in "Euripides' Pharmacy: Derrida, Deconstruction and Dionysian Drug Dealing," *Site* 25 (2009).
[30] Cf. "Plato's Pharmacy," 130.
[31] Cf. ibid, 87.
[32] Cf. Ibid, 166.

tured by exclusion of its other in a violent confrontation with an archaic past—a polarization of reason against the mythical experience, coinciding with *logos'* orientation around its own solar core. In this movement, under the threat of its other's shadow, indefinitely exceeding its own bounds, madness will be expelled, deported to silence and sent into exile. The solar caesura excludes madness from *within* reason, in a fundamental operation of metaphysics, as the struggle is confirmed and authorized in the attempts to *seize* and *appropriate* the thought of Plato, *following* Plato, but not arrested in a structural force until *after* Plato.[33]

If the "ancient quarrel" is articulated as a struggle between myth and reason, between poetry and philosophy (or philosophy and its other), the *two* suns in the *Bacchae* also become a premonition of how the struggle (during the classical period) will come to an end; but Plato, in his attempts to master the *pharmakon*, knows it is a struggle without a decisive settlement. On the contrary, since the *pharmakon* will defy any attempts of assimilation because of its subversive potential, in always being double and repeating its other, Plato had to expel the poets in an effort to exclude mad poetics from the *Republic*; but it is at the same time a division concealing another madness: the madness of philosophy.

In the *Bacchae*, as mentioned earlier, Nature (*physis*) joins in on the movement of the maenads in an all-consuming revelry: "all the mountains and its wild creatures joined in bacchic worship [*pan de sunebakcheu'*], and nothing remained unmoved by their running" (726–27). Through invocations to Dionysus "the whole land shall dance" (113–14) and in the *Phaedo* (69c–d) Socrates claims to have "striven in every way" to become a bacchant (*bakchos*), a "true philosopher" as he puts it, but where does that leave philosophy? What is this madness of philosophy? In the *Symposium* (218b) we are told that Dionysian and philosophical frenzy has a common root; it is a "shared" madness, just as in the *Bacchae*: "You were made mad, and the whole land was possessed by bacchic frenzy [*exebakcheuthê*]" (1295). The passage in the *Symposium* reads: "every one of you has had his share of philosophic frenzy and transport" (*pantes kekoinônêkate tês philosophou manias te kai bakcheias*) (218b). Philosophic madness (*philosophou manias*) and Dionysian frenzy (*bakcheias*) shared (*kekoinônêkate*), leaving the origins of philosophy founded in the same inexhaustible resource as poetry. Socrates. Mad. Again.

---

[33] Cf. ibid, 130f, 165.

Divine madness as the primordial reserve for Western thought? A reservoir *shared* and evidently poured in rich profusion? And if so, where does this leave the origins of early Greek thinking?[34] If we pull those strings once more, an uncanny design is revealed: philosophy, exceeding its own boundaries, emerging as the *shared* frenzy of a Dionysian *thiasos*—the archaic ritual ceremony that eventually turned into the shape of Greek tragedy. The "ancient quarrel" was silenced, poetry became philosophy's other, violently separated, but still—despite efforts to conceal it—Greek philosophy, sharing the same origin, tapped into the poetics of madness in a coinciding gesture with Greek tragedy, as they both emerged through the frenzied revels of divinity.

With Plato's efforts to consolidate philosophy's concepts, the stage is set for a new origin, a metaphysical degree zero, *beyond* Being (*epekeina tês ousias*). What follows is a structural arrestment, a Platonic prison if you will, harboring the metaphysics of light in all its decisiveness to Western thought.[35] The *other* sun, the hidden source of *logos* (and yet another inexhaustible reservoir) is a concealed, blinding sun, illuminating the origin of the ideas—a *hidden* sun beyond Being (*epekeina tês ousias*).[36] This Platonic origin, leading beyond the light *of* Being, is the violent point of departure for a metaphysical heliocentrism (a heliological gesture emerging from, and always returning to, if ever leaving, this Greek site) eventually culminating in Nietzsche's zenith:[37]

---

[34] Cf. Plato's *Laws* (967b–c), where the Athenian confer some views of early Greek thinking: "These were the views which, at that time, caused these thinkers to incur many charges of atheism and much odium, and which also incited the poets to abuse them by likening philosophers to 'dogs howling at the moon,' with other senseless slanders. But today, as we have said, the position is quite the reverse" (967c–d).

[35] Cf. Jacques Derrida, "Violence and Metaphysics," in Derrida, *Writing and Difference*, trans. Alan Bass (Chicago: The University of Chicago Press, 1978), 85f.

[36] "But did not the Platonic sun already enlighten the visible sun, and did not excendence play upon the meta-phor of these two suns? Was not the Good the necessarily nocturnal source of all light? The light of light beyond light. The heart of light is black, as has often been noted." "Violence and Metaphysics," 86. Cf. "Plato's Pharmacy," 88f.

[37] "Plato himself concretely illustrates the basic outline of metaphysics in the story recounted in the 'allegory of the cave' [...] Plato's thinking follows the change in the essence of truth, a change that becomes the history of metaphysics, which in Nietzsche's thinking has entered upon its unconditioned fulfilment." Martin Heidegger, "Plato's Doctrine of Truth," in Heidegger, *Pathmarks*, trans. Thomas Sheehan (Cambridge: Cambridge University Press, 1998), 235f.

(Noon; moment of the briefest shadow, end of the longest error…).[38]

* * *

In the 1961 preface to the *History of Madness* Michel Foucault—"beneath the sun of the great Nietzschean quest"[39]—addresses the possibility to write a history of madness *itself*: not following "a confrontation below the language of reason" as a horizontal becoming, but "to retrace in time this constant verticality" beyond an "original division."[40] Through this verticality he aims for a "degree zero" in the history of madness, an "undifferentiated experience," in order to localize an "organizing role" for our concept of madness: "The caesura that establishes the distance between reason and non-reason is the origin" and we must "speak of this primitive debate without supposing a victory."[41]

This caesura extends all the way back to Greek thought (a trace only briefly alluded to by Foucault), as the expulsion establishing the distance between *logos* and its other, between reason and what Foucault referred to as limit-experiences: "At the center of these limit-experiences of the Western world is the explosion, of course, of the tragic itself—Nietzsche having shown that the tragic structure from which the history of the Western world is made is nothing other than the refusal, the forgetting and the silent collapse of tragedy."[42] In emphasizing this experience—"which is central as it knots the tragic to the dialectic of history in the very refusal of tragedy by history"—we have reached the common ground of all dissensions (departing from within *logos*): the gravitating center of an "original division."[43]

Through the dialectics of the Western world, the silent trace of this caesura (or *Decision* as Foucault puts it) is depicted as limit-experiences, with the tragic itself at the centre, designated by Foucault as an "archaeology of silence." Possibly diverging from Foucault I would suggest a "degree

---

[38] "How the 'True World' Finally Became a Fable. The History of an Error," in Friedrich Nietzsche, *Twilight of the Idols*, trans. Walter Kaufmann (New York: Penguin Books, 1981), 486.
[39] See Michel Foucault, *History of Madness*, trans. Jonathan Murphy and Jean Khalfa (New York: Routledge, 2006), xxx.
[40] Ibid, xxix.
[41] Ibid, xxviii.
[42] Ibid, xxx. Foucault, rather puzzlingly, declares: "the Greek Logos had no opposite." See Jacques Derrida, "Cogito and the History of Madness," in *Writing and Difference*, 39.
[43] *History of Madness*, xxx. Cf. "Cogito and the History of Madness," 39.

zero" at the dawn of Platonism, at the end of philosophy's own struggle—already, as we have seen, referred to as an "ancient quarrel" in Plato's *Republic*—if we want to trace the origin of what could be depicted as an archaeology of silence: that mirror of negativity, which throughout Western reason, in a numb verticality, delineates its outline against the void.[44]

An archaeology of silence—keeping in mind, but not fully submitting to, Derrida's haunting critique of Foucault's enterprise—could possibly be situated from an alternative perspective: the history of metaphysics as vertical negativity, the empty negation of reason's own monologue on madness. But these two thousand years of dialectics—constituted by a continuity of violent exclusions—will place Plato and Nietzsche side by side. Seemingly at an infinite distance from the Greeks—or at the end of metaphysics if you will (as it runs from Plato to Nietzsche)—it is the original division that unites Plato and Nietzsche, since the reason that once expelled madness rediscovers (from within its own interior) madness as an internal possibility. Nietzsche's madness, situated at the end of metaphysics, harbors (in this particular sense) a limit-experience that opens a path to the modern world.

The emergence of madness in modern literature is not a madness returning to language, but a language that allows madness to emerge from within reason. In a modernity made possible by Nietzsche (through the internal disturbances of historical reason, operational in the works of Sade and Goya), reason rediscovers madness as its own, radical possibility: "the Western world rediscovered the possibility of going beyond its reason with violence, and of rediscovering tragic experience beyond the promises of dialectics."[45]

Madness, as Foucault stresses, is not located in the interstices of an oeuvre—it is the *absence* of a work: "*Where there is an oeuvre, there is no madness.*"[46] Madness is unreason—"an absolute rupture of the oeuvre"—but madness is not outside the oeuvre. The absence of madness resists reason's own monologue: the presence of this absence opens into an abyss of

---

[44] Ibid, 536. Derrida's critique of Foucault's position in the *History of Madness* initiated an interesting debate, but since Foucault himself in later works left this early position (and because of that not really addressed Derrida's critique in his reply nine years later) it would be worthwhile (and possibly from an alternative perspective prolific) to re-establish the still not exhausted (or rather inexhaustible) dialogue between Foucault's enigmatic preface from 1961 and the equally sublime and cryptic ending of this early work.

[45] Ibid, 535.

[46] Ibid, 537.

indefinite repetitions, delineating its outer limit against the void—the tragic experience of silence as the oeuvre's profound and inexhaustible resource.[47]

[47] Cf. Derrida, "Cogito and the History of Madness," 54.

Ghostly Reason: A Phenomenological Interpretation of Paul and Pneumatology

Hans Ruin

What is spirit? Is there really spirit? The question could also be expressed as follows: is it possible to give a *rational* account of spirit? Does reason have access to spirit, or is spirit what reason should refrain from in order to remain reason, and not madness, as in Kant's famous critique of Sweden-borg, as the seer of spirits and ghosts, the *Geisterseher*? Or is there in the end something irreducibly spiritual also in reason? And if so, does this mean that reason itself contains something of un-reason, or even non-reason, perhaps that a certain madness belongs not outside but also inside reason itself? Or is spirit in fact the highest and hidden form of reason, its ultimate telos?

How could we ever begin to answer such questions? Are they even meaningful as questions? Yet, as inheritors of the great philosophical systems of reason, from Hegel to Husserl and into the present, we cannot ultimately avoid them. For they have already been posed and addressed to us, as promises and as enigmas to decipher and interpret. The question of spirit and the spiritual is not a theme external to philosophy, but one that belongs to its root meaning and to its self-understanding in its highest speculative faculty.

Here I will attempt to explore the meaning of this inheritance through a critical retrieval of the sense of the spiritual—the *pneumatikos*—in some of the key texts of Western pneumatology, the Pauline Letters. This reading will lead us toward some of the most complex issues in Jewish-Christian theology, but it will ultimately do so not in order to restore philosophy to its religious-theological inheritance, but rather in order to reopen the question of the spiritual as in fact pointing to some of the most demanding issues in contemporary philosophical thinking—namely the meaning of history, tradition, and of the ancestral—and as a domain where the precarious border between reason and its other is enacted and disclosed. In the First Letter to the Corinthians, Paul writes of how "the God's Spirit dwells in you" (3.16) which is then followed by the declaration that "Do not deceive yourselves. If you think that you are wise in this age, you should become fools so that you may become wise. For the wisdom of this world is foolishness with God" (3.18–19). In Paul the *pneuma*/spirit marks the intersection and reversal between madness and reason, as being both destruction and foundation at once. For as he also writes: "Those who are unspiritual do not receive the gifts of God's Spirit, for they are foolishness to them, and they are unable to understand them because they are spiritually discerned. Those who are spiritual discern all things, and they are themselves subject to no one else's scrutiny" (1 Cor 2.14–15).

Here I will try to show how this spirituality can be read and interpreted as a metonym for interpretation itself, as the means for surviving in and through tradition, even for going mad, and precisely in and through this madness to have access to reason.

Phenomenological spirits (Husserl, Heidegger, Derrida)

In his so-called Vienna lecture from 1935, "The Crisis of European Humanity," Edmund Husserl gave a condensed version of his cultural-philosophical legacy, only a few years before his death.[1] In this partly dismal assessment of the intellectual situation and fate of Europe, one word carries a special weight, namely "spirit," in German *Geist*. The essay opens with the declaration that what is needed today is a "purely self-contained and universal science of the spirit."[2] Contemporary culture is threatened by a "naturalism" that draws the spiritual into the causal network of material being, blinding man to the autonomy of the spiritual. In the end even the sciences of nature are in themselves "spiritual" phenomena, and should be interpreted as such.

What Husserl here calls the "spiritual image (*Gestalt*) of Europe" includes its intellectual development from the earliest known cultural en-

---

[1] "Die Krisis des europäischen Menschentums und die Philosophie," first published as an appendix to *Die Krisis der europäischen Wissenschaften und die tranzendentale Phänomenologie, Husserliana* vol. VI, ed. Walter Biemel (The Hague: Nijhoff, 1954), 314–348.

[2] Husserl, *Krisis*, 317f. Trans. Quentin Lauer, in Husserl, *Phenomenology and the Crisis of Philosophy* (New York: Harper, 1965), 153, 155.

deavors but with a particular emphasis on the discovery of theoretical knowledge as an open-ended quest. This is also the birth and shape of rationality, as it emerges, develops, and is transmitted from the Ancient world into Modernity. Yet, it is not simply in the form of a reinstalled commitment to rationality that Husserl sees a solution to the present loss of orientation. On the contrary, the problem with which we are confronted is a "mistaken Rationalism," a *verirrenden Rationalismus*.[3] He is not referring primarily to the emergence of irrationalism in the political sense in the form of totalitarian self-mythologizing fascist movements, but to an inner perversion of the rational itself in the form of "objectivism" or "naturalism," and in particular in the logically inconsistent "naturalization of spirit."[4] In the very last lines of the essay Husserl carries his hopes of a new spiritual awakening through a new science of universal spirituality to its highest pitch, as he states: "for the spirit alone is immortal."

Husserl's call for a "spiritualization" of rationality, and for the need of retrieving the spiritual origin of rationality, has its conceptual-historical lineage. Its emergence as a philosophical-scholarly term had been prepared in Herder and in Fichte, but it was with Hegel that it truly entered the stage of modern philosophy. With the publication of the *Phenomenology of Spirit* from 1807 *Geist* is established as the central theme of his speculative philosophy of humanity and its development, and as the most general term under which it was possible to describe the evolution from simple awareness through self-awareness to reason, to culminate in the idea of "absolute knowledge."

"Spirit" thus occupies a specific position in the Hegelian genealogy and architectonic between reason and religion. But more importantly it is the name for the overall framework of this entire speculative philosophy, a name for that which is "in and for itself, and which is at the same time actual as consciousness and aware of itself," as his definition reads at the outset of the section with this title.[5] In the course of the nineteenth century, and partly as a direct consequence of Hegel's usage, *Geist* was established as a general term in German for the study of humanity in all its expressions, in the *Geisteswissenschaften*, "the spiritual sciences," which is the term used by

---

[3] Ibid, 337/179.
[4] Ibid, 339/181.
[5] Hegel, *Phenomenology of Spirit*, trans. A. Miller (Oxford: Oxford University Press, 1977), sec. 263.

Dilthey to contrast them with the sciences of nature, a distinction recalled verbatim by Husserl in his Vienna lecture.

In 1987 Derrida published an essay entitled "On Spirit" (*De l'esprit*) with the subtitle "Heidegger and the Question."[6] The reference to "the question" was intentionally ambiguous. This was a time when the discussion about Heidegger's politics had exploded again, and Derrida had been invited to speak at a conference where the theme was "Heidegger and the open questions." He chose to address these open questions not straightforwardly but rather obliquely through the interpretation of a theme that hitherto had received minimal attention in the literature on Heidegger, that of *Geist*.

The standard conception at that point was that "*Geist*" belonged to an older philosophical-humanist vocabulary from which Heidegger had departed, which had been argued by Beda Aleman among others. Polemicizing against this simplified reading, Derrida showed in this interpretation that, whereas in *Being and Time* Heidegger distanced himself from the use of "spirit" as a way of describing and analyzing human existence together with that of the "psyche" and "subject," he had in fact returned to this vocabulary only a few years later. Moreover, he not only returned to it, he emphatically embraced it in some of his most politically charged texts, notably the "Rectoral address" from 1933, but also *Introduction to Metaphysics*, as well as in several of the interpretations of Hölderlin and also in his later essays on Trakl. The task Derrida thus set forth was to determine the more specific meaning of and rationale behind this re-introduction of *Geist* by Heidegger as a philosophical-political category in the work from the early thirties onward.

In the course of this exploration, he discovered a multidimensional field of related topics in Heidegger, somehow united by recurring references to *Geist*. First of all, it had to do with the question as such. The spiritual in Heidegger has to do with a way of living in and through the ethos of the question. But *Geist* also resurfaced in relation to the problem of animality, as well as to technology. In both cases it pointed toward the attempt to delimit the human being from the animal and from the technical. The references to *Geist* also seemed to open Heidegger's discourse to a certain non-Christian, humanist teleology. Finally, as a response to the question "what is spirit?" Derrida found repeated references to the element of *fire*

---

[6] *De l'esprit: Heidegger et la question* (Paris: Galilée, 1987). Trans. Geoffrey Bennington and Rachel Bowlby, *Of Spirit: Heidegger and the Question* (Chicago: Chicago University Press, 1989).

rather than air, wind, or breath as the original Greek *pneuma*, of which *Geist* is a translation. In the end this explicit distance toward the Greek *pneuma* also indicated a more profound—and, in this particular context, more troublesome—avoidance of the most original shape of *pneuma*, namely the Hebrew *ruach*, "breath" or "wind," rendered as *pneuma* in the first line of Genesis in the Septuagint translation.

Through his analysis of the problem of spirit in Heidegger, Derrida had also opened the way toward a deeper questioning of the role and meaning of the spiritual in philosophy and in rationality. We could even say that he had made pneumatology valid again as philosophical and phenomenological concern. In retrospect we can see how in the context of his own work it pointed toward his subsequent preoccupation with the problem of the ghost, as the other facet of *Geist*, which he would develop in *Specters of Marx* some years later, and which would continue to reverberate in remarks on revenants and hauntings in the last writings. In different ways these analyses open new conceptual avenues for exploring how reason and rationality intermingle with their dialectic doubles, with non-reason, obsession, transposition, invasion, and excess, and thus also with figures for different forms of madness.[7]

What then is the spiritual in reason? What is its relation to thinking, to philosophy, and what does it tell us about rationality and its self-perception? Oftentimes it is as though reason, through the very reference to spirit, opens itself to invasions, possessions, and to transmissions. To study spirit and spirituality therefore involves a series of difficult methodological considerations. It is always possible to try to trace the emergence and transport of a concept through time, according to standard conceptual historical procedures. But spirit is itself concerned precisely with the limits of both historical methods and their objectifications. When Husserl recalls *Geist* as the culmination of his philosophical mission, it is precisely as a name for that which refuses historicization, and as that which in itself should mark a limit against the attempt to "naturalize" it, to defer it to the status of a corporeal body and a position in space-time.[8]

---

[7] Elsewhere I have elaborated the notion of the spectral, by tying it closer and more systematically to the phenomenon of history and the experience of transgenerational life. See my "Spectral Phenomenology," in Siobhan Kattago (ed.), *Ashgate Research Companion to Memory Studies* (Farnham: Ashgate, 2015), 61–74.

[8] In his analysis of *Geist* in Heidegger, Derrida also traced in particular the blending of terms and conceptual orders between the *geistig* and what is *geschichtlich*, "historical," showing how Heidegger at certain point would even refer to what is *geistig-geschichtlich*,

Against the background of these precautions, I would like to phrase my hypothesis as follows; namely, that spirit—*pneuma*, *ruach*, and *Geist* through the entangled history of translation—from its very inception is connected to the experience of what I will call ancestrality, an experience of the effect of past humanity upon the present. The spirit emerges at decisive junctures of tradition, as a way to poetize the traditionality of tradition and thus its historicity. References to the *pneuma* often seem to work as a name for that present absence of a living force that has shaped the present, and thus as the inner life and dynamism of tradition. To recall a *pneuma* is then equivalent to seek support in the experience of a sur-vival through time.

With these formulations I am only indicating a general framework for an interpretation that I will try to develop in what follows, in a reading of some of the founding pneumatological documents of the Western tradition, namely the Pauline Letters, in particular First and Second Corinthians, Galatians, and Romans. In a concordance that list the references to "spirit" in the Biblical writings, there are approximately five hundred entries, around one fifth of which are found in Paul's Letters. Paul stands out as the greatest pneumatologist in Biblical literature. Alongside the Gospel of John and the Acts of the Apostles, Paul is the paradigmatic pneumatologist in the sense that it is in his letters that a pneumatological theological discourse is first installed.

In the First Letter to the Corinthians we read: "these things God has revealed to us through the spirit [*pneuma*]; for the spirit searches everything, even the depths of God" (2.10). And in the Second Letter to the Corinthians, he writes of God who has given him the capacity to serve a new covenant/testament which is "not of letter, but of spirit [*pneuma*]; for the letter kills, but the Spirit gives life" (3.6). What can we learn from this pneumatological hermeneutic, from a *pneuma* that is not just a religious theme among others, but the very vehicle of insight and enlightenment, and the restoration of life in the face of death, and as the human capacity of reason that not only transcends reason and rationality, but which in its very essence challenges this same reason in its rationality?

In attempting to read the Pauline letter from a phenomenological-hermeneutic standpoint, I am moving on well-trodden ground. Over the last two decades, Paul's relation to philosophy has become a growing theme

---

spiritual-historical, especially in the "Rectoral address," but also in *Introduction to Metaphysics*. See *De l'esprit*, 61ff.

in contemporary continental thought, partly inspired by the publication in 1995 of Heidegger's 1921 lectures on the philosophy of religion, then expounded through books by Agamben, Badiou, Zizek, and Taubes, and explored in several collections on this theme.[9] It is, however, a notable trait in these attempts to read Paul from a secular-philosophical standpoint that the theme of *pneuma* is mostly absent. This absence is notable not only in view of the extraordinary weight that Paul himself attaches to this particular theme, located at the very heart of this message, but also in view of the remarkable weight of this concept in modern continental philosophy, from Hegel to Husserl to Derrida. There seems to be a certain coyness surrounding this particular theme in Paul, as if his academic readers—not only the philosophers but also the theologians and religious historians—tend to shy away from this territory.[10]

When Derrida wrote *On Spirit*, Heidegger's lectures on the phenomenology of religion had not yet been released from the archive. But in the lectures Heidegger did in fact address the Christian and Pauline concept of *pneuma*, opening a trajectory that was not available to Derrida at the time. Another book that came a few years after Derrida's analysis, and that was partly inspired by it, was a study by Alan Olson, *Hegel and the Spirit: Philosophy as Pneumatology*.[11] In this study Olson traces Hegel's understanding and use of spirit to its religious-political background, to Luther in particular and generally to a pietistic religious Lutheranism that was part of Hegel's upbringing. By "spirit" Hegel is said to seek to think the philosophical vehicle of "infinite mediation and differentiation." Olson does not pursue the topic back to Paul, but stresses the religious inheritance of the concept, back to the (Pauline) Luther.

The studies of Derrida and Olson confirm the relevance of exploring the narrative of Western rationalism and rationality as also narratives of spirit, and thus as part of what I would call a pneumatological inheritance. Such

---

[9] See, e.g., John Caputo and Linda Alcoff (eds.), *St Paul Among the Philosophers* (Bloomington: Indiana University Press, 2009), and Peter Frick (ed.), *Paul in the Grip of Philosophers*, (Minneapolis: Acumen Books, 2013).

[10] This silence with regard to spirit/pneuma is also notable in James D. G. Dunn (ed.), *The Cambridge Companion to St Paul* (Cambridge: Cambridge University Press, 2003) which has no article on it and lists only one instance of the term in the index.

[11] See Alan Olson, *Hegel and the Spirit: Philosophy as Pneumatology* (Princeton: Princeton University Press, 1992). Throughout the enormous secondary literature on Hegel there has been surprisingly little attention to the specific role and meaning of "spirit" itself.

an historical exploration is of particular relevance when one considers the particular aura that surrounds this concept also in modern thought. For the spirituality of reason is not a neutral name. When it is recalled and put to use, as in the aforementioned examples, it is as the name for the highest possibility and potentiality of reason. It is often recalled and situated where rationality appears to be threatened by itself—more precisely, by the inner repression, loss, and even death of itself.

As Derrida suggested, as Olson argues in his book on Hegel, and as any dictionary of conceptual history will validate, the root of the philosophical concept of *Geist* in modern thought leads back to Christian and ultimately Jewish religious sources, to *pneuma* and *ruach*. To state this is to state the obvious. But what is more difficult is to determine the inner relation and structure of this correlation. This requires more careful hermeneutical strategies. Here I will present a kind of double recursive reading, one that leads from philosophy to theology and back, from Heidegger and his early interpretation of Paul to an examination of *pneuma* in the Pauline letters, taking us beyond the implicitly Christian confessional framework of Heidegger's reading to where it permits us to understand the pneumatic as a metonym for thinking the traditionality of tradition as such.

Genealogies of the pneumatic

If we open the great archive of Western pneumatology, we are led back to Paul, as perhaps the greatest pneumatologist of them all. But he is not alone. For an exploration of this theme there exists a large body of conceptual-historical research. In Ritter's *Historisches Wörterbuch* the heading *"Geist"* contains some hundred pages of detailed references to its different meanings and to the relations between *Geist, spiritus*, and *pneuma*. How then could one address philosophically this theme without losing oneself in the endless trajectories of conceptual history? In what follows I will nevertheless provide a condensed version of such a history, guided by the more specific philosophical reading to follow.

Etymologically, the concept Geist has been traced back to a Indo-European root **gheis-*, meaning to "shudder," and also a West Germanic word *ghoizdo*, meaning "supernatural creature." In Old High German and Old English, *Geist* and *gast* appear respectively as translations of the biblical Latin *spiritus*, while also remaining a synonym to the more modern *Gespenst*, meaning simply "Ghost." The King James Bible speaks indistinguishably of "holy ghost" and "holy spirit" when translating the Latin *spiritus sanctus*, which in turn corresponds to Greek *pneuma hagios* in the original New Testament texts. Both *spiritus* and *pneuma* retain a connection to breath and breathing, which is one of the original senses of the Hebrew *ruach*, but also of *nephesh*, that in the Septuagint Greek translation were both rendered as *pneuma*.[12] When Luther translated the Old Testament he used *Geist* as the translation also of the passages when the sense is more literally the "breath" of God, thus infusing the German word with a connection to the act of breathing.

A specific hermeneutic problem surrounding spirit concerns the impact of Christian/Jewish rivalries, and also the relation between Christianity and Greek religious and philosophical sources. A central questions remains: is the pneumatic in Paul primarily Jewish, or is it specifically Christian? Or is it in fact a stoic concept, and thus part of the "rational" Greek inheritance? Or does it instead belong to a legacy of Greek mysticism and thus to a certain Greek irrationalism, dating back to the mystery Cults?

Before trying to read and elicit the sense of the pneumatic in Paul we need to rehearse briefly these two principal sources of its usage, the Jewish religious writings and Greek philosophy. Paul's letters and their impact would not have been possible had it not been for the Septuagint Greek version of Jewish religious writings which had already circulated for several centuries as the uniting document of Judaism in its diaspora throughout the whole Mediterranean area. When the seventy Jewish scribes (from whence the title of the text: LXX) translated the first book of Moses as *Genesis*, they fixed the first line as: *en arche epoiesen ho theos ton ouranon kai ten gen. he de ge en aoratos kai akatoaskeuastos kau skotos epauno tes abyssou kai pneuma teou epephereto epauno tou hudatos.* In the English translation: "In the beginning God created the heavens and the earth. Now the earth was a formless void, there was darkness over the deep, and God's spirit hovered over the water." And in the second account of creation, which follows immediately upon the first, where God molds man out of clay and then blows the "spirit of life" into his nostrils, the original Greek text has *pnoe*, which already in Homeric Greek has the meaning of wind and breath, from the same verb *pneuo*, as *pneuma*. From the earliest parts of the Jewish myths of creation the idea is thus articulated that God acts in and through a "spirit," a

---

[12] Both the words in the Hebrew texts that were rendered as *pneuma* in the Greek translation, *ruach* and *nephesh*, originally referred to concrete meanings of wind and breath, but gradually came to signify "spirit" and "soul."

pneuma, as both a manifestation of the creator, and a force in and through which God interacts with human beings. *Pneuma* is fixed in the mythical narrative as a poetic articulation of life in its vitality, creativity, and influence. Throughout the subsequent texts in the Jewish literature, that were eventually gathered in one volume, references to *pneuma* abound, especially in the prophets Isaiah and Ezekiel. In Isaiah 11.2 we read, for example, in an important passage prophesizing about the coming king: "A shoot springs from the stock of Jesse, a scion thrusts from his roots: on him the *pneuma* of Yahweh rests, a *pneuma* of wisdom and insight, a *pneuma* of counsel and power, a *pneuma* of knowledge and of the fear of Yahweh (the fear of Yahweh is his *pneuma*)." This is just meant to give one example of how firmly rooted in the language and style of the older Jewish-Greek literature the reference to *pneuma* and to a pneumatic understanding of humanity was at the time of Paul.

A parallel intellectual background for Paul is the widespread reference to *pneuma* and the pneumatic in Greek philosophical and medical treatises, from Anaximenes onward, highlighted in the (disputed) Aristotelian treatise *Peri pneumatos*, "Of the life spirit," and recalled in numerous sources at the intersection of medicine, religion, and philosophy, many of which belong to various schools of Stoicism.[13] None of the Stoic treatises have survived intact but there are numerous references to the general idea that the *pneuma* of humankind was regarded as connected to the *pneuma* of God, and thus that it serves as an intermediary of divine and human life and power. In many treatises *pneuma* and *psuche* are used interchangeably to designate the life force in man, as well as that which survives death, as explored early on by Nietzsche's friend Erwin Rhode in his classic work on Psyche and the Greek belief in afterlife.[14] In short, at the time of Paul, *pneuma* is a well established metaphorical and poetic representation of the force and flow of life, which reaches deep into the scientific and medical

---

[13] For a survey of ancient theories of *pneuma* in the intersection between medicine and philosophy and religion, see, e.g., Marlene Putscher's *Pneuma Spiritus Geist: Vorstellungen von Lebensantrieb in ihrer geschichtlichen Wandlungen* (Wiesbaden: Steiner Verlag, 1974).

[14] *Psyche: Seelencult und Unsterblichkeitsglaube der Griechen* (Freiburg: Mohr, 1898). Trans. W. B. Hillis, *Psyche: The cult of souls and the belief in immortality among the Greeks* (London: Routledge, 2010).

literature, as well as in esoteric doctrines, and which unites the main philosophical and religious sources of both Jewish and Greek culture.[15]

Following the question of the two legacies, we also face the question of the Pauline influence on German idealism and, from there, its influence on subsequent German philosophy. Is it marginal, or in fact essential? Is it perhaps the hidden and fundamental link between German philosophy and Christianity that Nietzsche always claimed was there? Or is it, on the contrary, the proof that even the most advanced articulation of European philosophical rationality is tied at the root to the mystery cults, and thus that its rationalism is in fact already interwoven with a certain irrationalism? Is there even a way to come to terms with these questions in a "rational" way?

To enter the scholarly question of pneumatics and its history is also to step into a territory where the borders between scientific and missionary spirit intermingle to the point of becoming indistinguishable. Here radical forms of evangelical Christianity take on the shape of intellectual history and vice versa, as in a recent academic-historical study of Paul and pneumatology published in a respectable series at Mohr Siebeck and written by Finny Philips, an Indian-American bible scholar but who is also a leading minister in India's Philadelphia Church, and responsible for the Native Missionary Movement.[16] It is as if the very attempt to specify the content of this thought and doctrine brings us so close to the very force and application of Pauline doctrine that the border between scholarly analysis and confessional commitment becomes irresistibly interwoven, in a way that actually has its particular interest in the context of our question.

---

[15] To trace the Pauline notion of *pneuma* to all the possible sources from which it emerges and from which it draws its appeal and its authority could easily lead to an interminable quest. An examples of an early such study is Hermann Gunkel, *Die Wirkungen des heiligen Geistes, nach der populären Anschauung der apostolischen Zeit und der Lehre des Apostels Paulus: Eine biblisch-theologische Studie* (Göttingen: Vandenhoeck & Ruprecht, 1888).

[16] Finny Philip, *The Origins of Pauline Pneumatology* (Tübingen: Mohr Siebeck, 2005). After an impressive summary of previous research on *pneuma* in Paul from the early nineteenth century onward, Philip launches the thesis that in the last 200 years of scholarship no one has genuinely seen and appreciated the importance of Paul's own conviction that he is called on to preach to the gentiles, and that he thereby expands the Jewish doctrine to a universal message following his conversion. So in the end, and despite the scholarly sophistication, we are back again in the Hegelian, idealistic universalism, with all its traps and flaws, and its always latent anti-Judaism. But this only shows how complex and difficult this issue is to balance and to master intellectually.

The problem of discursive borders and delimitations not only concerns the Christian confessional side of research on pneumatics, but also its philosophical developments. The soteriological dimensions of *Geist* in both Hegel and Husserl bear ample testimony to this predicament. Just to speak of the spirit, is somehow to engage a force, to respond to a call, from within the force of spirit itself. Thus the very problematic of *pneuma* and the pneumatological puts us in a similar position as with regard to the question of the holy, inviting awe and disbelief at once.[17]

Trying to use Paul as a way to access the problem of pneumatology in modern idealist philosophy also involves a complex hermeneutical situation. The Hegelian use of spirit as a metonym for the highest, redemptive potential of consciousness appears to have contributed to the theological reception of Paul throughout the 19th century, most clearly exemplified in writers such as Otto Pfeiderer and Bruno Bauer. In Pfeiderer's book *Paulinismus*, from 1873, the argument is developed, in a Hegelian vein, that it is through the doctrine of the *pneuma* that Paul invents an entirely new ethical system, in contrast to the Jewish law and also to the individual, material and bodily in human beings. The *pneuma* is the carrier of the universal in human beings through which they break free from the earlier constraints of restricted ethnical confession. While Pfeiderer was eager to promote the Greek element in Paul, he also wrote as a theologian with his own confessional commitments and duties.[18]

For early Christian theology, the role of spirit in the Pauline sense constituted a conceptual and political challenge that somehow had to be contained. It was Tertullian who, in the third century, first used the model of a *triados* to bring together the more spontaneous polyphonic theologizing at the time.[19] It was transformed into doctrine by the religious bureaucrats of Nicea in 325, and approved as dogma in the form: "the one

---

[17] On the general logic of this hermeneutical problem, see the editor's preface in Jonna Bornemark and Hans Ruin (eds.), *Ambiguity of the Sacred: Phenomenology, Politics, Aesthetics* (Stockholm: Södertörn Philosophical Studies, 2012), 5f.

[18] It is generally the case that studies by German evangelic scholars on spirit do not distinguish the practical confessional content from the historical and philosophical question of its meaning. See, for example, Eduard Schweizer, *Heiliger Geist* (Stuttgart: Kreutz Verlag, 1978). It argues that for Paul it has to do primarily with an experience of the early Christian community of Christ on the cross, and thus with the soteriological force of the doctrine.

[19] Already the gospel of Mathew 28.19 expresses the call to the disciples that they "teach all nations, baptizing them in the name of the Father and of the Son and of the Holy Spirit," but this is still not part of anything like a Trinitarian doctrine in the Nicean sense.

God exists in three Persons and one substance, Father, Son, and Holy Spirit." Throughout the ages independent theological thinkers have tried to historicize this awkward formula, notably Joachim of Fiore, but they were regularly condemned as heretics (e.g., by the Fourth Lateran Council in 121315). In order even to begin to think through this problem and its philosophical implications, it is therefore essential that one first adopts a healthy distance to the councils and their conceptual-political exercises, in order simply to read the texts, and first of all the texts of Paul.[20]

Heidegger's Paul

In the introductory remarks to his course on phenomenology of religion from 1921, Heidegger insists that the phenomenological question of method is not a question of the appropriate methodological system, but of access, of how to find the way to a "factical" (*faktische*) life experience. A phenomenology of religious life, he writes, should not be a theory about the religious conceived of as an object of study in the standard mode of a science of religion, but rather as a way of entering the religious, in under-standing, as a form of meaning-fulfilment or enactment (*Vollzug*).[21] It is not a psychological theory of religious experiences, but an explication of the meaning of religion, which therefore does not immediately need to take sides along confessional lines. Instead the confessional, as the meaning of devotion, is itself among the phenomena to be investigated. Nor does it take a definitive stance in regard to the distinction between rationality and irrationality, as if the religious, once and for all, could be located in the latter. The phenomenological understanding lies beyond this distinction. To such a phenomenological analysis belongs the preparedness to allow that the basic, organizing concepts remain "undecided." It is on the condition that we do not force a conceptual structure onto a phenomenon that this phenomenon can begin to speak and have sense on its own terms. Such an

---

[20] An avenue which would have deserve an extensive treatment in this context is the way in which Hegel, toward the end of *Phenomenology of Spirit*, does include a lengthy treatment of the meaning of the doctrine of trinity providing also an implicit connection between the original Christian doctrine and his own understanding and usage of the term (see sections 769–755).

[21] Martin Heidegger *Gesamtaugabe* vol. 60, *Phänomenologie des religiösen Lebens* (Klostermann: Frankfurt am Main, 1995). Trans. Matthias Fritsch, *Phenomenology of Religious Life* (Bloomington: Indiana University Press, 2004).

explication can also permit the non-understandable to be understandable, precisely by letting-be (*belassen*) its non-understandability. Speaking in the terms of Husserl, we should try to investigate these phenomena by "bracketing" their realist, or metaphysical, implications.

Referring to the contemporary interest in philosophy and phenomenology of religion in general, and specifically in regard to Rudolf Otto's recently published book *Das Heilige* (from 1917), Heidegger comments on the attempt to delineate the religious sphere with reference to the category of "the irrational" (*das Irrationalen*) in contrast to the rational:

> But with these concepts nothing is said as long as one does not know the meaning of the rational. The concept of the irrational should be determined from the contrast to the concept of the rational, which still remains notoriously unclear. This conceptual couple should therefore be abolished. The phenomenological understanding, according to its basic meaning, lies completely outside this contrast, which only has a very restricted validity, if any.[22]

Heidegger's main interest is the sense of time that animates the Pauline discourse, which he explores by focusing on the formulations of a life in faith as one of hope, waiting, and wakefulness, of an open, finite existential horizon for the unexpected.

Toward the end of the lectures Heidegger himself briefly addresses the problem of *pneuma* in Paul. He speaks of it in the context of its "*Bezugsinn*," its "relational significance," or the meaning of its relation to a world. *Pneuma*, just like *psuche* and *sarx* (flesh), should not be seen as entities, he argues. Instead they should be seen as "*zeitliche Güter*," as temporal goods, to the extent that they constitute a lived temporality. The "original Christian life" that he finds in the Pauline letters is one that cannot be interpreted with the help of categories that designate a continuous harmonic life, for they involve a sense of "being shattered."[23] Heidegger therefore also rejects the very idea of Paul as a mystical "pneumatician" (*Pneumatiker*) as had been suggested by the biblical scholar Richard Reitzenstein in a recent study

[22] Ibid, 79 (my translation): "Aber mit diesen beiden Begriffen ist nicht gesagt, solange man den Sinn von rational nicht kennt. Der Begriff des Irrationalen soll ja aus dem Gegensatz zu dem Begriff des Rationalen bestimmt werden, der sich aber in notorischen Unbestimmtheit befindet. Dieses Begriffspaar ist also völlig auszuschalten. Das phänomenologische Verstehen liegt seinem Grundsinn nach völlig außerhalb dieses Gegensatzes, der, wenn überhaupt, nur ein sehr beschränktes Recht hat."
[23] Ibid, 119.

on Hellenistic mystery religions. In terms of the "objective historical circumstances" the thesis may be valid, Heidegger says, but in terms of how *pneuma* functions in the Pauline text it adds nothing to the interpretation.[24]

Taking his lead instead from the famous quotation from 1 Corinthians 2.10f. of how it is through spirit that the depth of God is sought, and that it is only through spirit and not through worldly wisdom that understanding can be had, Heidegger states that *"pneuma bei Paulus ist die Vollzugsgrundlage, aus der das Wissen selbst entspringt,"* that *pneuma* is a position of knowledge, a way in and through which knowledge is brought about. For the same reason, what is essential in Paul is not to be spirit, but to have spirit (*pneuma echein*). For Heidegger it is important to distance Paul from the so called mystics, who are said to use artificial means to access the divine, whereas the supposedly genuine (Pauline) Christian position is to remain "awake and vigilant."

A significant lacuna in Heidegger's interpretation concerns his understanding of the historical situation of the Jewish communities within which Paul was formulating his discourse. There is a kind of prevailing Lutheran ideological bias in Heidegger's preoccupation with the very idea of "original Christianity," as has been argued recently by Ward Blanton in a critical study on the reception of Paul in theology and philosophy.[25]

An interpretation of the Pauline letters needs to transcend the horizon of Paul as "Christian" in the sense that this word was applied only later. Paul was—and this has become more and more of an accepted view in more recent and confessionally unfettered literature—primarily a Jewish reformer of the inherited Judaic religion, who experienced his own historical situation and teaching as truthful to this tradition and its inner meaning at this decisive historical juncture. It is also from this perspective that the genuine significance of his pneumatology makes sense. This is not the case in Heidegger's interpretation, which is why the reading I propose here goes beyond the horizon of his conclusions while relying on his basic hermeneutic approach.

---

[24] Richard Reitzenstein, *Die hellenistischen Mysterienreligionen nach ihren Grundgedanken und Wirkungen* (Leipzig: Teubner, 1920, 2nd rev ed).
[25] Ward Blanton, *Displacing Christian Origins: Philosophy, Secularity, and the New Testament* (Chicago: University of Chicago Press, 2007).

Pneuma in the Pauline Letters

Pneuma in the Pauline letters is not one thing. It is itself the unifying principle, the one that Paul frequently recalls, in order to secure the unity of his own message, as when he writes in 1 Corinthians 12.13, of how we are all by "one *pneuma* … baptized into one body, whether we be Jews or Gentiles, etc." *Pneuma* is here the metonymic figure of the unity of the congregation, a unity for which he is struggling, at times desperately, as the Letters clearly demonstrate. But the fact that *pneuma* is recalled to forge a unified congregation, does not make it a unified entity in itself. On the contrary, it works along several parallel trajectories in the Letters: at once as a manifestation of God and as identical to God's essence (2 Cor. 3.17); as a means of human knowledge to reach the truth (Eph. 6.17) and as truth itself (ibid); as a source of goodness (Gal. 5.22) and as distinct forms of comportment (Rom. 8.15); and as an independent force that takes possession of life. Throughout the Letters, it moves as a resource from which the discourse draws support, in and through which it inhales and exhales the force needed to communicate its message. *Pneuma* thus appears as partly a performative concept, as it is recalled at decisive junctures to secure the force and the legitimacy of the discourse itself—as when Paul says that "we have the same *pneuma* of faith that is in accordance with scripture [...] we also believe, and so we speak" (2 Cor. 4.13), and also that what is spoken is itself secure as a communication of *pneuma* (2 Cor 3.6).

Pneuma occurs frequently in the Letters as an oppositional concept, in opposition to matter, to body, to the finite in general, and directly in opposition to death. "But you are not in the flesh; you are in the Spirit" (Rom 8.9). Also in Romans it is said that "if you live according to the flesh, you will die: but if by the Spirit you put to death the deeds of the body, you will live" (8.13). *Pneuma* is thus fixed as a name for that which sur-vives, but also for the very possibility of survival, as a possible victory over mortality. What it promises is that there is survival, that there is a way to leave earthly bonds and thus to liberate oneself. The ultimate symbol of this promise is Jesus, who is taken to have vanquished death, and to have done so precisely in virtue of *pneuma* (Rom. 1.4).

Leaving aside the belief in resurrection, and the explicit contrast between a supposedly a-temporal spirit and temporal matter, we can see how the pneumatic carries a more general promise of a life liberated from destruction and also from being enclosed and entrapped, existing not outside time, but precisely in time, in a transformed time. In 2 Corinthians 3.17 there is a important passage that expands the conception of spirit in this direction. It speaks of how "where the *pneuma* of the Lord is, there is freedom." The whole context of this passage is worth reading, for it pushes the meaning of the *pneuma* toward another contrast, which in the end is more important than the one with mortal flesh, namely with literal tradition. Paul writes here of how the standard reader of the "old covenant"—i.e., the inherited body of Jewish literature—has a "veil [...] over their minds" (3.15), a veil that can only be lifted by the working of Christ as the vehicle of spirit. At this point *pneuma* thus emerges explicitly as the metonym for a practice and means of interpretation, as the capacity of gaining a more genuine access to tradition.

From here we can see the real significance of the fact that in many examples in Paul, spirit is not primarily contrasted with body or flesh (which it is too of course), but with "the letter," as when he writes in 2 Corinthians 3.6 that it is not of the letter but of the spirit, *ou grammatos alla pneumatos*. The spirit is then that by means of which a reader is supposedly enabled to move beyond the surface of what is read. It is not posited as entirely opposed to the *gramma*, but rather as being in the service of the *gramma*, as in the sense of "what is really said." It is, again and in short, *a capacity for living and receiving tradition*. It is a capacity to speak and communicate a message that is at once a part of tradition and in excess of tradition, as the second covenant is not "of the letter, but of the *pneuma*" (2 Cor. 3.6).

The same passage is followed by the remarkable conclusion "for the letter kills, but the *pneuma* gives life." Here the transition is established seamlessly between the problem of life and survival, and the very mode of how tradition is transmitted. And *pneuma* is at the heart of it all. If we abide by the letter we die, whereas the spirit will guarantee that we live. What then is this survival, for which the pneumatic reception is so central? How is it that we can die in and of a literal reception of tradition, whereas a pneumatic reception of it will enable it to live in us, and we through it? We need to phrase the question in this way in order to truly see what kind of herme neutics is at work in Paul, and how his preoccupation with the pneumatic is motivated by an attempt to orchestrate the destruction and the resurrection of tradition at once. In the end, the resurrection of Christ works as a metonymical promise of another resurrection, which is the resurrection of the individual and the community within the transmission of an inher-itance. Or as he writes in Romans 8.11: "If the *pneuma* of him who raised

Jesus from the dead dwells in you, he [...] shall also give life to your mortal bodies by his *pneuma* [trans. modified]."

The extent to which *pneuma* essentially has to do with how tradition is transmitted is highlighted most visibly perhaps in the second chapter of the first letter to the Corinthians. This is the passage where Paul presents himself as someone who comes not with "lofty speech or wisdom" (*sophia*), but with words of *pneuma* and power or strength (*dunamis*), that should guarantee that the listeners do not "rest in the wisdom of men but in the power of God." This pneumatically secured wisdom is then qualified in a temporal-historical way, by saying that it is "not of this time" (*ou tou aionos toutou*) but that it comes "before the ages" (*pro ton aionon*). This teaching or wisdom is then again qualified by *pneuma*, for it is what has been revealed through the *pneuma* (*dia tou pneumatos*), which is then followed by the formulation quoted earlier, of how the *pneuma* is what searches everything. In other words, *pneuma* is a means and vehicle of knowledge, communicated and transmitted through time. It acts so as to preserve what was there from the beginning, but which the passage of time itself tends to forget and dissimulate. Its knowledge is free, and it is also what brings about freedom. It is a force from ancient times that brings the present in touch with the past, to the extent that this present is already open to the past.

It is also at this particular point that the logic of Paul's pneumatics reaches its most intense moment in the entire corpus of the letters, as he writes of how we are "taught by the spirit, interpreting spiritual truths to those who are spiritual" (*alla en didaktois pneumatos pneumatikois pneumatika synkrinontes*). What he is reaching for here—this is the interpretation I am suggesting—is an articulation of the ideal of a truthful transmission of tradition, a tradition that can only be taught from within itself, in accordance with this itself, to those who are already open to it, and yet in contrast to the current cultivation of its message in the world.

In this particular passage, readers have often stopped short before what appears to be a strict demarcation between the spirit of the world (*pneuma tou kosmou*) and the spirit of God (*pneuma tou theou*), ending up in fruitless disputes concerning to what extent Paul is pointing beyond this world and its obligation and toward an entirely different world, which must then be countered with all his remarks of how we should still be committed to this world, to a love and concern for our immediate community, and more. But this discussion leads away from what I think we should see as the underlying motive of the entire narrative, namely to secure—metaphorically and poetically—that his audience remain open to the possibility of living the truth of tradition through time, across and against the constraints of the present.

In the following and final passage of this letter on learning, interpretation and transmission, the different types of intelligence are differentiated in a remarkable way. For here Paul writes that the ordinary human soul (*psuche*) does not reach into the *pneuma* of God, for these truths are only accessible through *pneuma* as the supreme and indisputable source of certainty. For the pneumatic man, he adds, is judged by no one. And in the last sentence he asks how we can reach into the reason or the *nous* of God's own self, answering that this is possible through the spirit and reason of Christ. For we have, he concludes, the mind or reason—the *nous*—of Christ.

The very formulation of "having the mind of Christ" (*noun Christou echoumen*), as a secured means of access to the *nous* of God can easily invite a reading of Paul as a mystic, particularly since he has referred earlier in the same passage to the "mysterious wisdom of God" (*en mysterio sophian theou*). But as Heidegger rightly points out in his lectures in relation to this particular passage, it is misleading to read Paul as a mystic in the conventional sense of the mystery cults.[26] His remarks are to the point, and they therefore lead in the direction of the interpretation that I have tried to develop here. Yet, in his urge to rid Paul of the label "*Pneumatiker*," Heidegger shuns away from the possibility of truly asses sing the weight and implication of the pneumatic in the Pauline letters, and thus also of reaching a more philosophically reflected understanding of pneumatics as such.

Once we have secured access to the phenomenological meaning of the pneumatological, as a "poietics" of historical existence and transmission of inheritance, we can also go further into the edifice of Pauline theology, and discern its structure. I am thinking in particular of the specific antagonistic framing of the pneumatic that runs through his discourse, where the

---

[26] GA 61, 123f. Here Heidegger recalls how this passage in particular was used to describe Paul as "*Pneumatiker*," according to which man himself is god, and thus connecting him to the Hellenist mystery cults "*Es besteht ein tiefer Gegensatz zwischen dem Mysten und dem Christen.*" But this conclusion, he adds, is misguided, *verfehlt*. To this he adds that the *pneuma* in Paul must be understood a basis for the realization of knowledge, a *Vollzugsgrundlage, aus dem das Wissen selbst entspringt.* This is then followed by a further rejection of a "mystical" understanding of Pauline Christianity. "*Der Myste wird durch Manipulation aus dem Lebenszusammenhang herausgenommen; in einem entrückten Zustand wird Gott und das All gegenwärtig gehabt. Der Christ kennt keinen solchen 'Enthusiasmus', sondern er sagt: 'Laß uns wach sein und nüchtern'.*"

pneuma is consistently acted out not just against the letter, but also against the law (*nomos*). We find an important passage to illustrate this constellation in Galatians 5.18, where it is written: "if you are led by the *pneuma*, you are not subject to the law." But not to be subject to the law is not equivalent to having left the law behind or to be law-less. On the contrary, and this is central to the Pauline message, it is only by not being subjected to the law that the genuine meaning of the law can be fulfilled. Or as it is stated in Romans 8.4: "that the righteousness (*to dikaoima*) of the law might be fulfilled in us, who walk not according to the flesh, but according to the spirit." Again we see how *pneuma* works to secure the access to the genuine meaning of the tradition, against the plain obedience, which looks only to current practice and interpretation. As a means of hermeneutic access, it establishes a link between past and present.

The same logic characterizes the passages that contrast *pneuma* and *gramma*, spirit and writing, that occur on several occasions, e.g., in Romans 7.6, that speaks of the delivery from the law as under a spell of death, and how life is made possible again not through the "oldness of the letter" (*palaioteti grammatos*) but through "the newness of pneuma" (*kainoteti pneumatos*). Here again the temporal dimension gives the clue to the interpretation. *Pneuma* is a newness of the old, that which comes before and through the times, whereas the letter is the oldness of the new. While the letter—that which is written—could seem to carry the weight and the truth of tradition and thus of what is living, it is in fact an inheritance of death. In contrast, the *pneuma* is what guarantees the life and liberation of the old, but of an oldness that in its newness is older than the old.

The event of Christ is for Paul a hermeneutic event, one that makes the ancient doctrines legible and valid again. The pneumatic understanding of this event and of its tradition is meant to secure access to this inheritance in understanding. Christ guarantees this access through his resurrection. The defining moment of his existence is not the fact that for a moment he was dead, and then again living, but that he through his example has shown how the tradition can become alive again as a promise. This is the matrix according to which Paul understands the relation to the tradition and the law (*nomos*), namely that it has become imbued with death, but that it can again—through *pneuma*—becoming living and thus also remain living.

With this in mind we can also make better sense of some of the most complex and troublesome statements on the relation to existing (Jewish) tradition. When we read in Romans that "a person is a Jew who is one inwardly; and real circumcision is a matter of the heart—in the *pneuma*, and not in the letter" (2.29), this makes perfect sense in relation to the suggested interpretation. It is not through the outer, material mark, nor through obedience to the written law, that one is true to one's tradition, but this is something that takes place through the connection between the *pneuma* of the law and the *pneuma* of the individual, in other words that one experiences oneself as attached, joined, and committed to one's human-intellectual inheritance.[27] This passage should therefore not be read primarily in the context of the subsequent controversies between Jewish and Christian communities, where it has worked its disastrous effects over the centuries, for this is not really what is at stake. What is at stake is, again, the attempt to grasp "poietically" the nature of a living bond to tradition, first of all for the Jews, and indirectly for anyone who is able to access it.

Concluding remarks: Pneuma as the life of traditionw

I have tried to show how we can and should read Pauline pneumatics as in fact a discourse primarily concerned with the problem of tradition and inheritance, and thus of the temporal condition of understanding. But it is indubitably the case that a central aspect of Paul's pneumatology is that of the triumph of life over death. In Romans 8.2 he writes that it is the *pneuma* of life in Christ that has liberated him from the law of sin and death. In Romans 6.23 the gift of God is said to be "eternal life" (*zoen aionion*), and to be "pneumatically minded" (*phronema tou pneumatos*) is equated with life, as opposed to being "bodily/carnally minded" which leads to death (Rom. 8.6). The examples could be multiplied. *Pneuma* is connected to life, and to the possibility of triumph over death. It is a word for survival, for the securing of survival, but also a name for that which survives. Tradition and legacy presupposes death. It is a law of history that the testator shall die, but also through his testament survive.[28] Second Corinthians 4.11 speaks of the

---

[27] The basic content of this image is repeated in 2 Cor. 3.3, where he writes of how the Letter from Christ is not one written with ink, but with *pneuma* of the living God, and "not in tables of stone," but in "the fleshy tables of the heart."

[28] In the letter to the Hebrews 9.13–20 (which according to standard biblical scholarship was written not by Paul himself but by a later follower) this connection between life, death, and inheritance is developed even further. It declares that in order for there to be a testament there must be the death of the testator. In the letter the death of the testator is given a sacrificial meaning, where the death of Christ becomes a sacrificial death through the eternal spirit, and one through which this spirit lives on in a new testament. For a more extended analysis of the role and meaning of sacrifice in Paul, see my

life of Jesus that is to be made manifest in the mortal flesh; in other words, it speaks of an infusion of life into the mortal body, and there is "victory" over death (1 Cor. 15.54).

But from whence does this life come? What is Paul here speaking about? A way of phenomenologically understanding this statement is that he is poetizing the experience of survival of an original impulse of life and capacity, as the memory of an original promise moving through time and history, countering the law of death. The *pneuma* is not just a position from within which the individual subject speaks, but it is the attempt to name that in tradition, which survives as a possibility for an unlimited future. It is the life in death, and the life across death. In 2 Corinthians 3.6 it is said that they have become "ministers of the new testament" (*diakonous diatekes*) not through the letter, but through the *pneuma*—for the letter kills, whereas *pneuma* gives life. The caretaking of the tradition is made possible by spirit as a principle of life and of survival.

It is in this sense that I believe that we should read what the Pauline letters speak of as spirit/*pneuma*, that it is an original reworking of the original sense of spirit as a transgenerational and ancestral force, operating through tradition and thus maintaining tradition. Paul understands himself as someone who transforms this inheritance, where spirit/*pneuma* is the name of his hermeneutical experience. It designates the genuine inheriting of tradition, in permitting the life of this tradition to be operative in himself and his community, but also a questioning of its inherited claim. This is also why he, as the carrier of a new and happy message, a *eu-angelos*, is also the one who must perform a "destruction" of that very same tradition. In Second Corinthians 10.4 he writes: "I destroy buildings of thought" (*logismous kathairtontes*; in Latin, *concilia destruentes*). This urge to destroy in order to remain living is also the point and source of his "madness." It is performed by an individual who in the next passage explicitly acknowledges himself to have a bit of madness (*aphrosynes*) within himself (2 Cor. 11.1). It is a spiritual madness, one that is said to serve the power and the spirit of a god, who also grants this power to his servant.

"Sacrificial Subjectivity," in Peter Jackson and Anna-Pya Sjödin (eds.), *Philosophy and the End of Sacrifice: Disengaging Ritual in Ancient India, Greece and Beyond* (Sheffield: Equinox, 2015).

We have reached the end of this attempt to interpret the role and meaning of *pneuma* in the Pauline letters. We have seen how it surfaces as a way of designating the enigma of tradition and of inheritance. Spirit is the locus of a "madness" in regard to reason precisely in that it refuses the legitimacy of reason only in order to make it possible for this reason to emerge again. It designates the way in which Paul secures his own access to a supposedly genuine message of a tradition that he is at once seeking to overthrow and to reclaim.

Matter, Magic, and Madness:
Giordano Bruno's Philosophy of Creativity

Jonna Bornemark

Religion, the limits of reason, and madness

Analyzing religion, philosophers have for a long time explicitly reflected upon the limits of rationality. Especially in phenomenology of religious experience, the relation to radical alterity has been explored most intensively. What can we per definition not know? How is subjectivity characterized by its not-knowing? And how is all knowledge related to the limits of knowledge? In this essay, I will not investigate these questions further; I will instead suggest that, through a reading of Giordano Bruno, madness can be understood as another side of this discussion on limits. Instead of focusing on what is impossible, we can with Bruno understand a similar basic structure of lack of overview not as a lack, but as a structure within which an infinite creativity is possible. This creativity goes beyond rational control, hierarchy and order; and therefore deserves to be called mad.

But why do we need this shift of perspective? Let us look a little bit closer at the phenomenological philosophy of religion. As I have discussed elsewhere I would argue that a limit of cognitive knowledge and of the reach of rationality is discovered in Husserl's analysis of inner time-consciousness.[1] In this analysis, the living stream of consciousness discovers the impossibility of having itself as an object. This is a very central place in modern phenomenology and its legacy is of crucial importance not least for French

---

[1] Jonna Bornemark, "Religion at the Center of Phenomenology: Husserl's Analysis of Inner Time-consciousness," in *Impossible Time: Future and Past in Philosophy of Religion*, eds. Marius Timmann Mjaaland and Ulrik Houlind Rasmussen (Tübingen: Mohr Siebeck Verlag, 2013).

phenomenology where radical alterity has been a key theme. In this discussion the divine easily becomes connected to transcendence and to a "beyond" (whatever one means by that). In a similar way there is no possibility for cognitive knowledge to fully know itself, as that would demand that it at the same time would be the object of knowledge and the subject of knowledge—and subjectivity cannot be transformed into objectivity without losing something central. In this way Husserl, and especially the tradition after him, has concluded that there is a certain transcendence in subjectivity as it evades any scientific (i.e. object-directed) knowledge. This evading of subjectivity has been connected to religious concepts such as "the divine," or "God." Transcendence here is an epistemological transcendence (even if it, as in Henry's case, is formulated as an immanence) in relation to an object's intentionality. But my fear is that there is something about the starting point in intentionality, in the transcendental Ego, and in the experience of the individual, that still lurks in phenomenology and that results in the strong divide between thematized object and transcendence. There is also, of course, another line of thinking in phenomenology, an a-subjective or non-individualistic approach found in thinkers like Max Scheler, Jan Patočka, Eugen Fink, and Maurice Merleau-Ponty, where the analysis of experience does not start with the experience of individuality. Here radical alterity becomes less important. Maybe this kind of phenomenology also opens up other kinds of religious experiences.

The phenomenological tradition has had a vivid dialogue with mystic strains of religion—and especially Christian mysticism.[2] Mystics often have been understood (rightly or wrongly) as having a religious tradition of transcendence and of a transcendent immanence (since what is most intimately me, the living stream, is not accessible to knowledge). But maybe this dialogue has been at the cost of other religious expressions, and maybe readings of other religious traditions would show us something different. My suggestion here is that one religious tradition of interest for an a-individualistic philosophical approach, which focuses on the living stream of experiences (which is one central concept from phenomenology that I wish to continue thinking with), and without the focus on radical alterity,

---

[2] See for example Jean-Luc Marion, *In the Self's Place: The Approach of Saint Augustine* (Stanford University Press, 2012); Harold G. Coward and Toby Foshay (eds.), *Derrida and Negative Theology* (Albany, New York: State University of New York Press, 1992); Anthony Steinbock, *Phenomenology and Mysticism: The Verticality of Religious Experience* (Bloomington: Indiana University Press, 2007).

might be a philosophical magic. In the ontology of Giordano Bruno there is a creativity that is not hindered by a radical alterity, but which in its embracement of itself, instead develops a certain madness of reason—far away from any kind of irrationality.

Giordano Bruno

But we have some work to do before we can come to this point. Giordano Bruno (1548–1600) provides us with an exciting intersection of Christian mysticism, Neo-Platonism, early science, and hermetic magic as he is inspired by Nicholas of Cusa, Plotinus, Copernicus, and Hermes equally.[3] Since Frances Yates (who wrote her famous work on Bruno 1964), it is accepted that he was part of, or at least deeply influenced by, a Renaissance magic tradition. His magical practice was probably limited to his specific art of memory, but his universe is animistic and magic—and this is what I want to explore in the following.

Just as early science did, and in contrast to Christian mysticism, Bruno understood the desire to create and control the world as something good rather than as something blasphemous. But the magic strain of his philosophy was nevertheless too provocative for the church and probably played a significant role in his conviction by the inquisition and death at the stake. Nevertheless, renaissance magic has also been understood exactly as an attempt to control the world, and thus as a proto-scientific attitude. This closeness to the rationale of science also condemns it as the most irrational of all religious attitudes. Within a scientific framework the modern verdict is hard: magic is the most irrational of all religious expressions and a mere superstition since it "doesn't work."

---

[3] I will draw on the following works by Bruno: *De la Causa, Principio et Uno* (1583), trans. Sidney Greenberg as *Cause, Principle and Unity* (henceforth: CPU), in *The Infinite in Giordano Bruno, with a Translation of his Dialogue Concerning the Cause, Principle, and One* (New York: King's Crown Press, 1950); *Del'infinito Universo et Mondi* (1584), trans. Dorothea Waley Singer as *On the Infinite Universe and Worlds* (henceforth: IUW), in *Giordano Bruno: His Life and Thought* (New York: Henry Schuman, 1950); *De magia* (written 1588, unpublished until 1891), trans. Robert de Lucca and Richard J. Blackwell as *On Magic* (henceforth: OM), in *Cause, Principle, and Unity* (Cambridge: Cambridge University Press, 1998), and *La Cena de le Ceneri* (1584), trans. Stanley L. Jaki as *The Ash Wednesday Supper* (Henceforth: AWS) (The Hague: Mouton, 1975).

But Bruno has also been understood as a precursor to the modern and scientific understanding of the world. He was impressed by Copernicus (1473–1543); furthermore, Galileo (1564–1642) picked up on Bruno's ideas. Just like Copernicus, Bruno had a heliocentric worldview where the earth rotates around its own axis and, like the other planets, circles the sun, rather than the sun circling the earth. But whereas Copernicus considered the stars motionless and "fixed" and his universe was, as in Ptolemy and Aristotle, a finite and rigidly bounded whole, Bruno's universe was infinite. The earth did not only lose its role as the center of the solar system, but also the solar system lost its central role as there is no fixed center in Bruno's infinite universe. In this way he plays an important part for the end of a Ptolemaic universe.[4] In Bruno there are no distinctions between physics, metaphysics and religion, and his discussions touch upon the physical world as well as upon ideal entities and religious goals. This has made it difficult for twentieth-century scientists to know how to read him: is he a (proto-)scientist, a philosopher, a mystic, a magus, or founder of a new religion? These positions have been separated during later centuries, but during his time they could all be included in one coherent vision of one's place in the world.[5] Bruno did contribute to a scientific understanding of the world, but his animism and vitalism, and his understanding of human beings as deeply interconnected with each other and the world, as well as part of the creativity of life (rather than a distant and objective spectator) is what science in modernity got rid of. Bruno might even have identified proponents of rationalistic modernity, as it came to be developed, as "Grammarians" or "Pedants"—his worst enemies, as he criticized all mechanistic thinking and logical rigidity. His universe is enchanted, but not irrational, it is rather the product of an infinitely creative rationality that continually finds new ways.

In many of Bruno's texts, there is a rationalistic tone—an Aristotelian rationalism that most often argues against Aristotle. But this rationalism is a drifting rationalism. It is impossible to find any fixed metaphysics, especially if one is looking for a unity within several of his works. But finding such a fixed metaphysics would be the desire of the Grammarians, and we do not want to belong to that category. Instead there is a movement going on here, a movement that goes deeper than any of his particular concepts. His concepts

[4] See Alexander Koyré, *From the Closed World to the Infinite Universe* (Baltimore and London: The Johns Hopkins University Press, 1957).
[5] This has been discussed in Ernan McMullin, "Bruno and Copernicus," *Isis*, Vol. 78, No 1 (March 1987): 55–74.

should always be understood in relation to each other, in a mutual co-dependence. Sidney Greenberg, translator and commentator of Bruno's work, states that without knowing how to distinguish without separating, one will never understand Bruno.[6] This becomes most apparent in the key distinction between cause and principle in *Cause, Principle and Unity*.

Principle and cause

The distinction between cause and principle is of great importance to Bruno's philosophy. The close relation between these creates a position we might call panenteism. But let's take it from the beginning. Bruno explains the difference between cause and principle in the following way: a principle contributes to the creation of a thing (or rather of some-thing) and remains within it; a cause, on the other hand, likewise contributes to the creation of some-thing, but is other than the thing. In the first one, the action is intrinsic; in the second, it is extrinsic. Bruno claims that when we call God (or the universal intellect) cause or principle, we point toward the same thing, but from different perspectives. God is first cause, to the extent that all things are different from it: all things, beings and worlds taken together do not add up to the creative power of world-creation. But as universal intellect it is neither different from things, beings nor worlds. It creates from within, constantly calling forth new forms in letting matter take new shapes. As extrinsic its efficiency is not one of the things that is produced, and as intrinsic it does not operate outside of matter—and since it is only its operation, it does not exist outside of matter.

This emphasis on a creation from within has recently led to a comparison of Bruno with Gilles Deleuze. Eliot Albert tries in his thesis to point toward some similarities. Unfortunately he does not undertake any close readings of Bruno's texts; nevertheless, he picks up some central themes. Both Bruno and Deleuze develop an ontology of becoming, production, and self-organization where there is a multitude of forces which affect and are affected, without center and without periphery. They both describe how the one and the multiple hold together, as the many are modal differentiations of one matter. As we will see in Bruno, matter is intelligent and intelligence material. They also have similar enemies as they argue against all-too-fixed

---

[6] Greenberg, *The Infinite in Giordano Bruno*, 40.

logical identities and in favor of a metaphysics of an irreducible pluralism, in which concepts also are in movement.[7]

But in contrast to Deleuze, there is for Bruno still room for a concept of God, even if it is not a transcendent God. Here God as first cause is not a substance either in a physical or a metaphysical sense, but as the "coming forth" of everything. It is a living, creative movement through which everything takes shape. This living movement is one and the same for everything existent, as it is the movement of coming into existence. Of course this living movement, God or universal intellect, is neither any of those beings that come into existence nor all of them taken together nor something separate or transcendent from those beings. It is intimately connected as intrinsic principle, but not exhausted in the world, and thus is an extrinsic cause. Maybe the difference from Deleuze's philosophy on this point is simply conceptual, as Bruno's God is a working force rather than a transcendent power. We find here neither scientific materialism nor theology or apophatic mysticism, but rather a magic, living universe. Maybe it could be called a magic materialism.

Matter

What then is matter here? It is not a Khora, which is unreachable for perception and understanding, as it is not beyond being and sensibility. It is no "absolute bare substratum" as Plotinus would have it. On this point Bruno is rather inspired by Cusa's idea that matter does not exist outside of God. Matter is in Bruno rather the *taking form* of life. No part of matter is without form since it is the form-taking. It is the *capacity to exist*. Matter is potency in its constant change of forms. It is the receiver of forms, but the forms does not exist somewhere else beyond matter, rather "all the forms together must be taken merely as various dispositions of matter, which come and go and cease and renew themselves" (CPU 134). There is no "dead matter" but only living bodies that, Bruno tells us, have three aspects: "first, the universal intellect inherent in things; [as it is comprehensive], second, the vivifying soul of all [being part of the living movement of "coming forth of forms"]; third, the substratum [the capacity to exist]" (CPU 135). To talk about form and matter

---

[7] Eliot Albert, *Towards a Schizogenealogy of Heretical Materialism* (Coventry: Warwick University Prress, 1999), 23, 25, 95, 161.

as two principles conceal their interdependence. Form is the disposition of matter; matter is the capacity to take form, i.e. to be. There is here a multitude in an indivisible being as Bruno says: "I will call matter that in which all those forms are united" (CPU 149). In addition, potentiality and actuality are interwoven in matter. Matter is the capacity to be formed (i.e. a passive potency) whereas form is the capacity to form (i.e. an active potency). Matter is a potency through which everything is in actuality. It is act in its capacity to be (CPU 138, 151).[8]

Potency is also central to understanding the relation between the human being, the universe and the divine: the human being is what she can be, but *not all* that she can be. The universe is *not yet all* that can be. Absolute potency (i.e. God) is *all* it can be in its creating force. These three positions try to formulate the pure act in matter taking form, and divides it into: 1) pure act—or absolute potency—since the divine is where the separation between potency and actuality is dissolved; 2) the sum of everything produced (the universe); and 3) the produced producing, living created—of which humankind is one (CPU 139f).

Bruno continues by stating that matter is not only corporeal, since not only corporeal beings can come into existence. As a spiritual and intellectual matter, intellects constantly take form in ideas (CPU 151). Matter in itself is not extension and measurable, but it can become extension in its taking form. Or, rather, it can be measurable, but its measures will be different and changing.

As Bruno proceeds in his analysis of matter, it becomes more and more interconnected to spirituality, intellect and the divine. It becomes abstracted. Act and potency coincide more and more in matter as the capacity to take form and thus at the same time the giving of form. From a starting point in *Cause, Principle and Unity*, it could even be claimed that intellect and form are concepts born from the capacity of matter to take form, and when this capacity is separated from the mere *potentiality* to take form, matter (the potentiality to take form) and form (the actual form-taking) develops into two concepts that become opposites of each other.

---

[8] Maybe Isabelle Stengers and other contemporary materialists who search for a materialism that is not reductionistic, and in which thinking, life and experiencing does not remain a mystery, would find a precursor in Bruno. For this quest in contemporary philosophy, see for example Isabelle Stengers "Diderot's Egg – Divorcing Materialism from Eliminativism," in *Radical Philosophy*, No. 144 (2007): 7–15.

Discussing matter, therefore, also includes a discussion on intelligence, soul and form. In discussing cause and principle, Bruno distinguishes between three forms of intelligence: "the divine which is all things, the mundane which make all things, and the other particular ones which become everything" (CPU 113). All forms are what Bruno calls soul, and thus everything is animated. In the dialogue he also immediately gets the objection: but the table does not have a soul! No, Bruno answers, not *as* table. But as a natural thing it has both matter and form; no matter how small it is, it still has part of a spiritual substance. All that has soul is not animal. Everything is part of soul and life, even if it does not act (CPU 117f). Life does not take place as isolated intellects, human or animal: life includes all and is rather the living bond between individuals. The intellect thus binds us together; just like matter, the intellect is what we share.

Bruno therefore also argues that spirit, consciousness, and life cannot be extinguished, since it is what exists; only outer forms can be erased—but erasure of one form involves the origin of a new form (CPU 118f). Intellect is thus, just as is matter, a movement, but the movement of a *calling forth* of forms in matter. Intellect is not ready-made forms that can be *taken on* by or infused in matter as if it were extrinsic to matter.

Matter in this way tends to include all the other concepts: intellect, form, idea, etc. And this tendency is also explicitly met in the dialogue:

- Why do you wish that it includes all, rather than that it excludes all?
- Because it does not come to receive the dimensions from without, but sends them out from and casts them out as from her womb (CPU 153).

Here matter is spoken of in more and more female categories as it becomes more and more active, and no longer a pure potency: "the pregnant is without progeny, which she sends forth and obtains from herself" (CPU 153). It is also explicit from the start of the dialogue that the discussion on matter is a discussion on the female (maybe not as women and sex, but rather as a principle, and thus as gender).

Bruno also concludes the discussion on matter with a note on the woman. Matter

> does not desire those forms which daily change on her back, because every well-ordered thing desires that from which it receives perfection. What can a corruptible thing give to an eternal thing, i.e. an imperfect thing such as the form of

sensible things which is always in movement—to something so perfect that if it is well contemplated is a divine being in things (CPU 158).

Without matter (i.e. the woman), the form (i.e. the man) loses all its power to exist. Matter continually throws off individual forms that it plays with for a short while. All of a sudden we find Bruno in a heterodox position, presenting a view somewhere between asexual reproduction where the male is superfluous (as matter brings forth forms by herself) and procreation with non-stable, promiscuous partners (where matter is constantly united with new and different forms). This position shows the strong heretical capacity of Bruno. It shows his capacity to throw things upside down and, at the same time, to work in continuity with tradition. He explicitly wants to think beyond duality—or rather continue thinking—through showing the mutual dependency of opposites, up to the point where the opposites coincide. There is a oneness beyond, or rather within, the infinite multiplicity of the world, and this is the key to his concept of infinity.

Living infinity

Infinity is often said to be the main subject in Bruno's thinking, not least since this is Bruno's contribution to the scientific tradition, as stated above. When it comes to infinity, Bruno once again draws on Nicolas of Cusa as he argues for an infinite cosmos without center and periphery, with no absolute position or circumference, where everything is moving, the earth as well as the stars. This position is also inspired by a Neo-Platonic universe where one Whole, God, or universal Nature is perfect and continuously emanating. But Bruno also disagrees with Plotinus on the notion that everything that can exist exists; instead Bruno argues that it is more perfect to continue being creative. Neither, therefore, does Bruno agree with the idea that the One is one in itself beyond its production of the world's intellect as it is emanated into the world; in this way Plotinus emphasizes a transcendence and the One as an external cause. For Bruno, God has no limits—i.e. his faculties of creation have no limits—and thus the universe has no limits and there is no limit to what could exist. God is an infinite divine potency which always also is its actuality. As such God also consists of numberless worlds with an infinite number of beings in an infinite time.

Bruno here also argues against dualism and against the idea that infinity and finitude are opposites: that there are two worlds, the finite and the divine infinite. Bruno tries to conceptualize of them together and formulates this as infinitely many finite worlds and beings. But he also understands infinity as the order and relation between all these worlds. Bruno emphasizes the simultaneity and co-dependence between finite beings, infinite numbers of finite beings and infinity as perpetually giving birth and infinite form-taking.

Bruno here tries to find a position between Aristotle's understanding that infinity has to do with quantity, which is always calculable and thus not infinite, and the Christian idea where infinity excludes extension and only can be understood as a transcendent God. He builds upon Cusa's idea that the universe has a kind of infinity since it is the greatest of all created. Also in line with Cusa, the infinity of the creating power should not primarily be related to a lack of knowledge and indefiniteness, but be understood as one perfect movement. The oneness of the movement binds together this infinite creativity with the created and infinite universe since the universe is the living reflection of the infinite substance. This infinite substance has no parts, but is rather a constant generativity. There is thus an extensive and an intensive side to infinity. The universe is extensive infinity since it has no margins or limits, even if its parts can have margins and limits.[9] And what he calls infinite substance, intellect, God, etc. is the intensive side in its infinite creativity.

Both the extensive and intensive infinity is one, unmovable, and without limit and end. It is the unchangeable aspect of the continual change (IUW 269). "[I]t is form in such a way that it is not form; it is matter in such a way that it is not matter; it is soul in such a way that it is not soul—because it is all indifferently and, in short, is one; the universe is one" (CPU 160). The surroundings are not different from what is surrounded, as a container is of a very different category than the things contained. In Bruno the universe is moving, and a plenum, rather than a void (IUW 254f). This also means that there is one and the same order everywhere. There are infinite numbers of parts and an infinite variety, but only one universe: one in its source, life and laws. As there is the same order everywhere, there is no special place for the human being. In this way also Bruno's philosophy is a threat against the Christian faith. God should here be understood as the nature of nature, or nature in its capacity of becoming nature (*natura naturans*), in contrast to natural beings (*natura naturata*). Divinity is the all-synthesizing principle

---

[9] This is discussed in Greenberg, *The Infinite in Giordano Bruno*, 12ff, 45ff.

that is revealed in nature. God is thus immanent in nature, but at the same time transcending it in its creative power.

There is thus an implicit and an explicit infinity, where the implicit infinity could be understood as the womb of the explicit (see, for example, IUW 361). Birth and the womb here become central categories, and life and vitalism are never far away.

The universe is alive, and even if its life is different in degree, it is still present everywhere. Everything moves because of its own intrinsic desires: humans, animals, planets, and things. Gravity is the movement of things to strive toward the center of its world. Iron desires the magnet. Instinct is nothing but the desire of the animals, and more (AWS 211f). Bruno sometimes describes planets as great animals, wandering about in the sky (AWS 155). Here "animals" should be understood in connection to its root "anima." They are living since life is here intimately connected to movement, and especially to bodies moved by their interior principles. Just like an animal, the earth has its inflow and outflow: the ocean is its intestines and the air is its lungs (AWS 157, 161). Today we might call it an eco-system. As a living whole, we are part of this organism; matter keeps picking up new forms, and the form (for example of a body) keeps picking up and getting rid of new matter, in an eternal flux beyond individual death and birth (AWS 223). Therefore, Bruno's philosophy has also been called an animist philosophy.[10] Such a philosophy of course also has a deep impact on how human understanding is possible.

Human understanding

As noted above, Bruno's concepts should not be understood as fixed; instead they slide into one another. He uses the image of how a point moving itself becomes a line, and a line moving itself becomes a surface, and a surface in its movement becomes a body.

It is necessary, then, that in the infinite, the point does not differ from the body because the point, running away from being a point, becomes a line; running away from being a line, it becomes a surface; running away from being a surface, it becomes a body. The point then, since it is in poten-

[10] For example by Guiseppa Candela in "An Overview of the Cosmology, Religion and Philosophical Universe of Giordano Bruno," *Italica*, Vol 75, No 3 (Autumn 1998): 348–364.

tiality a body, does not differ from being a body, where the potency and act are one and the same thing (CPU 161f).

In this way, Bruno explains how everything in the universe is interconnected, and in a similar way sense perception, cognition, and understanding move into each other. This also means that opposites are separated only in relation to each other: love for one thing is hate towards another (for example, a threat toward the loved); and coldness is the absence of heat (CPU 170ff). This interconnectedness also results in every being in its own mode comprehending the whole world-soul, although not totally. The universe as extension is thus not a container of individual beings, but an interval and space as everything moves within and through this understanding, preserving, moving, efficient cause and principle (CPU 164). The position of everything can only be defined in relation to another object. The coinciding of contraries means that each thing is within every other; they only exist in relation to each other. This is also why we can understand the world, since the world is in us and we in the world as a nesting micro- and macrocosmic structure. Therefore, to understand is to distinguish without separating.

Bruno is part of a metaphysical tradition and, in his attempts to describe and be part of a living world, he also implicitly shows how a living name-giving turns into fixed concepts and substances. When he uses a concept such as "substance" it is not yet a metaphysical substance as complete in itself. He rather shows the intrinsic connections between concepts such as "Substance," "Matter," "God," and "Soul," and how they can only be understood in relation to each other as attempts to distinguish specific aspects of the movement of a living stream.

Human understanding strives toward perfection. But exactly what such perfection would be is an important question to Bruno. Once again he argues against Aristotle who claims that perfection includes limitation and self-completeness. Bruno instead asserts that perfection means that which never reaches its fulfillment. There is here an indefiniteness of overflowing and inexhaustibility, and Bruno's influences from negative theology become apparent. But in Bruno such an overflowing is formulated in positive terms since the infinite understanding is an *understanding without end*, rather than a focus on the *limit of understanding*. (This is perhaps a concept of infinity that more resembles Spinoza than Plotinus.)[11] Such an ever evolving understanding could also be found in science, but what is lost in science, from a philosophical point of view, is Bruno's nuanced and multifaceted analysis of the relation between ratio and the infinity of cosmos. This infinity is not reachable through the senses—or only through an interpretation of the senses—but demands fantasy in dialogue with the sorting capacity of reason.[12]

Bruno's *Eroici furori* tells us more about the human desire for knowledge, which he claims can never be satisfied in finite truths. Yates tells us that desire is central in hermetic magic where love binds everything together. In this sympathetic magic the magus acts through participating in a divine love and through lines of sympathy that bind things together.[13]

Since we are part of the infinite birth-giving process, we desire to become all in all things, and are thus directed toward the infinite. Since we are part of this movement, the infinite is not only the extended world around us, but also intrinsic within us, and we desire to fulfill this intrinsic infinity by having infinite knowledge that would include the extended world. This insatiable hubris can be characterized as a madness of reason. But this does not necessarily mean that we desire to have knowledge of every object as an object with its specific relations (which would be the scientific way to fulfill this desire), or to understand the driving, birth-giving oneness of all objects as a divinity on its own (which would be the theological way to fulfill this desire), but rather to follow this infinite generativity in "becoming world."

But this is also what is impossible since the human mind can become everything; that is, it can understand everything but one: the absolute act.

> [B]ecause the intellect, when it wishes to understand, must form the intelligible species, assimilate it, measure itself with it, and make itself equal to that: but this is here impossible, because the intellect never is such that it cannot be greater, the other, however, inasmuch as it is in every sense and from all sides immeasurable,

---

[11] For a discussion on perfection in Bruno, see John Powell, "Perfection as a Cosmological Postulate: Aristotle and Bruno," *The Philosophical Review*, Vol 44, No 1, (Jan 1935): 57–68.

[12] Dorothea Walay Singer "The Cosmology of Giordano Bruno," *Isis*, Vol 33 (June 1941): 187–196, 194. Fantasy is also a central component in his art of memory as a magical practice. I discuss this further in "Giordano Bruno's Mnemonics: A Deleuzian Reading," in *Monument and Memory*, eds. Jonna Bornemark, Mattias Martinsson, and Jayne Svenungson (Berlin: LIT-Verlag, 2015).

[13] Frances Yates, *Giordano Bruno and the Hermetic Tradition* (London: Routledge, 1978 [1964]), 142.

cannot be greater than it is. There is therefore, no eye capable of approaching and having access to this highest light and this deepest abyss (CPU 141).

I find this a very interesting way to formulate the limit of human reason. In short, the absolute act cannot be greater and the human intellect can always be greater. This shows Bruno's radically affirmative position. Of course we find here an affinity with negative theology, and in this sense there is room for an epistemological transcendence in Bruno, but at the same time it is formulated in such a way that the human intellect in its infinite creativity takes on the infinite act, whereas the absolute act is immovable and thus betrays its constant creativity. Human understanding is something born (and not infinite), but born as always giving birth to understanding. As giving birth, it can mirror the continual changing, and thus the standing, of the pure act, but it cannot give birth to this standing. However this is not a loss, but rather a mad overcoming of the position. This standing is not what should or ever could be comprehended; exactly on this point the human intellect should embrace its own creativity and become a magus....[14]

Magic

The magus affects the world and uses its characteristic of being composed of all things woven together, as a magician is "a wise man who has the power to act" (OM 107).[15] Magic manipulates parts of the living universe by, for example, evoking its desires to move in a certain direction. And since every being contains everything else, it is possible for the magus to entice

[14] Also on this point, we can find a certain alliance between the philosophy of Bruno and that of Deleuze. In *Bergsonism* he argues that the human being has a specific place in the movement of life as she has the possibility to go beyond her own plane and have a relation to that which lies beyond her (109). This capacity is not the ability to correctly represent the world beyond, but to a certain kind of creativity in relation to it. As creative the human being uses a certain intuition that is in atunement with that which is not human. This creative emotion does not arise in all human beings equally, but more in certain individuals than in others. Its arising goes beyond the pressures of society and connects the person to a cosmic memory "in order to make him a creator, adequate to the whole movement of creation" (111). This connection to the virtuality, and memory of the world is not an act of contemplation, but of creativity since that which one connects to is a movement of constant creativity (111). To go beyond oneself here, as well as in Bruno, is thus not a movement of erasing oneself, but of continuing the creating movement which we all are made up by. Gilles Deleuze, *Bergsonism* (New York: Zone Books, 1991).
[15] *On Magic*, 1588.

the desired form into existence. Matter is the womb of any form, and continually changes form. This changing of form is what the magus wishes to be active in. The practice of magic is thus a practice of bonding, and of binding together in order to influence.

Bruno's living universe includes all kinds of living beings. Only through such a basic understanding of the living world can we understand inter-action within this world, and also between things that are far apart from each other. Neither what we call matter nor what we call soul or ideas (form) can, as we have seen, exist separately from each other (OM 116). Thinking is not one kind of sphere outside, or beside, matter. It takes place within matter, and influences it just as other kinds of movements in matter influence thinking. Through this life that goes through us, we are also bound together. Just as one life in the human body causes vision in the eyes, hearing in the ears, or taste in the mouth, the soul of the world produces different subjects and different actions (OM 111). Vision can only grasp what is distant immediately and without motion since it belongs to an outspread soul (OM 112). Magic includes understanding the intertwine-ment of beings, and the different expressions of one and the same, as well as being an active and acting part of the intertwinement and its expressions.

Bruno specifies different kinds of magic and orders them into three types: physical, divine, and mathematical.

1. Divine or theurgical magic includes controlling demons, gods, heroes and other spirits. These spirits can here be understood as part of this living world; we experience them as ideas, emotions, thoughts and ideas—in short as *Wesen*, beings that move around in the world inde-pendent of (individual) humans, but affecting humans. "[S]pirits fluc-tuate from one matter to another, and matter fluctuates from one spirit to another" (OM 125). That everything has its spirit means that it has its sense and is part of the form-taking nature of matter, and this is not limited to human minds. To be a spirit, or be a part of spirit, does not mean to be thinking or experiencing, but rather to be part of experi-encing just as something experienced is also part of an interwoven, living net. Human minds are of course part of this living net, and as living spirits we reflect the whole in our own way.
2. Physical or natural magic includes practices that we would understand as science, but here they are put into a magical framework. Examples of such practices are the use of magnets, or any kind of medicine or

chemistry. Even physically pushing things could be a kind of magic if this were an attempt to awaken the soul of an existing thing.

3. Finally there is a mathematical magic. The term "mathematical" might surprise us, but it is mathematical, Bruno explains, since it uses figures and symbols like geometry does, it uses chants like music does, it uses numbers and manipulation like arithmetic does, and it is interested in times and motions like astronomy is (OM 108).

Surprisingly, Bruno states that only the last kind of magic can be both good and evil, whereas the first two can only be good (OM 107). It is quite difficult to see from the text why this might be so, but he argues in the following way: the highest one, divine magic, works on the plane of ideas (for example, friendship and strife); the second one is the physical, which emanates from the first one (for example, water and fire); emanating from this second one is the lowest type (for example, light and darkness—as a dualism). I understand these three steps as: 1) the living flux and intrinsic infinity; 2) nature as extrinsic flux; and 3) mathematics as locking things up in their substantiality, keeping things within locked-up opposites, and thus hindering flux. In a similar way, he argues that the invention of letters, which would be included in a mathematization of the world, "resulted in a tremendous loss, first of memory, and then of divine science and magic" (OM 115). He contrasts our alphabet with the hieroglyphics, which are open to different and fluid representation, and as such they are closer to natural objects and individual things. The adoption of letters betrayed this kind of symbolism as they seek to fix meaning and betray individual sensitivity.

Magic needs to include a sensitivity to what is singular and specific in each situation: "not all things are influenced by everything else, and not all effects happen to everything in the same way. To give a proper explanation, the reason must be found in individual effects and cases. The occult forms and differences in things do not have their own names" (OM 134f). They are beyond perception. Just as different harmonies bind different persons, different magicians bind different spirits (OM 135).

Conclusion

From Bruno's perspective monotheism drains nature of life, separating life, form, and intellect from matter and nature. Bruno's magic materialism is an attempt to bring them together, as he argues against any fixation of radical alterity and for an affirmation of a creativity of rationality and intellect, because matter constantly is taking form. This takes us to a mad and rational measurability in motion, one in which mind and matter are not separated and where continual creativity takes place, far beyond the Grammarian's attempts to lock the world up.

Just as in phenomenology, there is an epistemological transcendence or radical alterity in Bruno's philosophy: the pure giving of the world, which earns the name "God," cannot be fully known. But this negativity is in Bruno transformed into infinite creativity. It is not an experience of impossibility but of infinite possibility. In relation to the impossibility to fully make subjectivity into an object for cognitive knowledge, what is emphasized here is not the impossibility to know subjectivity, but rather the non-fixated character of any knowledge as it is intimately bound to living, moving subjectivity. In relation to the radical alterity of the other person, this could be understood as the infinite possibility to understand one another, and not as the possibility to fully "own" or even be the other person (and experience exactly what the other person is experiencing). There is no static "experience" and no full experience of oneself; rather, there is a continual flux of which we are different parts. Understanding and experience move around and are not locked into one person who would have exclusive access to her own experiences. This does not open to irrationality, but to an enchanted rationality—i.e. not a calculating rationality, since there are no fixed substances that will stay in place while they are being counted, but an overflowing rationality that is constantly in motion as it keeps on reflecting itself, and as such is alive. It never has itself or the world under control or fully sees itself or the world, but keeps giving birth to the world as it keeps creating meaning. As such it also includes a certain kind of madness as its creativity always precedes any ordering rationality. In enchanted rationality, the capacity to order and control should instead be understood as a kind of creativity, a creativity that gives birth to its own rules of the game.

The limit of calculating rationality is not the limit of enchanted rationality: not to have a full overview is a problem and a lack for calculating rationality; but to enchanted rationality there are constantly new patterns to be investigated, and thus to be changed. Radical alterity or transcendence as a lack and a limit is only a problem to calculating rationality in its eagerness to see and control everything at once. To enchanted rationality what has been expressed as a radical alterity is rather an area to continue moving within.

The Unjustifiable in a Philosophical Rationality. An Example: Swedenborg in the Critique of Pure Reason

Monique David-Ménard

For centuries, Kant's readers in the university have maintained that critical and transcendental philosophy had its origin in an engagement with the ideas of Leibniz and Hume. Albeit, Kant himself wrote in the *Prologemena to any future metaphysics that will be able to come forward as science*: "I freely admit that the remembrance of David Hume was the very thing that many years ago first interrupted my dogmatic slumber and gave a completely different direction to my researches in the field of speculative philosophy."[1] However, if the book about spirit-seer Swedenborg is ascribed a certain place in the development of the Kantian system, it is usually in relation to practical philosophy. For example, what is studied is the structure of the drives, which can be connected with the categorical imperative, and the reliance of pure reason on Kant's interest for *Schwärmerei* (enthusiasm) is not highlighted in scholarship. Or rather, the relationship between metaphysics and enthusiasm is claimed only in very broad terms: for example Hartmut and Gernot Böhme remark that "spirit-seeing is for all intents and purposes the basis of experience for metaphysics, as metaphysics in return shows that spirit-seeing is possible." Yet they do claim, in reading the book about Swedenborg that "Kant was done with anything to do with demons, dreams or ghosts."[2] So critical philosophy is seen as a retreat onto safe ter-

---

[1] Immanuel Kant, *Prologomena to any Future Metaphysics that Will be Able to Come Forward as a Science*, trans. Gary Hatfield, in *Cambridge Edition of the Works of Immanuel Kant. Theoretical Philosophy after 1781* (Cambridge: Cambridge University Press, 2002), 57.
[2] See Hartmut Böhme and Gernot Böhme, *Das Andere der Vernunft: Zur Entwicklung von Rationalitätsstrukturen am Beispiel Kants* (Frankfurt am Main: Suhrkamp, 1983), 258.

ritory. But these remarks leave unexplained why in the same years, 1763 and 1764—thus before he got interested in the writings of Swedenborg—Kant worked on two different fields of research: on the one hand, delusion, and on the other hand, the logic of negation. In 1763 the *Attempt to Introduce the Concept of Negative Magnitudes into Philosophy* was published and in 1764 the *Essay on the Illness of the Head* as well as the *Observations on the Feeling of the Beautiful and Sublime*. The *Negative Magnitudes* put forth two different negations: contradiction is the destruction of the content of a thought. It is purely formal, however, and has nothing to do with reality, as opposed to the "real conflict" or "real repugnancy" or real opposition, an algebraic definition that constitutes something real. Everything that can be determined as real has to be constituted through the real conflict. If any idea cannot undergo this kind of negation—like for example the idea of God, which cannot contain any limitation—it is also impossible to define it as the concept of something real. On the surface, this problematic of negation has nothing to do with the observations on enthusiasm and delusion.[3] In the *Essay on the Illness of the Head* one can find a categorization of mental ill-nesses which cloud and trouble reason, judgement, or the senses. The senses also have to do with feeling and so with power of imagination, which he talks about in the third text. What the text about the illnesses of the head and the text about the sublime and the beautiful have in common is easy to see: the moral sense of the sublime is not far off from fanaticism and fanaticism is also connected with one of the illnesses of the head.

The two texts published in 1764 are thus related. One can observe that fanaticism is very close to enthusiasm in Kant's anthropological and moral writings. One could say that enthusiasm is the theoretical unfolding of fanatic empathy. But what does all of that have to do with negation?

The answer to that question is not given until 1766, in the *Dreams of a Spirit-Seer elucidated by Dreams of Metaphysics*: just as the negative magni-

---

[3] Apart from a comparison between contradiction and metaphysics and madness and illusion at the beginning of the book. Yet it is impossible to grasp the importance of this reference here, at the beginning of the book. It seems to be more of a rhetorical effect: "For learned nonsense cannot create the illusion of thoroughness here as easily as it can else-where. ... As for the metaphysical intelligentsia who are in possession of a perfect under-standing of things, one would have to be very inexperienced to imagine that their wisdom could be increased by any addition, or their madness diminished by any subtraction." "Attempt to Introduce the Concept of Negative Magnitudes into Philosophy," trans. David Walford, *The Cambridge Edition of the Works of Immanuel Kant. Theoretical Philosophy 1755-1770* (Cambridge: Cambridge University Press, 1992), 210.

THE UNJUSTIFIABLE IN A PHILOSOPHICAL RATIONALITY

tude resists the formalism of logical contradiction by determining something real, so the "waking dreamer" avoids the unlimited expansion of his
imagination by differentiating between "something" and his fancies.

> Hence, the images in question may very well occupy him greatly while he is
> awake, but, no matter how clear the images may be, they will not deceive him.
> For although, in this case, he also has a representation of himself and of his body
> in his brain, and although he relates his fantastical images to that representation,
> nonetheless, the real sensation of his body creates, by means of the outer senses,
> a contrast or distinction with respect to those chimaeras. As a result, he is able to
> regard his fantastical images as hatched out by himself and the real sensation as
> an impression of the senses.[4]

Does not the real opposition become the means to escape the endless and
shrewd game of feeble contradiction, just like the waking dream, in which a
"something" provides a contrast to the expansion of enthusiastic imagination?

The object is here, for the first time, depicted as that which makes the
unlimited expansion of mad imagination or the mad arguing of reason possible. That is maybe the most important point of intersection between the
description of the illnesses of the head and the new concept of negation:
something is defined as real if it limits the endless expansion of imagination
or of formal logic.

With this notion of the object we can now approach the *Critique of Pure
Reason*. Is Kant's relationship to Swedenborg only a youthful affair, which is
irrelevant to the construction of critical and transcendental philosophy, or
does his engaging with a theosophist actually pose a significant question,
making it a vital point not only in Kant's practical and anthropological writings, but also when it comes to the discovery of a new way of doing philosophy? In what way can the first *Critique* be described as a conceptual
separation from Swedenborg's thinking?

The name Swedenborg does not come up in the book any further. However, the engagement with Swedenborg's topics is not absent from the book.
I would like to present this ongoing occupation with him as one of the most
important sources for the separation between dialectic and analytic, between the new theory of negation and modality, and in general the concept

---

[4] *Dreams of a Spirit-seer Elucidated by Dreams of Metaphysics*, trans. David Walford, *The
Cambridge Edition of the Works of Immanuel Kant, Theoretical Philosophy 1755–1770*, 330.

of the object (*Gegenstand*) of knowledge as a result of his struggle with Swedenborg.

Maybe the struggle with another thinker is necessary in order to invent a new kind of philosophy. Such a struggle is not a simple dependency, but more like a kinship, which gets distorted into a new conceptual problem. Swedenborg's thought, Swedenborg's fanciful experience became a danger for Kant, from which the philosopher wanted to extract its theoretic possibility and on the path of this work the idea of philosophy itself changed.

The New Theory of Modality

First of all, let's look at the kernel of the engagement in the first *Critique*, which is the new concept of modality: the principles of Swedenborg's thinking get a precise description under the title of the first and second "postulates of empirical thought as such": possibility and actuality.[5] First, "What agrees (in terms of intuition and concepts) with the formal conditions of experience is *possible*." Second, "What coheres with the material conditions of experience (with sensation) is *actual*." These two definitions are necessary to be able to accord a status to a thinker like Swedenborg. Swedenborg is not called Schwedenberg as was the case in *Dreams of a Spirit-Seer*;[6] he is now "some."

His way of thinking is rendered very precisely in 1781 as in 1766 and can be located, as it were, between the newly definable modalities of possibility and reality:

> Consider a substance that would be present permanently in space, but without occupying it (like that intermediate something between matter and thinking beings which some have wanted to introduce); or a special basic power of our mind for intuiting (and by no means merely inferring) future events in advance; or, finally, an ability of the mind to stand in community of thought with other human beings (no matter how distant they may be). These are concepts whose possibility is entirely baseless. For we cannot base it on experience and its general laws. But without this experience and these laws that possibility is an arbitrary combination of thoughts; and although this combination of thoughts

---

[5] Immanuel Kant, *Critique of Pure Reason, Unified Edition*, trans. Werner S. Pluhar (Indianapolis/Cambridge: Hackett, 1996), 283.
[6] "In Stockholm there dwells a certain Schwedenberg, a gentleman of comfortable means and independent position." Immanuel Kant, *Dreams of a Spirit-seer Elucidated by Dreams of Metaphysics*, 341.

contains no contradiction, yet it cannot lay claim to objective reality, nor therefore to the possibility of such an object as one here wishes to think.[7]

Swedenborg forces Kant to grasp possibility and reality in a new way. First, Swedenborg does not trouble himself with the formal conditions of experience, which alone can create the objective validity of concepts. Thus, he neglects the middle step of experience, which is empty, but still forms the inevitable condition of an experience which has a content. Second, Kant postulates that his sensations—that is, the matter or content of his experience—cannot be classified under the transcendental principles. Those do not revolve around the emptiness of experience anymore—Swedenborg does have actual sensations and thoughts, but their matter cannot be classified by the principles of pure reason. That is why his material experience is nothing or unreal. Thus we find here already two of the four conceptions of nothingness, which can be found in the "table of nothing," namely *ens rationis* and *ens imaginarium*.[8]

The "danger of Swedenborg" one could say, also gives the philosopher some other cause for concern: it is indeed noteworthy that the way Swedenborg conceptualizes his existing sensations without a priori rules makes it impossible to understand that time and space take on a double role: the same synthesis is presupposed whether time and space are taken into account with empirical perceptions and sensations (thus for actuality) or they are developed as divisible forms in the mathematics of numbers and space (and thus for possibility). Swedenborg links his sensations in such a way that one becomes unable to explain the homogeneity of the synthesis, in the terms of empirical experience or in mathematical calculation.

To put this another way, Swedenborg's claims gave Kant the opportunity to better understand the role time and space play in these two cases: as elements of empirical phenomena, they do not appear as such. Nevertheless, they possess the same shaping necessity and whether they are visible in mathematics or whether they are indistinguishable from the matter of experience, they follow the same rules.

Only Swedenborg's error or delusion allows for the status of the usual non-appearance of space and time to be made clear.

One could contest this line of arguing by saying: is not this new theory of modality to be understood as engaging with the ideas of Leibniz and not

---

[7] Kant, *Critique of Pure Reason, Unified Edition,* 285–286.
[8] Ibid, 345.

only with those of Swedenborg? Indeed, Leibniz and Swedenborg are often linked in Kant's texts from the *Dreams of a Spirit-Seer elucidated by Dreams of Metaphysics* (1766) onwards. In the preface to the first edition of the *Critique*, for example, he talks about the "raving dogmatist's thirst for knowledge"[9] of metaphysics. Such a turn of phrase applies to Leibniz just as well as to Swedenborg, without having to spell out their names. When Kant, in the so-called "table of nothing," displays nothingness in the trans-cendental sense at the end of the analytic, both Leibniz and Swedenborg are present: "I.e., [nothing] is a concept without an object (*ens rationis*) as noumena are, which cannot be numbered among the possibilities, even though they must not on that account be claimed to be impossible; or as, say, certain new fundamental forces that are being thought are indeed thought without contradiction, but also without an example from experi-ence, and hence must not be numbered among the possibilities."[10] However, as we have just understood, when it comes to the distinction between reality and possibility, Kant communicates with Swedenborg alone: Leibniz, from Kant's point of view, does not mix the two determinations, rather, he traces possibility back to conception. Swedenborg is the only one who connects his sensations and perceptions in an unreal—that is, "badly arranged"—manner. So the first *Critique* was aiming at a clear distinction between the two thinkers, whereas in 1766 this distinction remained unthinkable. When Kant had this anxious encounter with Swedenborg's miracles and for that reason bought the strange book *Arcania caelestia*, he still believed what he remarked in a letter to Mendelssohn on the 8th of April 1766, namely that Leibniz and Swedenborg were, philosophically speaking, inseparable. The philosophical exercise of the first *Critique* had as its goal making this separation a philosophical deed.

The Construction of the first *Critique*. Dialectic conflict/real conflict (1781) as the legacy of enthusiasm/waking dream (1766)

We all know that the *Critique of Pure Reason* has four parts: transcendental aesthetic, analytic of understanding, dialectic of pure reason, and metho-dology. In addition, one usually begins by reading the first chapter. Yet

[9] Ibid, 9.
[10] Ibid, 344.

Kant himself writes in the "dialectic" that this arrangement may not be sufficient: "However, conversely, we can also draw from this antinomy a true benefit that, although not a dogmatic one, is yet a critical and doctrinal benefit: viz., we can by this antinomy prove indirectly the transcendental ideality of appearances—in case, perhaps, someone were not satisfied with the direct proof provided in the Transcendental Aesthetic."[11] What does that mean, understanding the theory of the object of knowledge in reverse?

When we start our reading of the *Critique* with the dialectic—Kant says "conversely"—we cannot separate aesthetic, analytic and dialectic anymore (the way one usually reads the book).

Aesthetic and analytic are rather the result of a limitation of dialectical reason. Philosophy starts with vain fancies and desires. If one can prove that the delusion of reason, by being a delusion, still follows a logic, one can also understand that the logic, which gives us a real object, is a small transformation of the dialectical logic of reason: dialectical logic, which is called "dialectical negation" in relation to antinomy, and the logic which for us creates a real object out of the dialectical object of reason is called, after the *Attempt to Introduce the Concept of Negative Magnitudes into Philosophy* (so since 1763) "real conflict"[12] or "real opposition."[13] In 1781 the same terms are called reality, negation, limitation, which are the categories of quality; and they repeat the same problem of confinement as in 1766. Every object is constituted as real, if it can be determined as an intensive quantity, and can be thought of as a conflict of forces, or a conflict of sensations or a conflict of thoughts, and so on. In the categories of quality then, negation plays the pivotal role: the sequence of an opposition of quantities can be determined as zero; yet the corresponding object to this determination is not at all nothing—it is something real that, for the algebraic formula, is a "zero." To determine something as zero is to think of this something as real. Something real is thus determined as a negative quantity. And if the alge-

---

[11] Ibid, 516.

[12] "In nature there are many deprivations which result from the conflict [*Conflictus*, V.K.] of two operative causes, of which the one cancels the effect of the other through real opposition." Immanuel Kant, "Attempt to Introduce the Concept of Negative Magnitudes into Philosophy," 223; "[A] real conflict [*Widerstreit*, V.K.] can only occur in so far as there is a second motive force connected with it, and in so far as each reciprocally cancels the effect of the other." Ibid, 215.

[13] "Consider the following question: Is displeasure simply the lack of pleasure? Or is displeasure a ground of the deprivation of pleasure? And in this case, displeasure, while being indeed something positive and not merely the contradictory opposite of pleasure, is opposed to pleasure in the real sense of the term." Ibid, 219.

braic sum of forces, sensations, thoughts etc. is not zero, then one has a limitation, the third category of quality. That's why there is a rigorous continuity from 1763 to 1781. And the concept of negative quantity is the means of this continuation. Still, following this one has yet to understand completely what a "depiction in reverse" of transcendental idealism means and also in what way Kant's engagement with Swedenborg is at the heart of this reversal.

In the *Dreams of a Spirit-seer*, Kant claimed that the waking dreamer was similar to the human being who uses reason, even if in his imagination some imaginary ideas or phantasms form. Something in his thoughts establishes "a contrast or distinction"[14] from the development of the imaginary. In contrast to that, the enthusiast is the one who lacks any limitation to the unfolding of the imaginary. That proof of contrast is lacking. That's why Kant calls an object not what one perceives directly but that which introduces a contrast for someone with an unlimited unfolding of the imaginary. And the real conflict is the logical formula of experiencing this contrast. That's why it is important to read and understand the text about negative quantities (1763) alongside the text about the enthusiast (1766).

In the *Critique of Pure Reason* the problem of this contrast is continued by determining in a more subtle fashion the logical content of the contrast between merely imaginary thinking—namely reason—and knowledge: it is now not only about the experience of "contrast or distinction," but also about the logic of experience, which can form a cognition or not. The counterpoint between enthusiast and waking dreamer, however, is transposed into the counterpoint between understanding and reason: what the syllogisms on the side of reason lack is the functioning of contrast which alone allows us understanding how to introduce a limitation on the delusion of reason. If the logical examination of contrast is lacking, only reason follows and we have the so-called "dialectical negation." A dialectical negation is the logical structure of an antinomy of propositions about the world as a whole, in which the negation is unable to form an object through real conflict. Remember when Kant explained, in the seventh paragraph of the chapter on antinomy, that two opposing propositions can both be false if the negation which expresses this opposition logically is constituting nothing; the logical determination of the infinite unfolding of reasoning is thus the dialectical opposition: "Thus of two dialectically opposed judg-

---

[14] Kant, *Dreams of a Spirit-seer Elucidated by Dreams of Metaphysics*, 330.

ments both can be false, because one judgment not merely contradicts the other but says something more than is required for contradiction."[15] And the solving of the antinomy consists in distinguishing between a "nothing" and a "something": "Thus no remedy remains for ending the dispute thoroughly and to the satisfaction of both parties, except finally to show that—since, after all, they can so nicely refute each other—they are disputing about *nothing*, and that a certain transcendental illusion has painted for them a reality where none is to be found."[16]

The logical determination of the infinite unfolding of reasoning is thus the dialectical opposition: Contradiction does not have any ontological power, only the real conflict or the category of negation and limitation has transcendental power. Thus, transcendental analysis is to be considered as the variation or modification of the dialectical rule of reason, if the constitutive power of negation is not used out of turn.

So since 1763—or even since 1762, when *The False Subtlety of the Four Syllogistic Figures* was written—Kant's reflections revolve around the logical means with which to determine the contrast between a delusion which is possible to delimit through a new kind of negation and a delusion impossible to delimit. And the logic of negation is a transposition of the difference between Swedenborg and Leibniz. The problem of the inability of contrast, in 1766, applied to Leibniz just as well as to Swedenborg. The exact expression in Kant's letter to Mendelssohn on was: April 8, 1766, even if he had not been confused because of the stories of and about Swedenborg, he still maintains that the difference between idealism and enthusiasm (*Schwärmerei*) remains indeterminable. But thanks to the logical deconstruction, the dialectical negation that is able to reveal "nothing" in terms of reason can be distinguished from the real negation (category of quality), which gives a "something" to our understanding, and thus Kant also gained the means to conceptually distinguish between Leibniz and Swedenborg.

[15] *Critique of Pure Reason, Unified Edition*, 515.
[16] Ibid, 513.

Does enthusiasm have no logic?

As a conclusion I would like to propose the following: in order to read Kant's texts as an ongoing debate with Swedenborg, one should not ask whether Kant or Swedenborg are correct, or if Swedenborg is the true thinker of the enlightenment despite the Kantian interdiction. The problem that poses itself is not anymore whether prophetism and religion are a higher truth than rationalism. The secularization of thinking or a "lay philosophy," in the sense that Freud talked about a "lay analysis,"[17] is the distancing from a belief that turns itself into a conceptual invention. Not all beliefs can accomplish such a transformation. There are also other trans-formations to a preliminary belief than philosophical displacement: logic, as it were—and in Kant the logic of negation was turned into the means to transform his anxious and passionate encounter with Swedenborg's person and way of thinking. So the conceptual exercise is a striving to distance oneself from a preliminary belief. Even if this distancing remains observable as in part a misrecognition of that which one is distancing oneself from.

Of course, one should still say something about this encounter-without-an-encounter between Kant and Swedenborg,[18] something that Kant was not able to clearly articulate: Swedenborg's experience and way of thinking are not just a lack of reason. Swedenborg's delusion also possesses a logic, or, to put it better, an arrangement. This is understandable with the help of Freud. A delusion, like a dream, has an inner structure that is different from the structure or logic of reason.[19] The condition to understand "dreamwork" is to first abandon the notion that logic, which pertains to both consciousness and reason, is to be considered as the original image. Along the way of this methodological abandoning, one can discover other rules which do not take the cognition of a "real world" as the aim of this thought anymore. So for a wish or a desire the principles of reason do not at all play the role of an

[17] Sigmund Freud, *The Question of Lay Analysis, The Standard Edition,* trans. James Strachey (New York and London: Norton & Company 1978).

[18] Monique David-Ménard, "L'Evidence d'un délire expliqué par l'évidence de la Métaphysique" in *Le Cahier du Collège international de philosophie, n°3* (Paris: Osiris éd., 1987). And *La Folie dans la raison pure. Kant lecteur de Swedenborg,* (Paris: Librairie Vrin 1997).

[19] Sigmund Freud, *The Interpretation of Dreams,* trans. James Strachey (New York and London: Norton & Company 1953), chapter VI.

original image. Dream and delusion should not be taken as a lack of reason any longer.

Thus, if one compares the logic of reason and understanding to the arrangement of the dream or of delusion, another task remains, a task that is different from Kant's task. Nevertheless, Kant experienced and conceptually proved that the logic of reason evolves close to the danger of delusion. Thanks to his philosophy, thanks to the transcendental concept of negation and modality, this closeness gains a philosophical meaning. So after reading Kant, and in a different way than after reading Plato or Erasmus, one can argue that philosophy is the discovery of a method of gaining distance from delusion (*Wahn*). The main themes of his philosophy—and maybe of philosophy in general—are to be understood as dependent on that source, and maybe the theoretical imaginations of philosophy remain grateful to that source, even if it manages to distance itself from that source. This would be, in my opinion, the status of a thought of laymanship or the secularization of philosophy.

Foucault, Derrida, and the Limits of Reason

Sven-Olov Wallenstein

The exchange on the status of madness in Descartes that took place between Derrida and Foucault cuts right into the heart of our present topic. Confusing as it may have been, and in some sense perhaps without any true point of contact, it nevertheless stakes out a series of paradigmatic positions. Is there is a limit of reason, and if so, in what way can the reflection on this limit also allow us to approach something which may be considered outside of reason? And if this is at all possible, to what extent can this be made into a source of thinking, and not just something that would condemn it to silence pure and simple? Or is any such approach already from the outset limited by the constraints imposed by the logic of discursive reason? The quarrel was phrased in terms of madness, although not just in terms of reason as an external opposition to madness, but of reason as constituted by a rejection of madness—which perhaps would amount to another kind of madness, a madness of reason itself that it must both perform and repress. But how can such a repression be undone, and in what language could it ever be expressed?

That this conflict was staged through a reading of Descartes can be taken as highly symbolic on another level also: at stake was the beginning of modernity and/or classical Reason, the very idea of the cogito as the source of clarity and rationality. As we shall see, the question whether the initiating Cartesian move that ensures itself of its transparency and self-possession is able to encompass the disorder of unreason, or whether it can only take place as a violent exclusion of unreason, extends beyond a historiographical question of the place of Descartes in seventeenth-century thought. It also comes to engage the status of philosophy itself, both as an institution related to other discursive practices, and as a claim to transcend all such finite and contingent institutional orders. In these exchanges, which occurred over some ten years, no simple answer was presented; rather, the question was gradually displaced, which may account for the sense that we may have today that this was a missed encounter, but also indicate the complexity of the question.

The three key texts that I will draw on here are Foucault's *Folie et Déraison: Histoire de la folie à l'âge classique* from 1961,[1] which was the occasion for the debate, Derrida's 1963 lecture "Cogito et histoire de la folie,"[2] and finally, Foucault's response in the afterword to the re-edition of *Histoire de la folie* in 1972, "Mon corps, ce papier, ce feu."[3] To this further documents may be added: Derrida's lecture from 1991, "'Etre juste avec Freud': L'histoire de la folie à l'âge de la psychanalyse,"[4] Foucault's explicit or implicit comments on Derrida scattered throughout his other books and lecture series, as well as a huge secondary literature. But even though all of these primary as well as secondary sources would need to be addressed in a more systematic reading, and would no doubt show that the exchange on madness is pursued and developed on many levels that go beyond the reference to the particular Cartesian moment, they fall outside of my rather limited scope here.[5]

Similarly, I will bracket out of the discussion whether any of the two opponents gets Descartes "right," in the sense of how their respective claims stand up when measured against more traditional historical scholarship.[6] In

---

[1] Trans. Jonathan Murphy and Jean Khalfa as *History of Madness* (London: Routledge, 2008). The French text is cited from the 1998 reprint of the 1972 Gallimard edition, *Historie de la folie à l'âge classique*. Henceforth: HM (English/French). Foucault's 1961 preface is not included in the later French versions, and is here cited from the *Dits et écrits*, vol. I (Paris: Gallimard, 1994). Henceforth: DE.

[2] In Derrida, *L'écriture et la différence* (Paris: Seuil, 1967); trans. Alan Bass in Derrida, *Writing and Difference* (Chicago: University of Chicago Press, 1978). Henceforth: WD.

[3] Not included in the later reprints of the 1972 edition. The French text is cited from DE, vol II; Eng. trans. in *History of Madness*, appendix II.

[4] In Elisabeth Roudinesco (ed.), *Penser la folie: Essais sur Michel Foucault* (Paris: Galilée, 1992). Trans. Pascale-Anne Brault and Michael Naas as "'To Do Justice to Freud': The History of Madness in the Age of Psychoanalysis," in Arnold I. Davidson (ed.), *Foucault and his Interlocutors* (Chicago: University of Chicago Press, 19979.

[5] For an attempt to reconstruct this dialogue on a larger scale, see Ronald Boyne, *Foucault and Derrida: The Other Side of Reason* (London: Routledge, 1990), which crosses many of my proposals in the following. For the exchange on madness, the Swedish-language reader can find a particularly rich collection of texts in *Arche* 34–35 (2011).

[6] For a discussion from this point of view, see Jean-Marie Beyssade, *Descartes au fil de l'ordre* (Paris: PUF, 2001), 14–38. As Beyssade notes with reference to the problem of whether Descartes encounters madness alongside dream and error (Foucault), or if it is already inscribed in the hierarchy of knowledge (Derrida), Descartes's text "authorizes both readings without any of them ever succeeding to wholly condemn the other" (19), which I think is valid for the entire debate. Beyssade however sees Foucault's two respec-

fact, even though the discussion between them at times appears to turn on precise philological points, even on the interpretation of certain Latin words and phrases, what is at stake is a much more general question of reading and interpretation as such, and of what it means for thinking to relate to its own past. By confining ourselves to these three texts, it will be possible to see three exemplary positions staked out, and also to gauge the extent to which Foucault's answer in 1972 changes the terrain, a shift that no doubt corresponds to the new perspective that had been opened up by his archeology of knowledge already underway since the late 1960s, as can be detected in the gradual transformation of the very idea of archeology.

Psychopathology and the truth of man

Foucault's early investigations grew out of his engagement with psychology and psychiatry, which also involved practical work at the Saint-Anne clinic. His first publication, the introduction to his and Jacqueline Verdeaux's 1954 translation of Ludwig Binswanger's *Traum und Existenz*,[7] drew on these experiences, and here we can see the emergence of an idea of ex-perience that incorporates the lessons of phenomenology and psycho-analysis, while also attempting to transcend them. Foucault's suggestion in the introduction is to show how Binswanger took his cues from Husserl as well as Freud only in order to transgress both of them, moving towards a different conception of consciousness. In Binswanger, Foucault locates a dialectic between experience and institution, or anthropology and social history, and his concern turns to how we might link them together: is there a common root, a shared historicity, belonging to these two modes of analysis, which would bring together the subjective and objective in a third dimension that does not treat them as fixed forms, but can account for their mutual and conflicted emergence? For Foucault this was the beginning of his extended and meandering analysis of the psychiatric establishment—which, as we will see, in 1961 will usher in the idea that madness harbors a profound experience of a limit, that it has an enigmatic substance, and does not simply amount to dysfunction, disorder, and deviation. In 1954, this

tive texts from 1961 and 1972 as basically proposing the same argument, which I believe to be misleading; his otherwise excellent analysis however focuses on Descartes, and not Foucault's development.

[7] See Foucault's "Introduction," in DE I, 65–119.

was still staked out in terms of a quest for a unity and wholeness that would have been objectified and thus missed by psychiatry, but may be grasped as the finite transcendence of Dasein, which is always under the threat of objectifying itself in the world, while still containing the possibility of retrieving itself.

However, in this early period there were rapid oscillations between opposing perspectives. In the same year as the introduction to Binswanger, Foucault published a book on psychopathology, *Maladie mentale et personnalité*, in which the concepts of the normal and the abnormal seem to be reduced to effects of institutional practices. Investigating the formation of modern psychiatry, Foucault at this point contended that sickness results from social conditions and conflicts, and he ended with a positive appraisal of Soviet-style materialist psychiatry, with Pavlov as the guiding reference. In a rather stark opposition to the text on Binswanger, we now encounter a critique of the "irrealization" of the relation to the world brought about precisely by traditional analysis of consciousness and its misplaced focus of the inner life of the individual. In 1962 there was a new edition of the book, where "personnalité" in the title had become "psychologie", and Pavlov was replaced by summaries of sections from the recently published *History of Madness*.[8] After this Foucault refused to have the book printed again, and he never referred back to any of these two editions, whereas the themes addressed in the essay on Binswanger will remain present in his work to the end. This arguably testifies to a more profound continuity, where the concept of "experience" can be taken as guiding thread,[9] although it is never wholly clarified, perhaps because this would have demanded a systematic confrontation with phenomenology that Foucault never pursued after his first attempts. As we will see, "experience" is one of the key concepts that organize the claims made in *The History of Madness*, even though it is an experience located at, and precisely *as*, the limit of what can be "reasonably" thought.

Nevertheless, both of these early texts, even though they appear to be diametrically opposed on one level, draw on the idea of a "true man." Regardless of whether we understand madness on the basis of social dysfunctions or existential impasses, there must be a possibility to conceive of an end of alienation, either through creation or social change, where human beings

---

[8] For a discussion of this, see Pierre Macherey, "Aux sources de *l'Histoire de la folie*: Une rectification et ses limites," *Critique* No. 471–72 (1986): 753–774.
[9] For a discussion of the continuity of the theme of "experience" in Foucault, see Timothy O'Leary, "Foucault, Experience, Literature," *Foucault Studies*, No 5 (2008): 5–25.

could recover their possession of themselves and achieve full existence.[10] It is precisely this theme, with its typical attempts to create a bridge between Marxism and phenomenology, which would be radically transformed in 1961, with the *History of Madness* signaling a new departure.

The history of madness

For the author of the *History of Madness*, there is no full essence of man waiting in the wings, no recovery of our being that would end the age of objectification or dominating reason. Madness is no longer a dysfunction to be surmounted, but fundamentally a dispossession, a disappropriation of any such essence that folds reason and subjectivity back into a radical out-side, or at least relates them to a fundamental limit, which nevertheless can be approached in a particular kind of experience.

Foucault would later distance himself from these claims, at least in their initial version, and suggest that the work on madness was marked by a particular kind of search for origins.[11] But in spite of this—or perhaps because of it—many of his later problems are contained in this book, though folded into each other.[12] This also applies to the idea of an experience of resistance,[13] which in fact can be taken as the very center of Foucault's methodological concerns: is there a different experience outside of the archives of knowledge and the relations of power, something that could work as a leverage for a thought that is *of* its conditions, and yet

---

[10] See Frédéric Gros, *Foucault et la folie* (Paris: PUF, 1991), 26.

[11] In 1969, Foucault assessed his earlier project in light of his current one: "We are not trying to reconstitute what madness itself might be, in the form in which it presented itself to some primitive, fundamental, obscure, scarcely articulated experience," and added in a footnote that "This is written against an explicit theme of my book *The History of Madness*, and that recurs particularly in the Preface." Foucault, *The Archeology of Knowledge*, trans. Alan Sheridan (London: Routledge, 1972), 47; *L'archéologie du savoir* (Paris: Gallimard, 1969), 64.

[12] Perhaps it would be possible to re-apply Michel Serres's description of the logic of Foucault's narrative to the place that the book holds within Foucault's own trajectory: it is a kind of dense overlay of "geometric" figures, whose reciprocal differences and relations will be gradually worked out as he proceeds. See Serres, *Hermès I: La communication* (Paris: Seuil, 1969), 167ff.

[13] For a reading that attempts to follow this question in relation to the theme of the body, see my "Foucault and the Body as a Site of Resistance," in Jasper Cepl and Kirsten Wagner (eds.), *Images of the Body in Architecture: Anthropology and Built Space* (Tübingen: Wasmuth, 2014).

cannot be reduced *to* them? How is it possible to let this otherness speak, or rather, as he says, to write an archeology of silence, without repeating the gesture of exclusion? Madness was the first entity that posed this question to its interlocutor, but it would be followed by others and, on a very general level, much of Foucault's subsequent work, at least up to the mid seventies,[14] would follow from it, in the sense that it attempts to trace an oscillation between the logic and rules of an already formed inside of discourses and a formless outside that haunts them. This outside is what supplies discourse with the element of power relations from which order emerges as a disciplinary ordering (discipline here being understood both as the regulation of conduct, and as the discursive entities called "disciplines" that it makes possible, the latter requiring at least semi-stable positions for observing subjects and observed objects), but also that which ceaselessly gives it an irreducible movement, by doubling the formal with a formlessness that makes truth into the result of a combat or a capture, rather than the discovery of a pre-given relation between a representation and its object.

The History of Madness pursues this task by, on the one hand, addressing the idea of a limit and an outside of reason (most substantially in the preface but also at various moments throughout the text) and, on the other hand, tracing the articulations and modalities of this inside-outside relation through a series of discursive determinations of madness, unfolding from the split between the renaissance and classical age to the late eighteenth century (which constitutes the main part of the text). A basic outline of the architecture of the book would read as follows:

1. The Renaissance still entertained the possibility of an exchange between reason and madness, which subsequently was cut, so that the exterior and the interior of reason came to be seen as simply divided. Before the event of demarcation, Bosch's *Ship of Fools* could show us the madman at the limit between exterior and interior, where inside and outside ceaselessly pass over into each other, and where the element of water provides the symbolism of an uncertain journey. Here madness is still an inner possibility of reason, either as the place of a radical truth-telling, as in Erasmus's *In Praise of Folly*, or as the prefiguration of the dissolution of reason, as comes across particularly in the visual arts. This experience of madness as a ubiquitous possibility, Foucault suggests, was born out of the

---

[14] See the Introduction in Jakob Nilsson and Sven-Olov Wallenstein (eds.), *Foucault, Biopolitics, and Governmentality* (Huddinge: Södertörn Philosophical Studies, 2013).

collapse of the medieval divine hierarchies, after which the drift of significations threatened to sink the world into a universal *furor*. Philosophy and
moral theory interpret this as the punishment of misguided learning, or as a
self-relation that has come out of joint; in none of them, however, was it the
absolute other of reason, but a continually present possibility.

2. The first major division, "the great confinement," occurred in the
middle of the seventeenth century, when the figure of exclusion was trans-
ferred from leprosy to madness, and it took institutional form in the
establishing of the Hôpital Général in 1656. For Foucault, this event com-
bines two aspects: it redefined an already existing material space, the lepro-
saria, by giving it a new content in the figure of the madman, who now
assumes the role of the excluded. This is obviously a highly complex process
that is played out on many levels, and in Foucault's book it is accounted for
in multiple ways; however, we may note that, whereas the description of the
earlier exchange between reason and madness (which admittedly is rather
brief and mainly functions as a foil to the subsequent analysis) largely draws
on literary and art-historical sources, the discussion of the confinement
makes use of explanatory models derived from social history—as when, for
example, Foucault emphasizes the ethical value of work, which places him,
at least tangentially, within a Weberian tradition. Parallel to this, he also
emphasizes the role played by a new perception or sensibility; what for us
seems like a mixture of incompatible grounds for seeing "unreason," for
Classical reason was a clear and distinct perception, for which the Cartesian
analysis provided a powerful model.

After this, there was constantly developing monologue of reason on
madness that takes on many guises. The details of this "classical" experience
of madness, and its subsequent transformations during the seventeenth and
eighteenth centuries, which occupy the substantial part of the book, must be
left out here, since we are only concerned with the overall architecture of
the investigation, which reaches its other main point of articulation in the
apparent "liberation" of the madman, just after the French Revolution.

3. This shift was signaled by another particular material event, the
moment of liberation in 1794, when the chains were removed from the
patients at Bicêtre; this liberation was then continued in the movement of
liberalization and humanization of the nineteenth century, through the
work of the great reformers, Tuke and Pinel. But, Foucault argues, what we
encounter in this is only liberation at the surface; at a deeper level, the mad
are further entrenched into a definition given to them by reason, so that
they now have to define their externality in their own speech. Instead of

chains, there is a moralizing demand for reflexivity codified in the manuals for treatment, and which gives rise to new forms of hermeneutic techniques, of which Freudian psychoanalysis will constitute a climactic point, even though its founding structures were established long before Freud.

4. But in this movement there is also an inverse possibility that for Foucault comes across in modern literature and art, where madness begins to circulate again: from Hölderlin and Nerval to Nietzsche, van Gogh, and Artaud, reason begins to once more discover madness as its most intimate and radical possibility—to be sure not as a madness that would *itself* return to language, but in allowing madness to be felt once more, from within reason's interior, as the murmurings of another language inside the discourses of deciphering and objectification.

For the Foucault of the aftermath of *The History of Madness*, the possibility of transgression was thus not related to a return to some previous moment in history, but was, at least for a period, able to takes its cues from an interpretation of modern literature and art. On the one hand, madness amounts to the absolute interruption of the work, the moment where it is abolished; on the other hand, it is the founding of its temporal existence. If it is the *absence of the work*,[15] this is not something simply negative, but a constitutive limit of the modern work, a moment of unreason that nevertheless opens the pathway to the undivided experience of division. Here we find the traces of another experience, a resistance that articulates itself by withdrawing into silence, into the margins of discourse, and rather than seeing madness as an entity constituted by being imprisoned in a medical institution, Foucault draws on a figure of thought inherited from romanticism: art as the bearer of another truth, a negativity that cannot be reduced to rational ordering. The infinity and excess of language transgresses reason and order, it scrambles and disassembles the law of the Father, and literary writing acts as the primordial reservoir for this resistance.[16] I have here dwelled on these motifs, since they indicate an import-

---

[15] See "La folie, l'absence d'oeuvre" (1964), DE, vol. 1; trans. as "Madness, the absence of an oeuvre," in HM, app. 1.

[16] The literary theme unfolds in a series of essays on, among others, Hölderlin, Bataille, Roussel, Flaubert, and Klossowski, all of which are reprinted in DE, vol. 1; the essays on Hölderlin, Bataille, and Flaubert are translated in Foucault, *Language, Counter-Memory, Practice*, ed. Daniel Bouchard (Ithaca: Cornell University Press, 1977). Foucault's literary essays may seem as asides in relation to his historical work, an yet, in all their obvious diversity, they display a cumulative movement that can be taken to culminate in the essay from 1966 on Blanchot, "La pensée du dehors," DE, vol. I; trans. in Foucault/

ant facet of the discussion, even though Foucault would later subject them to criticism—i.e. the possibility of a different experience—a form of resistance that undergoes many mutations throughout Foucault's work, and for which the 1961 *History of Madness* was a first cipher.

Returning to the *project* of *The History of Madness*, we can now see how it engages the idea not just of a particular *historical* limit, but also of a limit *of history* itself, both of which will be decisive in the following debate with Derrida. The task, Foucault suggests, cannot be to simply write a history of a certain phenomenon called "madness," but first, to write a history of reason from a negative point of view (how reason has become what it is through the exclusion of its other, in various shapes and forms), and then, more radically, to attempt to let madness itself speak through the system of exclusion, to write its own history. The first would be a history of the self-constitution of reason through exclusion, the second an "archeology of silence," a way to let otherness speak from its position of otherness. This language of otherness, he suggests, would demand a return to a moment before the division or Decision (*la Decision*, as he says dramatically), to a zero degree in history when madness was a still undifferentiated unity, a not yet divided experience of the division, as is stated in the book's opening lines:

> We need a history of that other trick that madness plays—that other trick through which men, in a gesture of sovereign reason that locks up their neighbor, communicate and recognize each other in the merciless language of non-madness, we need to identify the moment of that expulsion, before it was definitely established on the reign of truth, before it was brought back to life by the lyricism of protestation. To try to recapture, in history, this degree zero of the history of madness, when it was an undifferentiated experience, the still undivided experience of the division itself. To describe, from the origin of its curve, that "other trick" which, on either side of the movement, allows reason and Madness to fall away, like things henceforth foreign to each other, deaf to any exchange, almost dead to each other (HM, xxvii/DE I, 159).

To restore this communication, then, entails the creation of another language outside of the language of historico-philosophical discourse, a language that suspends the established forms of knowledge from historiography to psychopathology. This is however not done with a view to a

Blanchot, *Thought from Outside/ Michel Foucault as I Imagine Him*, trans. Jeffrey Mehlman and Brian Massumi (New York: Zone Book, 1987). In the latter he explicates this in terms of an idea of literature as the relation of language to the Outside (*le Dehors*), a dimension of emptiness that dissolves the subject into a space of pure dispersal.

teleology of truth and rationality that interprets the past as so many in-
complete attempts to attain a final reason, as would be the case of the
genealogy of scientific reason proposed in, for instance, Husserl's *Crisis*. If
there is a suspension and bracketing, its task is rather—and in this Foucault
comes closer to certain strands of Heidegger's thought—to uncover "that
gesture of severance, the distance taken, the void installed between reason
and that which it is not, without ever leaning on plenitude of what reason
pretends to be"; only a language that is "more original, much rougher and
much more matutinal than that of science" will be able to fulfill the task not
simply of harboring an analysis of the history of madness as a shifting
discursive object, during which "all those imperfect words, of no fixed
syntax, spoken falteringly" in which exchange once took place were gradually expelled from memory, but more fundamentally—and this is
Foucault's most daring and questionable proposal, where the debate with
Derrida will start—to "draw up the archeology of that silence" (HM,
xxviii/DE 1, 160). The proximity of these claims to some of Derrida's early
proto-deconstructive moves is obvious, which is no doubt also why he
would stake the difference between them with such polemical force.

The *arche* of this archeology implies a "vertical" relation that confronts
the "horizontal" becoming of reason with its "Exterior," a "limit-experience" that is also "something like the very birth of its history," and (drawing
on Nietzsche) a "tragic structure" (HM xxix, DE 1, 161). History, Foucault
suggests, would be constituted by the "refusal, the forgetting and the silent
collapse of tragedy" (ibid.), around which many other divisions would
cluster: dreams and conscious life, sexual prohibitions, morality and toler-
ance, desire—each of which promises many future inquiries that Foucault
would later undertake in very different ways, but which are here understood
in terms of a confrontation of the "dialectics of history" with the "immobile
structures of the tragic" (ibid.). The vocabulary of the horizontal and the
vertical, as well as that of birth, seems to signal an interplay or dialectic at
work between two dimensions which, though they are incommensurable,
are not entirely external to each other; the vocabulary of refusal, of
"Exterior," and of an immobile structure of the tragic, instead points to a
pure division between Reason and its other.

The decisive point here, however, is the analysis of a particular historical
limit, established somewhere in the mid-seventeenth century, which somehow not only echoes and resonates with other previous divisions, but also
provides them with their model and orientation. This is the moment of

Descartes, whose status is at the core of the debate between Derrida and Foucault.

The text on Descartes is admittedly brief (HM 44–47/67–70), and may be taken as an aside, or as a kind of initial setting of the stage for a sweeping historical overview of social and institutional structures in seventeenth-century Europe. But it also serves a strategic purpose; as the very opening of the analysis of confinement, it establishes a link to the Cartesian cogito, and does so through the category of a perception or evidence that would be common to the classical age, but which can be discerned in a paradigmatic form in Descartes. The move by which Descartes assures himself of the access to the cogito by pushing madness to the side is thus like a philosophical counterpart to the great confinement that would take on material and institutional form only a few years after Descartes's *Meditations*.

In Descartes's argument, the structure of this perception or evidence comes across in how the thinking mind assures itself of its own transparency by excluding madness in a gesture of unquestioned certitude. On the path of doubt, Descartes encounters error and dream, as well as madness, although they are overcome in very different ways. In error and dream, Foucault suggests, the untruth lies in the object, whereas madness relates to the subject itself, to the very possibility of thinking. Madness cannot form part of the Cartesian path of doubt; it does not contain any residue of truth that can lead to the overcoming of illusion, but must be "simply excluded." While the empirical person may be mad, the thinking ego cannot, *as thinking*, be mad; madness, Foucault claims, is not superseded in a structure of truth, but is expelled through an act of violence: "While *man* can still go mad, *thought*, as the sovereign exercise carried out by the subject, seeking the truth, can no longer be devoid of reason" (HM 47/70).

Derrida's critique

Derrida's 1963 lecture poses two fundamental questions, the first bearing directly on the reading of Descartes, the second on the general presuppositions of Foucault's archeology. The first is phrased in two parts, separated by the emphasis: does the Cartesian text have *this* historical meaning that has been assigned to it by Foucault (which is a problem of textual exegesis) and then, does it have this *historical* meaning (which is a problem of its relation to an institutional milieu and to the history of thought)? The second, bearing on Foucault's entire project, proceeds to ask whether this reading—or misreading, as Derrida will argue—can in fact be said to arise from the structure of the archeological investigation as such. At the center of both questions lies the question of historicity, of the relation between time and thought as such, and of whether thought can be entirely inscribed in a particular historical conjuncture.

Foucault wants to write a history of madness itself, Derrida claims, of madness before it has been caught up in knowledge, which occasionally seems to lead him to a rejection of the language of reason in its integrality in favor of an archeology of silence. But as Foucault himself notes—and Derrida here merely highlights and sharpens the paradoxes already named in Foucault's preface—this is an impossible project, since any history of silence must itself be phrased in a language: any archeology must itself be a *work*, and cannot pass over into the domain of the *absence* of work without silencing itself. Moreover, with the particular cases of psychiatry and psychopathology, both disciplines are as such part of a more encompassing structure of reason that can only be questioned from the inside; in short, with and against Foucault, Derrida contends that there is no history except the history of reason or of sense, and no leverage point to be had in some exterior position. Foucault on the other hand, Derrida suggests, is forced to argue as if he knew what madness is, as if it were contained in a radically different experience that would somehow be accessible through some suspension of sense, or of philosophy—a kind of counter-phenomeno-logical *epoché* that would open toward a phenomenology not of sense and the constitution of sense, but of the limit of sense.

Even if such an *epoché* would be possible, the question remains of the nature of the instance before which the conflict of reason and madness, sense and non-sense, could make sense, and the nature of the language in which it could be expressed. In any case, it can neither be the language of the mad nor that of the warden, which is why, Derrida suggests, the "decision" of which Foucault sometimes speaks (though not always—as we have seen, his vocabulary is on this point ambivalent) must rather be understood as a diremption, an *Entzweiung* inside the logos itself: its inside (is) its outside.[17]

---

[17] The same phrase famously recurs a few years later, although with the "is" written *sous rature*, in *De la grammatologie* (Paris: Minuit, 1967), 65, trans. Gayatri Chakravorty Spivak, *Of Grammatology* (Baltimore: Johns Hopkins University Press, 2nd rev. ed. 1998) 30. In both cases it points to the necessity of maintaining the terms of the tradition while subjecting them to a profound suspicion; they are at the same time insufficient and unavoidable. The crossing out of terms derives from Heidegger's *kreuzweise Durch-streichung*; see Heidegger, "Zur Seinsfrage," in *Wegmarken*, Gesamtausgabe vol. 9

The idea of such a diremption must in turn be interrogated in relation to a wider historical dimension which is only hinted at in *The History of Madness*. How are we to read Foucault's claims with respect to the tradition that, back through the Middle Ages, would take us all the way to antiquity, and within which the division occurring in the classical age can be nothing put a particular skirmish? Foucault briefly alludes to a breakdown of the hierarchy of significations at the end of the Middle Ages, which unleashed the threat of the world sinking down into universal *furor*; beyond this, he asserts the Greek logos had no opposite, while at the same time describing Socratic dialectic as "reassuring," which must mean that this dialectic must have taken place against the background of a division already present in the Greek logos (to this Foucault's reference to tragedy may be taken as an answer, although one that is hardly compatible with the claim of the absence of an opposite to the logos).

Furthermore, if the division between reason and madness is to be a condition not only of a particular conception of history, but of historicity as such—i.e. the condition of possibility of all types of history—how can this act of dividing itself have a history? How could it be located at a specific point in time? In short, how could we write the history of historicity?

All of these questions are brought together in the reading of Descartes, which, though brief, is placed as the introduction to the chapter on the great confinement, leading into the following argument. Now, Foucault focuses on a particular stage in the Cartesian argument that has generally been overlooked by commentators,[18] where he for a moment seems to entertain the possibility that he is mad. After the first step on the path of doubt, the insecurity of perceptions which refer to things at a distance, Descartes considers the case of things that exist in his immediate proximity—my body, this paper, this fire in front of which I, the meditating one, am seated—the sensation of which appears to give them an absolute certitude:

(Frankfurt am Main: Klostermann, 1976), and Derrida, *De la grammatologie*, 38; *Of Grammatology*, 23.

[18] Exceptions to this do exist, however, and already Pierre Bourdin, author of the seventh set of Objections to the Meditations, seems to have been aware of the problem: Foucault briefly alludes to him in the final paragraph of his reply (HM 573f, DE 2, 267). Observations on this particular passage, similar to those of Foucault although without any claims about a general history of madness, were also made by Harry Frankfurt, *Demons, Dreamers and Madmen: The Defense of Reason in Descartes's Meditations* (Indianapolis: Bobbs-Merrill, 1970).

Yet although the senses occasionally deceive us with respect to objects which are very small or in the distance, there are many other beliefs about which doubt is quite impossible, even though they are derived from the senses—for example, that I am here, sitting by the fire, wearing a winter dressing-gown, holding this piece of paper in my hands, and so on. Again, how could it be denied that these hands or this whole body are mine? Unless perhaps I were to liken myself to madmen, whose brains are so damaged by the persistent vapours of melancholia that they firmly maintain they are kings when they are paupers, or say they are dressed in purple when they are naked, or that their heads are made of earthenware, or that they are pumpkins, or made of glass. But such people are insane, and I would be thought equally mad if I took anything from them as a model for myself (*sed amentes sunt isti, nec minus ipse demens viderer, si quod ab iis exemplum ad me transferrem*).[19]

For Foucault, this last sentence means that madness is immediately brushed aside, it is not a possibility immanent to reason, but is excluded through a kind of decree, whereas for someone like Montaigne it was a constantly present inner possibility for reason. In this way, Descartes relegates madness to the outside of reason, and it cannot even be allowed as a feigned hypothesis.

In Derrida's reading, Foucault is mistaken about the general movement of doubt, in which madness is only one step, and not a decisive one; rather than being excluded, it is admitted and then intensified in the following case offered by Descartes, that of the dream. The dream argument amplifies the doubt applied to the level of the senses, then leads us to a consideration of the categories that would withstand even the dream (extension, form, quantity, place, time), since any dream must be based on a combination of existing things, before finally moving to the maddest hypothesis of them all, the *Deus deceptor* that allows me to doubt even the evidence of arithmetical truths, like $2 + 3 = 5$. It is only this metaphysical and hyperbolical doubt that can reveal the unshakable truth of "I am, I exist" (*ego sum, ego existo*): because I need to *be*, to *exist*, if I am to be deceived by an evil genius, no

---

[19] *The Philosophical Writings of Descartes*, trans. John Cottingham, Robert Stoothoff, and Dugald Murdoch (Cambridge: Cambridge University Press) II, 12–13. Latin text in *Oeuvres*, eds. Charles Adam and Paul Tannery (Paris: Vrin-CNRS, 1964–1974) VII, 18–19 [AT]. Duc de Luynes's French translation, approved by Descartes, and cited by both Foucault and Derrida, reads: "Mais quoi? ce sont des fous, et je ne serais pas moins extravagant, si je me réglais sur leurs examples" (AT IX, 14). One of the most meticulous recent French translations, by Michel Beyssade, gives: "Mais ce sont la des insensés et moi-même je ne paraîtrais pas moins privé de sens, si je me retenais d'eux quelque example pour me l'appliquer"; see Descartes, *Méditations métaphysiques* (Paris: Livre de poche, 1990), 33.

matter how powerful. The earlier hypothesis of madness, Derrida claims, is in fact only a rhetorical objection made from the point of view of a naïve and natural understanding that Descartes only feigns to accept in order to turn it around. In other words, Descartes is saying, "So you think I would be mad if I doubted these things in front of me? Well, then, let us take the dream as an example, since the dreamer is even more insane and might be mistaken about everything, whereas the madman is only mistaken about particular things." And then, on the level of hyperbolical doubt, the evil genius introduces the possibility of a complete and universal madness, where even the ultimate intelligible truths such as those of arithmetic may be doubted.

There is to be sure, Derrida acknowledges, a continual trust in something like the normalcy of language (and, we might add, a trust in the laws of logic—ultimately the law of contradiction that neither Derrida nor Foucault mentions), although this cannot be taken as specific to Descartes. Language, Derrida contends, has always belonged to the domain of logos and reason, which does not mean that we must reject the existence of a background of silence, nor that the origin of historicity contains violence and pain, only that it is impossible to locate these securely in the division between reason and that which it silences and represses at some particular event or point in time.

For Derrida, Descartes does not at all exclude madness; on the contrary, the level of hyperbolical doubt shows that the cogito is valid regardless of whether I am mad or not, since it is located outside of all intra-worldly and finite determinations of what it means to be reasonable. The cogito is a demonic, hyperbolic, and non-human transcendence that in fact can assume madness as the very possibility of its own freedom, and in this sense it stands in the lineage of the *daimonias hyperboles* perceived by Glaucon in *The Republic* (509c 1–2), when Socrates announces the idea of the good as beyond being, *epekeina tes ousias* (509b).

Foucault, according to Derrida, isolates one stage in the process of doubt and misses its fundamental point. In this he reduces the excessive dimension of doubt; he encloses the cogito in the world, and even in the institutions that it allegedly mirrors, like the Hôpital général. Derrida might here be said to reenact Husserl's critique of historicism in *Philosophie als strenge Wissenschaft*, casting Foucault as a latter day version of Dilthey, for which there is no truth to be had beyond changing worldviews; in the end, Foucault, by assuming a historicism that reduces the question of the origin of sense to a moment in history, is even said to undertake a confinement analogous to the one inflicted upon the mad.

Everything can no doubt be reduced to history in Descartes, Derrida admits, except the hyperbole, which constitutes the very possibility of a thought and a transcendence that we must not too soon enclose in the order of the epistemological. The hyperbole will no doubt almost immediately return to this order, when Descartes subsequently needs to reflect and preserve the cogito, and calls upon a metaphysical hierarchy in which God protects me from madness. It is here that Foucault's reading applies, when we need to be reasonable in order to speak and communicate our findings; it is here that we find the guidelines provided by natural light, the implicit axioms of hierarchies of perfection, the amount of reality in cause and effect, and more. This is why, Derrida suggests, the cogito must be distinguished from the deductive system in which Descartes ends up inscribing it, must even be protected from the positive interpretation that Descartes gives of it and which allows it to function as a cornerstone in the system of rationalism.

For Derrida, philosophical thought is precisely the interplay of hyperbole and finite totality, which is where the root of historicity must be located. Philosophy must at the same time imprison the mad—the discipline must communicate, locate, and justify its arguments in a particular order of reasons, as in the case of Cartesian rationalism—*and* liberate them, since it requires a transcendence that goes beyond any specific and finite order, although not by reaching the infinity of ideas, but rather by installing a differential relation that preserves the difference by constantly modifying, twisting, and reinstalling it. The relation between reason and madness—between reason as being tied to finite, bounded entities and as being indeterminate transcendence—must be one of *economy*, Derrida suggests, just as our relation to the violence inherent in reason and history.[20]

[20] "Economy" should here be understood as a way of balancing and negotiating impossible claims, and the term appears in many of Derrida's early writings. For instance, it appears in the reading of Levinas in "Violence and Metaphysics," which has a similar structure as the polemic against Foucault, with Levinas's claim about the exteriority of ethics in relation to ontology assuming the place of madness in Foucault; it appears also in the reading of Bataille and Hegel in "From General to Restricted Economy," where Bataille's ideas of expenditure and absolute sovereignty are as it were "economized" in relation to Hegel (both of them are translated in WD). There is no doubt also a relation to Freud's theory of the economy of drives, which Derrida would subsequently treat in detail in the much later essay "Spéculer—sur Freud," in *La Carte postale: De Socrate à*

Foucault's response

Foucault's response was eleven years in the making, and it first appeared as an appendix to the 1972 French re-edition of *The History of Madness*.[21] The argument dwells in great detail on the text of Descartes, but also engages principal questions about reading and interpretation, and as we have already suggested, it testifies to the transformations that Foucault's thought had undergone since 1961. This comes across particularly in the interpretation of Descartes, which does not so much supply arguments that a decade earlier were missing or implicit as much as it provides a new perspective that depends on a transformed understanding of archeology. In fact, the very form of attention directed to the text has changed, something only superficially due to the quarrel over philological details and more fundamentally to a new form of reading. For Foucault in 1972, Descartes no doubt still excludes madness, although the argument now bears on a series of moves that effect a transformation of the subject, rather than on a violent expulsion and the establishing of a singular and absolute limit. The task of archeology is no longer to reach something beyond reason, a silence withdrawn from discourse, but rather to locate the rules of what is being effectively said, which in turn stakes out a variety of possible subject positions, each with its own specific limit.

First, Foucault suggests that Derrida is mistaken in seeing the dream as having a stronger force of universality than madness: the point is that dreaming is something I often do, which is why it can function as a demonstration, and become available in the exercise of the meditations. This exercise returns us to the subject as practice, and it sets up a certain self-relation. The reference to the dream does not deepen the doubt that could have resulted from the example of madness, as Derrida claims, but provides it with a reference to and an effect in the meditating subject: I compare myself as meditating in the present to myself as dreaming in the past, so that I may continue to meditate even as sleeping and dreaming, whereas madness would have simply interrupted the movement of meditation. This is why the dreamer is not madder then the madman, and the difference is

Freud et au-delà (Paris: Flammarion, 1980); *The Post Card: From Socrates to Freud and Beyond*, trans. Alan Bass (Chicago: University of Chicago Press, 1987).
[21] A shorter version of the reply was published the same year in the Japanese journal *Paideia*. Here I will focus on the longer version. The *Paideia* essay has been translated as Appendix III in HM, 575–590; French text in DE 2, 281–295.

not that between a less and a more suitable example, but a difference in the *position of the subject*, which Foucault locates on four levels.

a) *Vocabulary*. In the example of madness it is a question of comparing (*comparare*) my present with a distant and unfamiliar example: I would be mad "if I took anything from them as a model for myself" (*si quod ab iis exemplum ad me transferrem*). In the dream there is always the memory of the dreamer that I was, and maybe still am; it is an identification by proximity whose point is to ensure continuity.

b) *Themes*. Madness means taking oneself to be another, believing one is dressed even though one is naked, or having a body made of glass. Madness transports the mind to another scene, whereas the dream indexes the same scene on which I am now present, but in a different way, through a kind of oneiric doubling of demonstrative pronouns (*this* hand, *this* paper, *this* fire).

c) *Test*. When I test the dream the difference vanishes. The hypothesis of madness, on the other hand, is never tested, but simply rejected without further ado: *sed amentes sunt isti*, for they are *amentes*, deprived of *mens*, reason.

d) *The result*. As Descartes says, I *would* be thought equally mad (*nec minus ipse demens viderer*) if I modeled myself on the fools. Here we should note the use of the conditional mood, which pushes the alternative into the counterfactual or non-real, so that to even carry out the test would be insane. In dreaming, on the other hand, I *am* surprised (*obstupescere*): the example takes root in me, in the present tense and indicative mood.

When Derrida says that Descartes does not speak of madness, and does not exclude it, Foucault contends that he overlooks the crucial difference between the *insani*, those who make simple errors in judgment, no matter how profound, and the *amentes*, those whoa are neither capable of nor entitled to perform legal or any other types of institutionally sanctioned acts, which is a disqualifying term, not a descriptive one. What Descartes claims, on this reading, is that I would be just as *incapacitated*, just as unauthorized to perform valid acts, as the *amentes* if I were to follow their example. What is at stake is not the truth of ideas (whether I am made of glass or not), but a qualification of the subject: I may without problem continue meditating as sleeping (as *dormiens*), but as insane (*demens*) I would not be able to continue and lay claim to stating anything valid.

To summarize: there is a difference in terms (*comparare* vs. *reminiscere*) between the reference to an alien example and the creation of continuity; there is a difference in thematic images (to sit by the fire vs. imagining oneself to be a king); and finally and most importantly, there is a difference in textual organization between the passage on the example that, if considered at depth, would have interrupted the course of the meditation as a valid practice and the passage in which we remember what it means to sleep in order to be able to continue meditating even though we might be sleeping in the present. The decisive outcome is the *qualification of the meditating subject* based on the difference in the quality of the act and in the effects these acts produce in the subject. For Derrida, Foucault says, what is at stake is rather the

> reduction of discursive practices to textual traces; the elision of events that are produced there, leaving only marks for a reading, the invention of voices behind the text, so as not to have to examine the modes of implication of the subject in discourses; the assignation of the originary as said and non-said in the text in order to avoid situating discursive practices in the field of transformation where they are carried out (HM, 573, DE 2, 267).

What the concatenation of Cartesian statements produces is on the one hand a system of philosophy, and on the other hand a new place—or a new distribution of possible places—for the subject. These two lines intersect at the point of madness, where the question is asked: under what conditions may I reasonably (*plane*) continue to doubt everything in the framework of the meditations as a practice? The example concerns the "system of actuality" of the meditating subject—what is *here* and *now* in the deictic form of *this* hand, *this* paper, *this* fire—and not on an extended and corporeal nature in general. How could I ever doubt this deictic presence? From the point of the system, the mad are indeed mistaken, but only about their actuality, and would in that sense not prevent doubt to proceed; from the point of view of the meditations as practice, the example they provide is as it were too exorbitant, too strong, since it renders continued meditation impossible, as is signaled by the term *demens*, which implies the impossibility of even feigning madness. The doubt produced by the dream is just as strong, or even stronger, with respect to its objects and in relation to the system, while it also establishes a continuity with my actuality and allows the meditation to pursue its rational course, thus encapsulating and neutralizing the all-too-insane deviation proposed by madness. The dream in this sense overcomes the obstacle by making the two lines, system and practice, converge, whereas madness causes them to diverge.

Foucault suggests that Derrida, in order to explain the detour through madness, instead creates a naïve, rustic non-philosopher who is made to intervene in the meditations by his exclamation "But these are fools!" According to Foucault, Derrida expels the madman three times: first, by denying that it is Descartes who speaks; then by ascribing the exclamation to the voice of naïve non-philosophy; and finally by disarming it through the alleged continuity with the dream argument. Derrida would in this way continue the Cartesian exclusion in a more insidious and invisible fashion, in saying that he, just like the hyperbolic Descartes, in fact welcomes madness, but only as an inner moment of a philosophical discourse, which then in turn can claim a kind of negative, hyperbolic—but in this also infinite—mastery, precisely by rejecting all determined orders of reason as so many factual and external restraints on the freedom of thought.

This initial farce is then continued at the most radical level, Foucault suggests, when Derrida perceives a more profound madness at work in the "*Deus deceptor*" argument, where it is not at all present; Derrida refuses to acknowledge madness where it is in fact present for a moment but only as excluded, in order to then introduce it at a later stage where it has already been disarmed. On the level of the metaphysical doubt, madness is not at all the issue, and what we see here is rather a highly controlled movement, in which I do not believe anything, since the hypothesis of the Evil Genius is precisely what allows for a suspension of all beliefs.

For Foucault, Derrida's inattention to these moves in Descartes's text is highly symptomatic: in transforming discursive practices to textual traces, he is able to interpret the latter as pointing toward a negative, indeterminate, and elusive transcendence that renders interpretation infinite, without ever connecting it either to the transformations of the thinking ego's positions or to the material structures that provide the meditations with efficacy in a given context. Rather than the closure of metaphysics, this is the apex of what Foucault in an unmistakably derogatory fashion calls a "little pedagogy" (HM 573; DE 2, 267), a mystifying interpretation of texts that endows philosophy with an indeterminate, but thus also infinite, authority located beyond all specific and determined conflicts and struggles.

Transcendence and discursive practice

It is important to see how Foucault's response shifts the terrain in relation to the claims made in *The History of Madness*, and does so in several respects. If one assumes that the answer provided in 1972 would merely support the claims made in 1961, the result would be confusing, and rather than simply locking the respective arguments up in an antinomic structure (madness as an *excessive* example in Foucault vs. madness as a particular and *not yet universal* example in Derrida) it is perhaps more productive to see this particular exchange as a way in which Foucault comes to reformulate the idea of archeology. This obviously does not mean that there might not be internal (and, for Foucault, probably more important) reasons for this shift in the progression of his own research, only that the exchange with Derrida proved to be an exemplary place for articulating them. To be sure, this is not what Foucault said, and the logic of polemics presumably prevented him from ever acknowledging it. However, the kind of retrospective view that I am proposing here need not be caught up in such a logic, but should be able to clarify the issues themselves without assuming any partisan stance.

To begin with, we must note that Foucault provides no answer to the specific historical charge made by Derrida, that there would be a kind of categorial mistake involved in the attempt to locate first a split between reason as such and its other, and consequently the origin of historicity, at particular points in time, for instance in the seventeenth century. Foucault drops without further ado the idea of a historically unique "decision" in the classical age; moreover, while it is true that he, at least in passing, also had referred to Greek and medieval thought, here too Derrida's criticism is left unanswered, and Foucault provides us with no explanation of why, for instance, the Greek logos had no opposite. The break in the seventeenth century could not be a unique event while still at the same time drawing on a long chain of definitions of reason that are themselves historically shifting and unstable.[22]

For Derrida, philosophy must be able to go beyond any given historical totality, and while he too is just as suspicious of any metaphysical claims to absolute truths, he rejects the attempt to reduce philosophy to being simply one among many discourses. We must uphold a transcendental ethos: philosophy must, and can, question itself with its own means, otherwise it falls prey to mere dogmatism, and the question of the origin of sense and rationality cannot be posed as a factual question to be answered by empirical investigations. It is true that the two opponents share a common

---

[22] It is highly significant that when Foucault at the end of the 1970s returns to Greek and Roman thought, in the two last published books on the history of sexuality, and in the lecture series on the hermeneutics of the subject, the governing of living beings, the governing of oneself and of others, and the courage to truth, he will stress long continuities in how motifs from ancient thought are taken up and transformed in modernity; the idea of decisive breaks will almost entirely vanish.

motif in the attempt to think something beyond the order of reasons set up by the Cartesian turn, and even something that metaphysics as such has repressed in order to constitute itself. For Derrida, this can however only be approached by way of pursuing the transcendental question beyond and against itself, although without letting go of the hyperbolic movement as such; whereas Foucault in 1961 appeals to an experience of an outside that is wholly other, without reflective mediation with the inside, and which therefore can only appear in the guise of brute factual events.

To this more general critique posed by Derrida—that Foucault's attempt to locate a radical outside or other of reason moves too quickly, and that it cannot account for its own condition of possibility but instead symptomatically ends up reducing the freedom of philosophy to a set of factual conditions—Foucault's answer is more oblique, and must be extracted from the new interpretation of Descartes that he gives in his reply. Looking back on his earlier argument, he takes a different step that aspires to locate a level of analysis situated transversally in relation to both Derrida's quest for *archi*-transcendentality *and* his own earlier claims for an *archeo*-logy of radical alterity. This will be the idea of discursive practices as ways of modifying the mediating subject's self-relation, which also comes across in the new understanding of archeology: it is no longer a quest for an abyssal ungrounding or unique limit beyond which reason would have no purchase, but an account of the variable positions of the subject in relation to the statement, of its various claims to authority and legality, and of what it means to be a responsible author for one's statements.

This problem of the subject and the statement had first appeared in systematic fashion three years earlier in *The Archeology of Knowledge* (1969), and would a few years after the response to Derrida be integrated into the analytic of power. In this sense the reply to Derrida is a crucial transitional text, not least by engaging in an implicit self-criticism that aligns Foucault's earlier position with Derrida's: the idea of madness as a radical alterity to be reached by way of a different type of discourse must be abandoned, since it harbors a nostalgia for a deep, savage being outside of categorial constraints, which is in fact—so Foucault can be taken as implicitly saying—also true of Derrida's hyperbolic transcendence, even though the vocabularies chosen to express it were different. Foucault's answer does not reiterate the former position, but approaches the problem from a different angle that also transforms the perspective adopted in *The History of Madness*.

The question now asked by Foucault is fundamentally not who or what imprisons madness, or what type of analysis might allow us to tap into its silence, both of which now prove, at least implicitly, to be in tune with the idea of a philosophy that could sustain a claim to truth radically outside of any context. The idea of archeology must be rethought along the lines of a discursive practice for which thinking begins not in a hyperbole, in a transcendence toward the unconditioned or abyssal, but in the experience of a *constraint* that must be explored, interrogated, and perhaps modified, but always from within a particular context.

Conclusion

For Foucault in 1961, there is an outside of reason, a depth that must be excluded if reason, which sometimes seems to be identified with the institution of eighteenth-century rationalism and sometimes extends all the way back to Greek thought, is to exert its power. The task of a history of madness must then be not only to identify a set of specific material and discursive structures that interrupted those exchanges between reason and unreason that Foucault here perceives as having preceded the moment of rupture, but also, seemingly in passing but with much larger consequences, to dethrone philosophy from its position as a discourse of first and funda-mental principles. Cartesian philosophy, according to Foucault, belongs to the same order as classical reason in general, which by implication suggests that philosophy should be brought down from the heavens and be wholly aligned with medical, legal, and other similar types of discourse, without any purchase on trans-historical truths. But as a consequence, his own project must then invent a different type of discourse, which cannot simply write the history of exclusions, but must attempt to go back to the division as such in order to grasp, paradoxically, the Other of reason before it has congealed into a determined other that can be located in a dialectical opposition. Foucault must create a counter-philosophical discourse that supports itself on empirical facts, and yet finds its resources in an experi-ence that radically subverts traditional modes of historical intelligibility that are founded precisely on an exclusion of madness.

Derrida's critique can be read as a defense of a transformed and yet still recognizable version of transcendental philosophy. Beyond all the empirical issues that surround Foucault's book on madness, there remains the fundamental question, Derrida says, of how we could ever aspire to return to the genesis of historicity *as such* within an empirical history. For Derrida, the motif underlying Foucault's investigation is not to critically dismantle metaphysics from within, but to simply circumvent it by reinscribing it into a set of factual conditions. The most notable case of this Derrida locates in the reading of the Cartesian cogito, which Foucault, according to Derrida, violently reduces to a reflection of a particular historical totality, the Classical age, and even more drastically to the "great confinement" of reason's other with the establishing of the Hôpital général in 1656. Against this, Derrida claims that we must retain the possibility for thought to transcend any finite constellation, not in the sense that it would be able to reach some positive infinity of ideas, but as a movement that makes it possible for the difference between finitude and infinity to appear at all.

In Foucault's response the terrain shifts. The question of reason—or more precisely of the subject as the bearer of rationality—as it appears in Descartes should not be posed to the history of metaphysics as a series of determinations of the being of beings that always relate to an excessive and withdrawn dimension of being: i.e. the trajectory that has become somewhat of a commonplace in certain strands of phenomenology, especially after Heidegger. It does not bear on something like the limit, end, death, or closure of metaphysics, but on how forms of truth and subjectivity are created in history through practices, in their turn linked to forms of power and institutional procedures of rationalization that are in principle open-ended and contingent, and cannot be understood as emanating from an initial sending or approaching some final limit. For Foucault this does not mean to reduce subjects and truths to mere effects, but to see them as always conflicted and temporary modes of action and reaction, resistances to and alignments with powers and discourses that are not simply outside of them. This shift, while obviously also grounded in Foucault's own research, was made possible by the exchange with Derrida, where the idea of an archeology of the limits of reason underwent a decisive displacement.

Light and Darkness:
Jan Patočka's Critique of the Enlightenment

Gustav Strandberg

One of the lines of thought running throughout the *oeuvre* of the Czech philosopher Jan Patočka is formulated around a question concerning the enlightenment, addressing simultaneously what the enlightenment really was, from where it originates and what it points towards in modernity. The way in which Patočka attempts to respond to these questions, however, harbor a certain ambiguity. At the same time as Patočka levels a relentless critique against the form of enlightenment that underwrites the cruelties of the past century and that continues to rest in the midst of "enlightened" reason, he also calls for a renewal of the enlightenment, one capable of responding to the "epoch of night, war and death", which defined the 20th century.

The purpose of this article is to describe so as then to draw out this tension in Patočka's writing by elucidating both his critique of the enlightenment and his scattered remarks on the possibility of its renewal. In order to approach this dual task one must, however, begin by trying to come to terms with the history of the enlightenment itself and its relation to what Patočka designates as the origin of history.

Care of the soul and the origin of history

In his second heretical essay, Patočka poses the question of what constitutes history and in what the specificity of history consists. The prevailing means of answering such questions is, as Patočka writes, by pointing at different instances of "collective memory which either first emerges with writing or has its strongest support in it."[1] The problem with this kind of explanation is, however, that it tries to deduce the meaning of a specific historical event from the meaning which a narrative about it gives us, while the meaning of an event is different from the meaning that is found within the narrative about it. Whereas the meaning of an event involves people who "act and suffer", the meaning enclosed in a narrative about historical events is found in "the logical formations pointing" to them.[2] The narrative of an event can thus accord us a "meaning" that is relatively independent of the context in which it arose and to which, moreover, we can return and understand in more or less the same way, independent of our present situation. The meaning of an historical event is, on the other hand, something that constantly transcends the description of it; its meaning lies, as Patočka concludes, in the very "development of the situation itself."[3]

The historical nature of an event is, in other words, not something enclosed in the history *about* it. This implies, in turn, that historical narratives can exist that do not "primarily and thematically [aim] at actual events in history", but that appear, paradoxically, as historical narratives without any real history, as an "a-historical" history.[4] This, according to Patočka, is the case with the annals and chronicles we find in Egypt and China, for example. The reason why these preserved writings constitute "an historical narrative without any real history" is, in Patočka's eyes, due to the fact that "its purpose and meaning was the preservation of the lifestyle of prehistorical humanity", a lifestyle completely absorbed by the preservation and securing of life itself.[5] These empires were, as he goes on to write, like grand "households" in which the question of meaning never need to "transcend the household and its cyclic repetition of birth, reproduction and sustenance":

> Annalistics captures the past as something important for the successful future comportment of the grand household which cares for itself in this sense; it is primarily composed of ritualistic writings, cultomantic records, observations of what is fortunate and unfortunate in events and acts. As long as humans live in such a way that this vital cycle of acceptance and transmission, of the preser-

[1] Jan Patočka, *Heretical Essays in the Philosophy of History*, trans. Erazim Kohák (Illinois: Open Court Publishing, 1996), 28.
[2] Ibid, 28.
[3] Ibid.
[4] Ibid.
[5] Ibid.

vation and securing of life, exhausts the meaning of what is done, we can say that it moves in the rhythm of perennial return, even though in reality tradition functions, inventions take place, and the style of life changes to the point of producing a change as fundamental as the collective memory just mentioned.[6]

The reason why Patočka rejects this early form of historical writing lay not in the writing itself, but rather in the society from which these events are written. Even though historiography is not the proper place of history this does not, however, entail that the question concerning the specificity of history is something we must relegate to the historicity of man. The historicity of human existence is, as Patočka notes, far too wide a concept, since it cannot account for the fact that there are, or at least that there have been, nations and civilizations without any proper history.[7] Neither historiography nor the historicity of man can thus explain the "a-historical" nature of these societies.

If the question concerning the origin of history is posed as one concerning the historicity of human existence then the question must therefore be articulated more precisely. We can, as Patočka writes, only speak of history when a rupture occurs through which life no longer is bound to itself and to its own reproduction, but is confronted with the world in its totality. What Patočka designates as the origin of history is, in other words, a specific form of experience in which the earlier form of life, with its traditions and myths, is disturbed:

> Such life does not seek to escape its contingency, but neither does it yield to it passively; since it has glimpsed the possibility of authentic life, that is, life as a whole, the world opens itself to it for the first time—it is no longer merely an involuntary background against which that which concerns us shows itself; rather, it itself can now stand forth, as the whole of that which opens up against the black backdrop of closed night. This whole now speaks to humans directly, free of the muting effect of tradition and myth, only by it do they seek to be accepted and held responsible. Nothing of the earlier life of acceptance remains in peace; all the pillars of the community, traditions, and myths, are equally shaken, as are all the answers that once preceded questions, the modest yet secure and soothing meaning, though not lost, is transformed.[8]

[6] Ibid, 29.
[7] Ibid, 28.
[8] Ibid, 39–40.

This disruptive experience is in fact the experience through which humanity is confronted with meaning as such—that is, with a meaning that does not belong among the different interests and objects within the world, but with a meaning that, on the contrary, only appears when all "inner-worldly" meaning has been lost: a form of meaning that can only appear through an experience of a loss of meaning. As Paul Ricoeur notes in his preface to the French translation of the *Heretical Essays*, this is a loss of meaning, but a loss of meaning "that does not descend into the 'meaning-less' but an access to the quality of meaning implied in the search itself."[9] It is, in other words, the experience through which meaning appears *as a question* for humanity, since meaning can, as Patočka indeed emphasizes, "only arise in an activity which stems from a searching lack of meaning."[10]

Patočka's descriptions of this meaningful loss of meaning are to a large extent indebted to Heidegger's analysis of anxiety in *Being and Time*. On Patočka's account, what Heidegger shows in his analysis is precisely that meaning only can appear in a "moment of crisis."[11] The principal difference between the two thinkers, however, is that Patočka understands this crisis as an historical experience, or rather, as *the historical experience* as such, whereas Heidegger would understand the crisis brought about through anxiety as one of the fundamental possibilities of human existence as such, not only in its "historical form." Phrased somewhat differently, we can thus say that the meaning of history, as Patočka understands it, can be relegated to neither the domain of historiography nor to a question concerning the historicity of humankind. Rather, Patočka tries to understand history in its very unfolding—not only as the history of events, but history *as* event. History can, in this sense, only emerge in and through an event in which the world has lost all meaning for human beings and when the world, by this very loss, is being transformed. When all that which is contained *within* the world appears in all its nothingness then, and only then, can the world appear as such.

Meaning does not, however, appear in the form of an epiphany, but as something to which human beings must constantly respond.[12] History is an

---

[9] Paul Ricoeur, "Preface to the French Edition of Jan Patočka's Heretical Essays," trans. Erazim Kohák, in Patočka, *Heretical Essays*, xiv.
[10] Patočka, *Heretical Essays*, 60–61.
[11] Ibid, 60.
[12] Patočka will speak of this "responsibility" by using the Czech word *odpovědnost* that has the meaning of responsibility, accountability and reliability, but which also contains

event, but an event for which humanity is held responsible. For even though the origin of history is characterized by our confrontation with something that lies beyond the mere labor involved in sustaining and reproducing our own lives, this repetitive dimension is, nevertheless, something that constitutes a fundamental part of our existence. Human existence is, in other words, permanently exposed to the possible threat of a return to a life entirely absorbed by its own reproduction, a life estranged from itself. Estrangement is hence a curious phenomenon, since human existence is estranged from itself precisely by being too close to life: when human beings are immersed and entangled in their own life they are, in fact, living at the furthest distance from themselves.

Human existence can thus be said to be in a state of decay or de-generation when life itself "loses its grasp on the innermost nerve of its functioning", when it is estranged from itself and keeps returning to this estrangement as something that is more "natural" and "pleasant" than its own being.[13] This decaying appears in the guise of a refuge among things and as a flight away from a person's imposed task of constantly enacting and realizing their own being—as a refuge from the fact that humanity after this disruptive and distressing experience is exposed in and for the world. This experience of interruption—through which meaning emerges for humanity—is concomitantly the experience through which the being of humankind becomes a question for people; the being of humankind is no longer something that can be found in life itself, nor can it be equated with the mere sustenance of it. Rather it appears as a question, as a question that human beings must respond to by themselves, without any form of support.

The meaning of human existence is, in fact, something that can only give itself "*through phenomena*", which is why it is completely dependent on the form in which these phenomena appear.[14] If the world is reduced to the appearance of a conglomerate of "things" that we use in different ways to prolong our own life, then human existence itself will be reduced to the same level as the things surrounding it—human existence will lose itself among things and become estranged from itself. In order for the question concerning the meaning of human existence to arise at all *as a question* it

clear connotations of response and answer. The Czech noun for answer and response is *odpověď* and the concomitant verb is *odpovědět*.

[13] Patočka, *Heretical Essays*, 98.

[14] Jan Patočka, *Plato and Europe*, trans. Petr Lom (Stanford: Stanford University Press, 2002), 28.

must transcend the "inner-worldly" domain; human existence must be confronted with the world, with that which renders the particular appearances possible—that is, with the world in its totality. Phrased somewhat differently, a man can, as Patočka writes, only discover himself when he discovers that he too "is *manifest as a part* of this world."[15] Patočka's reflections on the origin of history are, in other words, interwoven with his phenomenological analyses. The event of history is at the same time the event through which the appearance of the world is disclosed for humankind. It is this "light of the world", as Patočka writes, that distinguishes human existence from other forms of life, but it is also this privilege that "places duties before man" and forces him to respond to the historical event of the world.[16]

In contrast to the responsible form of existence—which time and again imposes the question of the meaning of its own being—estrangement is a form of life that appears as a refuge, binding human existence to life and threatening, moreover, to throw its own existence back upon a "pre-historic state." The estrangement in question can here be said to be a movement in which human existence is reified and in which the things themselves become animated—something that Patočka calls a "self-refusing self-extension."[17]

While the estranged form of human existence lives with a belief in itself as an autonomous subject, capable of controlling and mastering the world surrounding it, the responsible form of human existence is attuned to the fact that meaning is not something to be managed or controlled like the things surrounding it, but that meaning, by necessity, transcends both the surrounding world and our own selves. Meaningfulness is therefore not something that stems from or is produced by human beings, but on the contrary is—as Patočka tirelessly underwrites—something "problematic." For even if meaning can only co-appear with the world in its totality, this by no means implies that the world is something static and unchangeable. The world, in fact, never shows itself *"in the same way twice"*, but its appearance constitutes an historical movement. This, Patočka writes, constitutes the problematic nature of the world.[18] In this way, the responsible form of

---

[15] Ibid, 60.
[16] Ibid, 27.
[17] Jan Patočka, "K prehistorii vědy o pohybu" in *Sebrané spisy VII – Fenomenologické spisy II* (Prague: Oikoymenh, 2009), 198.
[18] Patočka, *Plato and Europe*, 73.

human existence can be said to consist in its continuous response to the world and, by implication, to the world's historical manifestation. Only by thus responding to the world does the question of the very being of human existence have any meaning for it. For these reasons the meaning of history can be something we define neither through historiography nor through a naive interpretation of the historicity of human existence, but is rather, as Patočka writes, "an openness for the shaking" that the confrontation with the world brings about.[19] This openness is, to be sure, an openness that we find in humanity. However, it is not to be interpreted as a trans-historical fact, but, rather, as an historical task to which human existence must continuously respond. This history of responsibility for the world can therefore, as Patočka notes, be said to be an "inner process" in which human beings gradually discover their own "proper and unique *I*": history is first and foremost the "history of the soul."[20]

What gives the "history of the soul" its distinctiveness, however, is a distinction more fundamental than that between the estranged and the proper way of life (indeed, it undergirds the latter through being more primordial): namely, it is the distinction between the profane or "the everyday" and "the exceptional" or the sacred.[21] This distinction counterposes the light of reason with the darkness of what Patočka calls "the orgiastic dimension" of human existence. Whereas "the everyday" is essentially the self-enslavement of labor, the orgiastic dimension of human existence both relieves and liberates us temporarily from this burden: not because it is a *flight from* responsibility (as is the case with the estranged form of life), but rather because we are *"enraptured"* through and by it; the orgiastic is the domain in which "something more powerful than our free possibility, our responsibility, seems to break into our life and bestow on it a meaning which it would not know otherwise."[22] It is, as Patočka continues, the domain of passion and the demonic in which we do not flee from our selves, but in which we are "surprised by something, taken aback and captivated."[23] Similar, then, to the responsible form of human existence— but remaining as its constitutive counterpart—the orgiastic dimension is furthermore a domain in our existence which confronts us with the world

[19] Patočka, *Heretical Essays*, 44.
[20] Ibid, 103.
[21] Ibid, 98.
[22] Ibid, 99.
[23] Ibid.

in its totality, with something that, in certain experiences, opens itself for us *by itself.*[24]

Not only is the orgiastic dimension a necessary part of human existence, but it also constitutes one of the few moments in which the world in its totality can appear for us. Since this dimension represents neither a flight from responsibility nor something that the responsible form of life can hope to overcome—or, even, completely subdue—it must be incorporated in responsibility. If, therefore, the orgiastic dimension is granted complete freedom (which is to say, if it is not incorporated within responsibility) it can intensify and augment the self-estrangement constantly harbored within itself as one of its possible forms. Whereas estrangement implies that life remains bound to itself and to its own reproduction, the orgiastic dimension appears as an alleviation from this laborious burden and, as a freedom from life itself, it appears as an ecstasy from the bondage of life to itself. Yet, while the orgiastic dimension can, from time to time, make itself known as a liberation from life, it is, nevertheless, not the proper place of freedom, according to Patočka. The momentary alleviation it can offer us is still rooted in that which it opposes. The liberation in question is, in other words, something that remains bound up with the reproduction of life and therefore subordinated to a sphere in human existence, which in the end remains blind to the question of meaning. The orgiastic dimension hence reveals the world for human beings, but in such a paroxysmal and rapturous way that the question concerning the meaning of human existence is eclipsed as soon as it appears.

In order for the question concerning the meaning of human existence to arise, this orgiastic penchant must be anchored in responsibility. According to Patočka, it is this "economy" between responsibility and the orgiastic dimension—between the everyday and the festive, between light and darkness—that can be found at the very base of the history of western metaphysics. History can only arise when human beings manage to rise "above decadence" and, in doing so, realize that human existence contains possibilities that are neither enclosed within the laborious struggle to reproduce one's own life nor in the orgiastic moments. This does not imply, however—and this is important to stress—that human beings in any way can

---

[24] Patočka speaks, specifically, here of the erotic, the sexual, the demonic and the fear inspired by the sacred; although, no doubt, the list can be further extended.

subdue these dimensions, only that they must learn to live *in and through this opposition*:

> We believe that the I in this sense emerges at the dawn of history and that it consists in not losing ourselves in the sacred, not simply surrendering our selves within it, but rather in living through the whole opposition of the sacred and the profane with the dimension of the problematic which we uncover in the responsible questioning in a quest for clarity with the sobriety of the everyday, but also with an active daring for the vertigo it brings; overcoming everydayness without collapsing in self-forgetting into the region of darkness, however tempting.[25]

The first explicit attempt to incorporate the darkness of the orgiastic dimension under the responsible light of reason is to be found in Greek thought. If we want therefore to locate the origin of western history, we must turn, according to Patočka, to the Greek question concerning the care of the soul (*epimeleia tes psyches*) and, more specifically, to Plato's understanding of this question. Citing Eugen Fink, Patočka writes that Plato's thought is "an attempt to think light without shadow."[26] The exit from the Platonic cave marks simultaneously a departure from the orgiastic domain and an exiting which proceeds along a "path of light" and leads, in the end, towards light itself in the form of the idea of the Good—an idea which, as Fink writes, gathers other ideas like "all the rays of light in the one and only sun."[27] Whereas earlier cultures had striven for a fusion or a confrontation between responsibility and the orgiastic dimension, Greek thought subordinated the orgiastic dimension to reason and its conception of the Good as the highest idea. Plato's thought thus represents, according to Patočka, the intrusion of a "mythology of light" in the history of the soul, an intrusion that would have enormous consequences for the history of western metaphysics.[28]

Light, which takes a position of prominence in Plato's thought, remains not completely un-refracted however. If the responsible light of reason would have subordinated and suppressed the orgiastic dimension completely, then the economic balance between the two dimensions would be disturbed: the orgiastic dimension would thus no longer be an incorporated part of responsibility, but instead only its subordinated other. The reason

---

[25] Patočka, *Heretical Essays*, 115. Italics added.
[26] Ibid, 103.
[27] Eugen Fink, *Metaphysik der Erziehung im Weltverständnins von Plato und Aristoteles* (Frankfurt am Main: Vittorio Klostermann, 1970), 107.
[28] Patočka, *Heretical Essays*, 106.

why the light which Plato's thought ushered into our history is considered such a paradigmatic event rests, according to Patočka, on its ability to unite and hold together these conflicting spheres. In part this depended on the constitution of Greek society: since Greek society was permeated by a number of orgiastic moments that challenged its everydayness, Greek philosophy could occupy the position as a completely "non-ecstatic" and "non-orgiastic" part of human existence.

There was, in other words, no need to fear that "the pathos of the everyday might overwhelm and choke out its opposite."[29] Greek society could thus harbor the contradiction between the everyday and the exceptional, between responsibility and its orgiastic counterpart. But if we for a moment disregard these historical circumstances we can also observe that there is, according to Patočka, something specific contained in Plato's thought that enabled this form of coexistence: Plato's understanding of the care of the soul is at the same time a "care for death" (*melete thanatou*). Indeed, Patočka writes that the platonic care of the soul goes thus beyond a care for life, to the extent that a care for one's own death remains "the true care for life."[30] The care for death is therefore—and this is important to emphasize—the most important part of Plato's teachings on the soul precisely because it is this relation to one's own finitude that enables the incorporation of the orgiastic dimension of responsibility.

All of the orgiastic moments in human existence—whether we are speaking about sexual and erotic experiences or religious ones—include a specific relation to one's own finitude. They are all experiences that take place on the limits of human existence, on the limit between life and death that intersect human existence as its untraversable boundary. In other words, if the economical balance between responsibility and the orgiastic dimension is to be maintained, it is necessary for the responsibility in question to contain a relation to the finitude of human existence. Plato's philosophy is thus a philosophy that still contains darkness: Patočka writes that the "darkness is there; the cave does not cease to exist."[31] According to Patočka, this tension between responsibility and the orgiastic dimension, between light and darkness, forms the basis of western history. It emerges for the first time in Greek philosophy and endures in Christianity, albeit in a different guise.

[29] Ibid, 103–104.
[30] Ibid, 105.
[31] Patočka, *Plato and Europe*, 139.

From Julian the Apostate's time on the Roman throne onwards, an important development in the relation between the orgiastic and responsibility takes place. The responsible life still remains and thereby encapsulates and controls its orgiastic counterpart, but the idea of the Good that functions as the guarantor for responsibility gradually changes. If the idea of the Good had earlier been an idea that human beings reach through an inner dialogue—and through an inner dialogue that constantly confronts each one with their own finitude—it is now something that is enclosed within the *mysterium tremendum* of Christianity, that is, in God.[32]

The truth about the soul is, in other words, no longer something that humanity can hope to attain through insight, but a truth that remains bound to its inescapable destiny, to an "eternal responsibility from which there is no escape *ad secula seculorum*."[33] As soon as Christianity makes its entrance into the history of the soul, the orgiastic dimension of human existence is therefore no longer something subordinate to responsibility—as was the case in Greek thought—but something that is "suppressed to the limit."[34] Christianity thus succeeded in preserving some of the insights contained in the Greek conception of the soul, but only at the price of an absolute suppression of the orgiastic moments in human existence. As a consequence, Christianity has, for Patočka, an ambiguous position in the history of the soul: on the one hand, it constitutes a continuation of the Greek heritage; on the other, it is a first step in the direction of a dislocation of the economical balance sought between responsibility and the orgiastic dimension—a dislocation that would only reach its completion in and through modernity. As Derrida has pointed out in *The Gift of Death*, the difference between Greek thought and Christianity can thus be said to revolve around two different forms of economy contained in the larger economy of western metaphysics. Whereas Greek thought represents an economy of incorporation, Christianity appears as an economy of repression.[35] What Derrida, however, fails to see—or simply disregards—in his reading of Patočka is the role that Patočka accords to Christianity in the

---

[32] Patočka, *Heretical Essays*, 106.
[33] Ibid, 107.
[34] Ibid, 106.
[35] Jacques Derrida, *The Gift of Death*, trans. David Wills (Chicago: Chicago University Press, 2008), 22.

movement towards the perversion of this economy that takes place through the enlightenment.[36]

The fusion between Greek thought and Christian faith, which takes place during the Roman Empire, finally leads to a synthesis that engenders something radically new in history. The transformation of humanity's relation to the Good, effectuated in and through Christianity, will lead concomitantly to the creation of a seemingly unbridgeable cleft between humanity and nature. Nature is transposed to an object at a secure distance from humankind and to an object that people can control and master in different ways with the help of reason—and with a reason that has its roots in Plato's thought. For example, Galileo was, as Patočka notes, if anything a Platonist.[37] This rationalism will at the same time find a close ally in the increasing emphasis being placed on human practice by Christianity: that is, in its estimation of practical values over and above contemplative ones. What Patočka is pointing to, in actual fact, is of course the radical transformation that the Reformation brought about and, more specifically, the consequences it had for the emerging form of modern natural science.

The mathematization of nature became something that no longer takes place behind the closed doors of science; it is a process that forms itself into an effective synthesis of science and technology, thereby constituting itself as modern natural science. The result of this process is, in the last instance, even more than the rise of a mathematical natural science, though: according to Patočka, modern natural science both supports and is supported by capitalism as an emergent form and power:

> The Christian attitude to life's practice, its valorization of practical life against theory, makes it possible to integrate even the Platonic "mastery" of nature into practical contexts and so to create a truly effective knowledge that is technique and science in one—modern natural science. Transformations in the Christian spiritual core itself, the transition first from a Christianity of and for the nobility to an ecclesiastical autonomy and then to a lay Christianity, made it possible for Christianity—with Reformation's ascetic attitude to the world and with the pathos of personal certification by economic blessings—to contribute to the rise of that autonomy of the productive process that characterizes modern capi-

---

[36] It is this elusion by Derrida concerning the question of Christianity in Patočka's work that enables him to claim that Patočka is, in fact, a Christian philosopher. Even though Patočka's relation to Christianity cannot simply be framed as a question revolving around the simple juxtaposition between "Christian" or "non-Christian", it is nevertheless clear that Derrida is pushing the proverbial envelope a bit too far here.
[37] Patočka, *Heretical Essays*, 111.

talism. That capitalism quickly sheds the constraints of its religious impetus and allies itself fundamentally with a superficial modern rationalism, estranged from any personal and moral vocation. It comes to be characterized by an immensely successful mathematical formalism. It's most successful aspect focuses on a mastery of nature, of movement, and of force. That is the modern mechanism which capitalism was only too glad to turn into a cult of the mechanical, so contributing to what came to be known as the industrial revolution.[38]

This development did not, of course, cease with the form of capitalism that industrialization engendered. It constitutes a veritable revolution that "penetrates throughout and ever more completely determines our lives", to the extent that we today "no longer [are] capable of physically surviving but for the mode of production that rests increasingly on science and technology."[39]

Thus, from the inception of modernity onwards the economy which earlier—albeit with some difficulties—managed to hold together and unite the responsible way of life with the orgiastic dimension became perverted. The care of the soul, which in Plato's thought had served as a bulwark against the irresponsible ecstasies of the orgiastic dimension, is now reduced, Patočka writes, "into the service of everydayness."[40] What in Plato's thought had once been a movement directed inwards—towards one's own self—and, moreover, had constituted a movement of questioning in which *the* question concerning the very being of existence and its relation to meaning had been at stake, is now turned outwards, towards things.

From the sixteenth century onwards we can observe how, according to Patočka, that which earlier was a care of the soul—a care of one's own being—is gradually transformed into a "care of having", into a care for the exterior world that in the end has the conquest of that world as its goal.[41] For Patočka, this transformation reaches its particular perspicuity in the thought of Francis Bacon. Even though Bacon was neither a mathematician nor an inventor in any revolutionary sense of the word, he was nevertheless the greatest methodologist of modernity:

---

[38] Ibid, 111. Concerning the development of Protestantism and its relation to both modern science and capitalism, Patočka is—as is obvious from his working notes—indebted to the groundbreaking analysis of Max Weber in *The Protestant Ethics and the Spirit of Capitalism*. See: Jan Patočka, "Evropa pramenem dějin" in *Sebrané spisy III – Péče o duši III* (Prague: Oikoymenh, 2002), 471.

[39] Patočka, *Heretical Essays*, 111–112.

[40] Ibid, 112.

[41] Ibid, 83.

Where the first thinkers, who had introduced the idea of a new historical era, spoke about the supremacy of the soul, Bacon announced the supremacy of man. The supremacy of man is the era in history in which the effective knowledge, by a continuous process, subjugates nature and places it in the service of man; the era in which effective knowledge through a methodical cultivation and exploitation with the help of a method becomes a tool for the true love of mankind, the love of genus humanum—the true philanthropy.[42]

What in fact take place during the inception of modernity are the first tentative steps towards a complete transformation of human nature. As soon as human beings appear everywhere on the face of the world, they concomitantly disappear from it. When human existence no longer has any real relation to its own being, or when this relation simply is turned around into a care for the domination of the world, the shape and figure of human-kind transforms itself. Human existence no longer cares for its own being, but appears as a "force", as one of the mightiest forces in the world.[43]

At a time when human beings no longer have any relation to their own being, the possibilities of living in a responsible way disappear along with it. The increasing hegemony exacted by techno-science—together with its as-severation that it is the only true relation to "that which is"—is accompanied by a dislocation of the economical balance that had once prevailed. The more dominant techno-science becomes, the crueler "the revenge of the orgiastic fervor" will be, Patočka notes.[44] If Greek thought was able to bridle the orgiastic dimension by offering it a responsible discharge in a renewed confrontation with the finitude of human existence, and if, for its own part, Christianity endeavored to suppress the orgiastic as far as possible, then modernity constitutes an attempt at eradicating, once and for all, the orgiastic dimension through the light of reason. When the incessant questioning of the being of human existence disappears, then humanity's relation to its own finitude will disappear along with that questioning—and thus the only responsible discharge for the orgiastic dimension will come to nothing.

[42] Jan Patočka, *Aristote, ses devanciers, ses successeurs*, trans. Erika Abrams (Paris: Vrin, 2011), 362.
[43] Patočka, *Heretical Essays*, 116.
[44] Ibid, 113.

The glaring light of the Enlightenment

However, each and every attempt at annihilating the orgiastic dimension entirely is doomed to fail. If one discharge is obstructed, its energy will only spring forth from another. The orgiastic dimension can thus be directed in different ways, but never can it be eradicated. Yet, this is precisely what the enlightenment sought to achieve, according to Patočka. The force and the depth of the enlightenment consisted of what earlier forms of knowledge—with their insistence on the inner life of the soul—had neglected: that is, an "efficient and fruitful knowledge."[45] This development did, of course, bring about a number of positive consequences—and Patočka himself is quite clear on this point—such as, for examples, the secularization of society, the rejection of earlier forms of hierarchy, and so on. Rather, the problem with the enlightenment lay with how this development unfolded at the cost of a form of knowledge that not only rejected tradition, but which excluded everything that failed to correspond to its own measure of truth. In the enlightenment, the only "source of life" is light and rational knowledge, while that which cannot be reduced to a form of this light is discarded as one of history's many leftovers.[46]

The "revenge" of the orgiastic dimension makes itself felt already during the nineteenth century in the form of the Napoleonic wars, the revolutionary events that transpired during 1848, and in the increasingly violent repression of the revolutionary moments during that century. The nineteenth century thus appears as a century of energy accumulation, a summoning of latent orgiastic energy that only emerges during the twentieth century. Patočka therefore concludes that the twentieth century is the truth of the nineteenth century.[47] He notes that Nietzsche had already foreseen the outcome of this withheld tension in Europe. In the first section of the posthumously published *Will to Power*, we can read:

> For some time now, our whole European culture has been moving toward a catastrophe, with a tortured tension that is growing from decade to decade: relentlessly, violently, headlong, like a river that wants to reach the end, that no longer reflects, that is afraid to reflect.[48]

[45] Ibid, 88.
[46] Ibid, 45.
[47] Ibid, 113.
[48] Friedrich Nietzsche, *The Will to Power*, trans. and ed. Walter Kaufmann (New York: Vintage Books, 1968), 3. Cited by Patočka in "Die Selbstbesinnung Europas" in

Though the enlightenment can be said to reach its tersest formulation during the latter half of the eighteenth century, it is only in and through the twentieth century that its full effects are unleashed. The rational light of the enlightenment denies the existence of the orgiastic dimension, while simultaneously perverting the care of the soul. In the aftermath of the enlightenment, therefore, the everyday has superseded the exceptional and reduced the orgiastic to the service of the everyday: freedom is reduced to leisure and to a leisure that serves only as the function and support of labor-time. Liberated from the shackles of responsibility and fused together with the everyday, the orgiastic dimension intensifies the estrangement of human existence; at precisely this juncture the orgiastic makes its appearance in the guise of the demonic. Human existence becomes, at this point *and* once again, reduced to a prehistoric level. It is the reproduction of life that remains at the centre of things, even if the form of its appearance alters during the enlightenment.

The orgiastic dimension, however, can never disappear completely. Rather, it is incorporated into the light of reason, which, in turn, will glare its darkness. It is, as Patočka describes this paradoxical phenomenon, the "same hand that stages orgies and organizes everydayness", and "the author of the five-year plan is at the same time the author of orchestrated show trials in a new which hunt."[49] The exceptional nature of feasts and rituals is now only an element among others in the equilibrial structure of the everyday, to the extent that human beings now, as Patočka notes, are paradoxically arranging feasts in honour of their labour.[50] For this reason, the many wars of the 20th century appear *simultaneously* as "the greatest undertaking of industrial civilization" *and* as a "release of orgiastic potentials which could not afford such extreme intoxication with destruction under any other circumstances."[51] In other words, war and destruction form the only discharge large enough to channel the orgiastic energy that the

---

Perspektiven der Philosophie, No 20 (1994), 245. The fact that Patočka at times turns to Nietzsche in this context does not come as a surprise. For even though some of his analyses of the history of western metaphysics are in line with Heidegger's descriptions of it, he seems at times to be closer to Nietzsche than Heidegger. That which Patočka is considering as the economy between light and darkness can be regarded, in this sense, as a form of Nietzschean genealogy, but a genealogy that perhaps would find its closest equivalent in the early Nietzsche of *The Birth of Tragedy*.

[49] Patočka, *Heretical Essays*, 114.

[50] Patočka, "La supercivilización y su conflicto interno," in *Libertad y Sacrificio*, trans. Iván Ortega Rodríguez (Salamanca: Ediciones Sígueme, 2007), 123.

[51] Patočka, *Heretical Essays*, 114.

preceding century had accumulated; they generate the only discharge that remains when all the barrages have been exhausted.

The wars of the twentieth century are not the first time in which the orgiastic dimension fuses together with such cruelty, according to Patočka. Previously in the religious wars of the sixteenth and the seventeenth century—that is, at the inception of modernity—such a fusion took place, but Patočka notes that the demonic has never before "reached its peak precisely in an age of greatest sobriety and rationality."[52] Hence the twentieth century is—as was mentioned earlier—"an epoch of the night, of war, and of death", but more besides: it is an epoch comprised of a darkness engendered by the very light of the enlightenment.[53] Enlightened rationality has, in other words, given rise to a universally prevailing light that *by* its very glare blinds man and *through* this glaring light transforms itself into complete darkness.

When Patočka declares in the pathos-ridden essay "Wars of the Twentieth Century and the Twentieth Century as War" that all attempts at understanding the twentieth century have failed because all of them "approached war from the perspective of peace, day, and life, excluding its dark nocturnal side", it is precisely this perversion of light into darkness that must be borne in mind.[54] These attempts are all doomed to fail, according to Patočka, because they have tried to understand the twentieth century through the ideas of the enlightenment, and are thus unable to see that the enlightenment itself has engendered the darkness in question. From this perspective, it is only possible to understand war in relation to the peace it is supposed to bring forth. To put it otherwise: war, with its unfathomable darkness, is paradoxically that which, in the end, becomes an instrument for peace; war appears as, in the phrase that H.G. Wells once coined, a "war to end all wars." Patočka describes this as follows, lending his voice to the advocates of peace:

> From this perspective, life, especially historical life, appears as a continuum within which individuals function as the bearers of a general movement which alone matters; death means a change in functions; and war, death organized en masse, is an unpleasant but necessary interlude which we need to accept in the interest of certain goals of life's continuity but in which we can seek nothing "positive". At most, as Hegel said (and Dostoyevsky repeated), it can serve as one

[52] Ibid.
[53] Ibid, 120.
[54] Ibid.

of the salutary tremors that civic life needs lest it become sclerotic and fall asleep in its routine.[55]

If we regard war solely from the perspectives of daylight and peace, then not only will we be led into a complete misunderstanding of the orgiastic "reasons" behind the war and of what constitutes its "meaning", but we will also find that the peace "produced" by the war remains but a continuation of it. Indeed, as Patočka remarks, the Second World War did not really end, but rather mutated into "something peculiar which looks neither quite like war nor quite like peace."[56] What Patočka principally has in mind here is, of course, the Cold War; yet his remark actually points to something more fundamental. Patočka is in fact suggesting that the orgiastic dimension of human existence remained repressed after both world wars and that it subsequently continued to avenge itself in different forms. Even though the bellicose discharge of the orgiastic dimension no longer stands to be found in the midst of Western Europe, this does not entail that it in any way has disappeared, only that it has been transposed to other places and structured along other frontiers.

This development resides at the very heart of the history of Europe. One of the distinguishing traits of the care of the soul—at least, as Plato formulated it—is its universality. Plato not only introduced a "mythology of light" into the history of the soul (as previously discussed), he was also responsible for introducing the idea of a universal reason, which, through its mathematical-geometrical conformity, is available to everybody at all times. According to Patočka (in line with Husserl's thoughts in *Krisis*), it is this universality that gives Europe its distinctiveness. At the same time, this very universality also paves the way towards its own demise. When reason shifts at the inception of modernity from forming the means by which human beings are said to relate in a responsible manner to their own being to a means for mastering and controlling the world, the very idea of European civilization is transformed along with it. Earlier civilizations could never have become "universal civilizations"—even if, in many cases, they had aspirations to do so. It was only when modern natural science found an ally in the emergent structures of capitalism that something completely new occurred in history. European civilization then became what Patočka calls a "super-civilization": a civilization that no longer has its abode in any

[55] Ibid.
[56] Ibid, 119.

demarcated territory or in any nation, but which only rests on the universality that modern natural science constitutes and which capitalism endorses. This "super-civilization" lives, as Patočka writes, according to the principle of reason alone, a principle that always strives towards the simple rather than the complex, always values clarity as well as penetrative knowledge over and above the mysterious. This principle, in short, gives priority to the light of reason over the darkness of the orgiastic.[57]

This principle is universal in nature, though it is founded upon a universality that contains a "non-totality" in its essence.[58] The universality of the super-civilization can only realize itself spatially in such a way that it constantly threatens its own universality: at the same time as its universality demands a continued expansion, each conquered area brings with it new tensions that destabilize the whole. Phrased somewhat differently, this super-civilization is, as a result of its universality, driven towards perpetual growth.

It is precisely at the moment in which the care of the soul is transformed into a care of having that Europe enters a process of ruination. When the care of the soul is turned outwards toward a mastery of things, Europe is swept along by a development that will both shatter its boundaries and overthrow its own hegemony. As Patočka writes, in the aftermath of two world wars, Europe—"that two-thousand-year-old construction"—is "definitely at an end."[59]

The repetition and renewal of the enlightenment

Patočka's descriptions of the care of the soul as the foundation of Europe can at times seem hopelessly Eurocentric. But even though some of his descriptions are doubtless marked by "Eurocentrism" it is important to underline that Patočka's descriptions of the demise of Europe *do not* contain any nostalgia for the Europe that once was. Patočka will, on the contrary, write that the collapse of Europe perhaps was "something that has had a positive meaning."[60] The fact that Europe gradually has lost its position of power in the world is thus not something that Patočka is mourning. The

---

[57] Patočka, "La supercivilización y su conflicto interno," 137.
[58] Ibid, 120.
[59] Patočka, *Plato and Europe*, 10.
[60] Patočka, "Doba poevropská a její duchovní problemý," in *Sebrané spisy II – Péče o duši II* (Prague: Oikoymenh, 1999), 40.

problem does not, however, lie in the being or non-being of Europe, but concerns the direction that the "Post-European" world has taken since the enlightenment. Even though Europe no longer exists as a world-hegemonic-power, its "spirit, which through the belief in a positive knowledge is laying so much to waste, still remains, and is striving to subject the whole world under it."[61] The question, therefore, is: how are we to relocate the point of equilibrium between light and darkness, which the enlightenment had so profoundly disturbed? How might we, as Patočka writes, be able to "*repeat* the care of the soul under different circumstances" without relapsing into a nostalgia for that which has been?[62]

These questions can, in fact, be reduced to a question concerning how we might recreate a responsible relation to our own finitude in a time when it is precisely this relation that has been lost. As Derrida might phrase it, how may we give ourselves death (*se donner la mort*) in a time when life has eclipsed death?[63] From the perspective of the enlightened individual, life is namely everything (Patočka quips); it is the only "value that exists."[64] From the perspective of the techno-scientific forces of the day, on the other hand, death is only a number in impersonal and statistical planning. It is precisely through this specific relationship that the powers of the day rule over human beings: they rule by a constant threat of death—that is, by threatening life as the highest value. In the war fought for the sake of peace, death is thus, paradoxically, something that is absent even though it seems to be present everywhere. For the individual, death exists only as a threat, while, for the powers of the day, it remains solely of statistical concern. This is why one must—as a preliminary step—break with the domination of both day and peace in order to be able to liberate oneself from war. According to Patočka:

> The will to war counts on generations yet unborn, conceiving its plans from their viewpoint. So peace rules in the will to war. Those who cannot break free of the rule of peace, of the day, of life in a mode that excludes death and closes its eyes before it, can never free themselves of war.[65]

---

[61] Patočka, "Die Selbstbesinnung Europas," 272.
[62] Patočka, *Plato and Europe*, 90.
[63] Jacques Derrida, *The Gift of Death*, 12.
[64] Patočka, *Heretical Essays*, 129.
[65] Ibid, 129.

The enlightenment must therefore be renewed—as Patočka emphasizes in an earlier text—and it must be renewed in its very foundations, but in order for this to be possible the enlightenment must be shaded in such a way that its rational light is balanced by an orgiastic darkness, and that life is balanced by death.[66] To say that the enlightenment must be renewed is, however, not the same as saying that it must be destroyed. On the contrary, it must, as Patočka writes, "at the same time remain the same" in order for the renewal to be possible.[67] The idea of a total renewal of the enlightenment—a complete transformation of it—remains as naïve as the attempt to reverse the course of history towards a previous stage. At stake for Patočka is instead an attempt to turn the enlightenment against itself, so that the darkness of the enlightenment can be used to illuminate its own blinding light.

This darkness must already be contained within the very economy of the enlightenment as such, since the enlightened techno-scientific form of capitalism is the only reality that remains *for* us. We must, in other words, find the point in the enlightenment in which the darkness, despite its repression, still finds an expression. This point resides in what, for Patočka, constitutes the "absurdity *par excellence*" of both day and peace, namely the experience of the battlefront.[68] At this point human beings can, as he writes, "glimpse something 'eschatological', something like the end of all of the values of the day", but it will, however, remain a mere momentary glimpse. The momentary experience of an eschatology directly turns the eschatology back towards "the context of the day." No sooner is it glimpsed than it is "sequestered" and put into service by the day.[69] Despite the momentary nature of this experience, we nonetheless have testimonies about it, according to Patočka. We find it, for example, in both Ernst Jünger's and Pierre Teilhard de Chardin's descriptions of their own experiences of the frontline during the first world war, but we also find it in literature, for example in William Faulkner's novel *A Fable*.[70]

---

[66] Jan Patočka, "Česká vzdělanost v Evropě," in *Sebrané spisy IV – Umění a čas I* (Prague: Oikoymenh, 2004), 31.
[67] Ibid.
[68] Patočka, *Heretical Essays*, 126.
[69] Ibid, 126.
[70] For the discussion of Jünger and de Chardin see Patočka, *Heretical Essays*, 125-136. The discussion in which Faulkner's novel is mentioned is to be found in Patočka's notes for the *Heretical essays*. See Patočka, "Koncept eseje 'Války 20. století a 20. století jako válka'" in *Sebrané spisy III – Péče o duši III*, 500.

What interests Patočka about the descriptions of combat experience of both Jünger and Teilhard de Chardin is their common insistence on its complete lack of meaning. All that was meaningful in the light of day loses its meaning in the dark trenches at the frontline. This is similar to the experiences that Patočka designates as the origin of history: a loss of meaning that allows for meaning to appear as a question for humanity once again. If the history of western metaphysics is characterized by the human exit from the darkness of the Platonic cave along a path that leads to the light of reason, we can in the cases of Jünger and Teilhard de Chardin observe a similar, but inverted, movement. The experience that enables a renewed confrontation with the question of meaning is no longer that which stands in the light of reason; rather, it is the opposite. The glaring darkness of the enlightenment changes the rules of the game irreversibly. It is no longer possible to locate light and darkness in the same way as before; light and darkness switch places at precisely the point in which the peace of the day appears as the darkest form of darkness.

In the writings of Teilhard de Chardin this idea of a meaningful loss of meaning is expressed in the thought of an "absolute freedom" from all the interests of the day and from life itself. It is an experience of freedom that does not receive its meaning from anything at all, but which only rests *in itself*. In the case of Ernst Jünger the idea concerns a specific feeling of meaningfulness, a feeling that Jünger himself had difficulties in expressing, but which remained for a long time after the war had ended.[71]

While both Jünger and Teilhard de Chardin can be said to express a certain "heroic" understanding of the war, what we find in Faulkner is an expression of precisely the absurdity of an experience in which peace and war seems to have traded places with each other. It is brought forward, perhaps most strikingly, in a passage in which two English soldiers are discussing the refusal of a French regiment to carry on with the war:

'One regiment,' the runner said. 'One French regiment. Only a fool would look on war as a condition; it's too expensive. War is an episode, a crisis, a fever the purpose of which is to rid the body of fever. So the purpose of war is to end the war. We've known that for six thousand years. The trouble was, it took us six thousand years to learn how to do it. For six thousand years we labored under

---

[71] See for example Jünger's reflections in "Der Kampf als inneres Erlebnis," in *Sämtliche Werke: Band VII – Betrachtungen zur Zeit* (Stuttgart: Klett-Cotta, 2002).

the delusion that the only way to stop a war was to get together more regiments and battalions than the enemy would, or vice versa, and hurl them upon each other until one lot was destroyed and, the one having nothing left to fight with, the other could stop fighting. We were wrong, because yesterday morning, by simply declining to make an attack, one single French regiment stopped us all.'[72]

Faulkner's novel seems, in fact, to capture precisely what is at stake in Patočka's understanding of the front experience. It points to the absurdity of a situation in which war is fought for the sake of peace, a situation in which the overwhelming presence of death is reduced to an instrument for life.

* * *

The frontline experience is thus the experience in the very heart of the enlightenment which, according to Patočka, gives testament to a rupture within its very economy. This rupture is an experience of human finitude, and one in which the orgiastic dimension reveals itself once more. In Patočka's eyes, only such an experience can restore the balance that has been lost as well as accord humanity a renewed relationship to the question of meaning.

The question is, however, whether or not the front experience really constitutes that specific form of experience which would enable a renewed confrontation with the question of meaning. This is, in fact, a question that Patočka himself poses by writing: "Why has this grandiose experience, alone capable of leading humankind out of war into a true peace, not had a decisive effect on the history of the twentieth century, even though humans have been exposed to it twice for four years?"[73] There are, of course, no simple answers to this question and Patočka does not provide us with one himself. However, Patočka does provide us with one of the most decisive challenges facing philosophical thought today: the challenge of reconceptualising reason itself.

Today this challenge seems more pressing than ever. The development towards a hegemonic fusion between techno-science and capitalism, which Patočka describes, has, if anything, only been intensified in the years following the publication of the *Heretical Essays* in 1976. It has been intensified to the point at which each and every form of resistance against this

---

[72] William Faulkner, *A Fable* (New York: Vintage, 2011), 80.
[73] Patočka, *Heretical Essays*, 129.

form of thinking either is forced to adopt its language or is discarded as irrationality. One of the pressing questions would thus be how to counter reason with reason itself—that is, to find the point in the edifice of modern rationality that makes it crumble and use this point as a lever against it. This is, to be sure, a challenge that we find in other thinkers as well, but Patočka's main contribution to this challenge is his insistence on the necessary part the darkness of human finitude and passion play in reason itself: it is only by insinuating reason with its purported opposite that a new form of reason can emerge.

Philosophy and its Shadow:
On Skepticism and Reason in Levinas

Carl Cederberg

In this text I will examine the role of skepticism in Emmanuel Levinas's late *chef d'oeuvre, Otherwise than Being*. I shall show that Levinas takes skepticism to be a close ally to philosophy, and that skepticism, even though it appears to be irrationalism and anti-philosophy, is essential to the movement of philosophy.

But what do we mean by skepticism? As with many human practices, philosophy often defines itself against its others: philosophy is not sophistry, literature, poetry, science, religion, etc. When defining itself within the philosophical field, one strategy is to define other thinkers as non-philosophers. Philosophy purifies itself by deciding that what it once thought to be pieces of itself are not parts of it, not philosophy, and to push them away from itself. Among these pieces, skepticism holds a special place. Skepticism is formulated in philosophy, but is believed by many philosophers to divorce itself from philosophy by denying the essence of philosophy, claiming philosophy's meaning to be void. Or, in its even stronger formulations, skepticism denies the truth of everyday experience and rationality upon which the possibility of philosophy rests.

One of the first things I learned as a student of philosophy is that skepticism is self-contradictory. When the skeptic says that there is no real knowledge about the world, we can say that this must be wrong. For if this statement would be true, then at least this statement would contain a truth about the world, which would make it untrue. A statement cannot at the same time be true and untrue; this would be against the law of non-contradiction. As a student, I recall having been rather happy with this turn of argument, and the promise it seemed to bear for philosophy. And I think this experience is, at least at some point in development, shared by many philosophers. The experience demonstrates a certain philosophical power.

Thwarting a lethal enemy of philosophy shows philosophy to have meaning despite everything. In retrospect, however, this seems about as meaningful as dry-land swimming. Defeating skepticism must be the wrong way to justify philosophy; if philosophy can be given meaning only through the threat of skepticism, itself only a movement within philosophy, philosophy becomes a mere game.

Moreover, these skeptics we claim to refute—do they really exist? Does anyone really radically deny the evidence of our senses of the outer world, or the testimony of our rational capacity? This, I take it, is more or less Heidegger's take on the refutations of skepticism in *Being and Time*. The consequent skeptic, says Heidegger, would have already killed himself. "[T]he skeptic [...] does *not even need* to be refuted. Insofar as he *is*, and has understood himself in this being, he has obliterated Da-sein, and thus truth, in the despair of suicide."[1] To be in the world is to understand meaning— not the overarching meaning of everything, but meaning from the stand-point of my situation. To consistently hold that there is no meaning in the world can be done only by leaving it. Then it would be true for this individual that there is no truth in the world, since the truth of the world is lived by us.

All this is under the assumption that skepticism amounts to a denial of meaning. Heidegger's interpretation of skepticism follows from his existen-tial interpretation of Kant's transcendental philosophy, and has a prehistory as far back as Descartes and Hume. Let us make a short—but for our pur-poses sufficient—recapitulation of the role of skepticism for these thinkers of modernity.

Originally, in the thoughts of ancient skeptics like Pyrrho and Sextus Empiricus, skepticism implied not the denial of meaning, but the suspension of judgement. Descartes' method of radical doubt can in this sense be seen as the reinscription of skepticism in modern philosophy. He views this skepti-cism as led by reason: "Reason now leads me to think that I should hold back my assent from opinions which are not completely certain."[2] Only by doubt-ing all knowledge can we begin to search for that which is self-evident and know it as such. Through this skeptical method, we can doubt many things,

---

[1] Martin Heidegger, *Being and Time*, trans. Joan Stambaugh (Albany: SUNY Press, 1996), 210.
[2] René Descartes, *Meditations on First Philosophy*, in *Selected Philosophical Writings*, trans. John Cottingham, Robert Stoothoff, and Dugald Murdoch (Cambridge: Cambridge University Press, 1988), 76.

but when we start to doubt the very fact of our own thinking existence, we end up by proving it, and it means also finding ourselves as essentially rational. As Descartes states, "I am [...] a thing that thinks; that is, I am a mind, or intelligence, or intellect, or reason—words whose meaning I have been ignorant of until now. But for all that I am a thing which is real and which truly exists. But what kind of a thing? As I have just said—a thinking thing."[3] This experience, the experience of *being intellect*, of *being reason*, then becomes the paradigm for rational procedure, to "simply refrain from judgement" where I cannot see clearly and distinctly.[4]

For David Hume, however, this skepticism did not doubt enough. Why would I be a thing? We should trust nothing but our experience, consisting of a never-ending stream of impressions. These impressions are associated according to principles of psychology to form ideas such as the ego and God. Descartes was wrong to see these ideas as substances. The findings of Descartes' meditations, and the fundaments of his reconstitution of a meaningful world, can be understood as mere effects of psychology. It is our nature to associate impressions which appear regularly and contiguously in time and space. The idea of the self appears from a bundle of such associated impressions, and God from another bundle. Even our understanding of causality is of psychological origin—a mere belief.

Immanuel Kant takes the Cartesian and Humean skepticism as a point of departure. Philosophy needs to show why we can trust there to be more than mere impressions. Like Hume, he says that our understanding of the world is of our own making. But this is not a cause for skepticism. The structure which we find permeating the world is not a contingent effect of the empirical psyche, but is provided by the transcendental subject. This means that we understand the world the way in which any rational creature would understand it as the world. Our experience of the world as governed by rational laws, such as that of causality, is possible because we are rational creatures. This is how we can understand Kant's statement about being awoken from his dogmatic slumber by Hume: his transcendental philosophy is awoken, ignited by Hume's skepticism. Even if this gives credit to Hume, he views his philosophy as a refutation of skepticism.

While Kant views this as a philosophical refutation of skepticism, Hegel sees skepticism and the overcoming of it as two intrinsic parts of phil-

---

[3] Ibid, 82.
[4] Ibid, 103.

osophy's movement. Positive philosophy cannot really overcome skepticism, but allows it to exist beside it. Hegel means that skepticism taken for itself cannot be refuted. Skepticism must be integrated into positive philosophy. Taken for itself, skepticism is nothing but a philosophical paralysis, but from the viewpoint of the movement of philosophical argument in history and in spirit, it is a necessary counter-move to the philosophy of mere positions.

When Kant's transcendental philosophy is given an existential interpretation, skepticism acquires the sense that we saw in Heidegger, a doubt in the meaning of the world that is constantly provided by Dasein, the structures of which *Being and Time* takes upon itself to analyze. Skepticism seems no longer to be a serious opponent or contributor to philosophy.

With Levinas, however, skepticism plays an important role, but no longer as the opponent of philosophy. This might, of course, come as no surprise. Often Levinas's position is viewed as a brand of religious skepticism, replacing philosophy with a moralist religiosity.[5] His philosophy circles around the notion of the other, and any effort to build up some rational system of knowledge seems to be a violation against this central, yet so ephemeral, concept. However, already in *Totality and Infinity* Levinas ascertained that "[t]he sense of our whole effort lies in affirming not that the Other forever escapes knowing, but that there is no meaning in speaking here of knowledge or ignorance."[6] No matter how subtle this difference might seem, it is an important one. Levinas is, in a sense, rationalist. In his critique of the traditional understanding of rationalism, he aspires to a new foundation of reason, in the subject as one-for-the-other. It is, we can say, a skeptic path towards reason. In *Otherwise than Being*, the final chapter before the final remarks is titled "Skepticism and Reason." Here, he is concerned with the way in which skepticism can show us a different understanding of reason than the traditional one. He starts:

> Reason is sought in the relationship between terms, between the one and the other showing themselves in a theme. Reason consists in ensuring the coexistence of these terms, the coherence of the one and the other despite their difference, in the unity of a theme; it ensures the agreement of the different terms without breaking up the present in which the theme is held. This co-

---

[5] See Alain Badiou: "In truth Levinas has no philosophy—not even philosophy as the 'servant' of theology. Rather this is philosophy [...] annulled by theology, itself no longer a theology, [...] but precisely an ethics" (*Ethics* [London: Verso, 2001] 22–23).
[6] Emmanuel Levinas, *Totality and Infinity*, 89.

existence or accord between different terms is called a system. [....] The flow of time does not break up this presence and this presentation; through retention, memory or historical reconstruction, through reminiscence, consciousness is a re-presentation, understood in an almost active sense, as in the act of rendering present anew and of collecting the dispersion into a presence, and in this sense being always at the beginning or free.[7]

This view of reason entails, as we see, both freedom and unfreedom: reason implies freedom because at the beginning it does not trap us in the chain of events determining us from the past, but brings them up to the surface of the present and allows rational scrutiny and self-reflection. On the other hand, a certain enclosed-ness is suggested. But what is it that is lost?

Levinas continues:

But the problem is that one can ask if a beginning is at the beginning, if the beginning is not already preceded by what could not be synchronized, that is, by what could not be present, the unrepresentable, if an anarchy is not more ancient than the beginning and freedom.[8]

The unrepresentable is of course the other, the neighbor, who signifies to me in what Levinas calls "proximity":

Proximity is a difference, a non-coinciding, an arrhythmia in time, a diachrony refractory to thematization, refractory to the reminiscence that synchronizes the phases of a past.[9]

But proximity is not therefore "unreason" or "irrational".

Proximity [...] signifies a reason before the thematization by a thinking subject. [...] It is a reason before the beginning, before any present [...] Proximity is communication, agreement, understanding or peace.[10]

Just like Descartes, Levinas is led by skepticism to understand the I as reason, but in a thoroughly different manner:

I am extracted from the concept of the ego, and am not measured by being and death, that is escape the totality and the structures. I am reduced to myself in responsibility [...] Reason is the one-for-the-other.[11]

[7] Emmanuel Levinas, *Otherwise than Being*, 165.
[8] Ibid.
[9] Ibid, 166.
[10] Ibid.

Thus, through discovering what reason fails to assimilate, Levinas is led to a new understanding of reason, where reason is no longer the assimilation of different terms but instead is the irreducible responsibility which lies at the core of all rational discourse.

But in what way is this insight led by skepticism? Why the reference to skepticism? The question that leads Levinas to skepticism is the question regarding the language which philosophy speaks. In *Otherwise than Being*, more than anywhere else, Levinas is concerned with the way philosophy expresses its insights. How can the critique of philosophy—the critique of conceptual reason—be philosophically expressed? The reason that this becomes a problem is that this is not a critique from which he in any way exempts his own philosophy. On the contrary, Levinas grapples exactly with the problem that the expression of a philosophical insight might contradict the function of a philosophical statement. Levinas discusses this problem under the labels of the saying and the said. Just as with any statement, a philosophical statement has a meaning, a certain content that it transmits and which resides in the meanings of the words and the structures of language—this is what Levinas refers to as the said. Yet this is not all there is to communication, not even to philosophical communication. Communication assumes a communicating subject, the possibility of a certain contact. The terms of communication and the concepts within a specific act of communication are made possible by this contact—this contact and this very communication is what Levinas refers to as saying. But even when he describes this as saying, he is giving it a philosophical content; it becomes part of language, a said. In this, the saying is inevitably betrayed. The act of showing this betrayal, what we could describe as the Levinasian rendering of deconstruction, is what he sometimes calls unsaying the said. But, since this unsaying of the said amounts to another said, is not this process hopeless? This question is what leads Levinas to introduce the moment of skepticism. Levinas asks:

> Can this saying and this being unsaid be assembled, can they be at the same time? In fact, to require this simultaneity is already to reduce being's other to being and not being. We must stay with the extreme situation of diachronic thought. Skepticism, at the dawn of philosophy, set forth and betrayed the diachrony of this very conveying and betraying. To conceive the otherwise than being requires, perhaps, as much audacity as skepticism shows, when it does not

[11] Ibid, 167.

182

hesitate to affirm the impossibility of statement while venturing to realize this impossibility by the very statement of this impossibility. If, after the innumerable "irrefutable" refutations which "logical" thought sets against it, skepticism has the call to return (and it always returns as philosophy's legitimate[12] child), it is because in the contradictions which logic sees in it "at the same time" of the contradictories is missing, because a secret diachrony commands this ambiguous or enigmatic way of speaking, and because in general signification signifies beyond synchrony, beyond essence.[13]

How can we unpack this dense statement? Let us start from the beginning. The question of assembling saying and being unsaid (*se dédire*), i.e. letting them be at the same time, alludes to the idealist view of the subject which Levinas holds to be misleading. The subject is not only that which assembles; first the subject is vulnerable, receptive, responsible. For sure, the subject is also this unit of assembling and gathering, but there is an aspect of that which is gathered which is lost. The contacted—the one before whom I am responsible—is not assimilated into the assemblage. Thus there is a distance between the description and what it aims to describe. Levinas here describes the encounter between these modalities in temporal terms, introducing the term "diachrony." When trying to put words on my responsibility for the other in a philosophical context, responsibility and the other become concepts among others, elements operating together in my thought.

But since philosophy aims to make things clear to thought, or to think things through, there is always the temptation that that for which one thinks and that which one thinks are the same, united in thought. The temptation of idealism as well as phenomenology is to think subjectivity, being in the world as encountering itself, as presence. Skepticism shows the possibility to see thought as breaking with this presence, introducing another attitude towards temporality:

> The periodic return of skepticism and its refutation signify a temporality in which the instants refuse memory which recuperates and represents. Skepticism, which traverses the rationality or logic of knowledge, is a refusal to synchronize the implicit affirmation contained in saying and the negation which this affirmation states in the said.[14]

---

[12] Translation altered: Alphonso Lingis, normally so accurate, mistakenly wrote the opposite of *enfant légitime*: "illegitimate child."
[13] Levinas, *Otherwise than Being*, 7.
[14] Ibid, 167.

In other words: when philosophers show that skepticism refutes itself while it refutes the possibility of general statements of the world, we should not be so quick to say that this shows skepticism to be void of meaning and importance for philosophy. Even if the contents of what skepticism utters contradicts the possibility of the truth of what it is saying—for the non-existence of true general statements of the world would itself amount to a true general statement of the world, would it be true—this does not deny the possibility of denying.

Skepticism helps philosophy to "loosen its grip on being,"[15] to put an interval between the saying and the said.[16] The "spiraling movement" of skepticism "makes possible the boldness of philosophy, destroying the conjunction into which its saying and its said continually enter."[17] Skepticism thus does not oppose philosophy; rather its movement belongs inextricably to that of philosophy. Levinas writes that "Philosophy is not separable from skepticism, which follows it like a shadow it drives off by refuting it again at once on its footsteps."[18] It is as if skepticism performs a sort of destructive groundwork, making it possible for philosophy to re-group, to reassess the very foundations of its existence, the idea of philosophical reason on which it grounds.

When the subject (be it Kantian, Hegelian, Husserlian or Heideggerian) experiences the world as meaningful, this is by a certain process according to which its understanding of being gradually becomes one with being itself. What Levinas finds in skepticism is a rebellion against the philosophical understanding that this assembling character of reason would be the end of the story, introducing instead the thought that it could be possible for philosophy to insist in resisting this self-complacence of reason. Does this make him into a skeptic? Not in the Humean or Cartesian sense, denying a certain ontology on the basis of a certain epistemology. But in some other sense?

It all depends on what we mean by skepticism. One way to decide the matter would be to compare him to the ancient skeptics. Levinas never worked extensively on the ancient skeptics; yet it might be interesting to look at possible parallels. Where to start? As far as we know, Pyrrho, generally held to be the father of skepticism, did not put any of his philosophy in print. The main written source of ancient skepticism is Eusebius

[15] Ibid, 44.
[16] Ibid, 168.
[17] Ibid, 44.
[18] Ibid, 168.

of Caesarea, who quotes large parts of Aristocles' *Peri Philosophias* in his *Praeparatio evangelica*. There, Aristocles presents the main doctrine of Timon, Pyrrho's most important apprentice. In order to lead a happy life, Timon is supposed to have held, we must deal with three important questions: 1) What exists? 2) What shall be our attitude towards what exists? 3) What shall be the outcome for those adopting this attitude?

1) The answer to the first question is that all things are fundamentally not differentiable (*adiaphora*), unstable (*astathmêta*) and indeterminate (*anepikrita*). In this context we are reminded of Levinas's notion of the "*il y a*", the sheer weight of inhuman, uninterpreted existence. 2) Because of the uncertainty of our grasp of the things, Eusebius says, we shall withhold our judgement on the things (*epoche*), hold neither that they are nor that they are not ("saying of every single thing that it no more is than is not, or both is and is not, or neither is nor is not"). This reminds us of the phenomenological *epoché*, even if this is not a term that Levinas often employs. Does not, however, the reduction from the said to saying assume an *epoché*? 3) As a result from this attitude, says Eusebius, we shall live in speechlessness (*aphasia*), tranquility (*ataraxia*) and, say some, happiness.[19] It is in the answer to the last question that Levinas seems to differ the most from the skeptics. Skepticism is therefore first and foremost an ethics, in the sense that it describes an attitude leading to a happier life. Levinas does not propose an ethics in this sense. In the first part of *Totality and Infinity*, which describes the joy of existence, he explicitly opposes *ataraxia* to happiness. We are happy to have needs. Such is the human predicament. But this is a mere starting-point; Levinas's philosophy is neither a road to *ataraxia* nor to happiness—nor to *aphasia*. For sure, we must speak and give judgements. Indeed, if there is an ethics in Levinas, it is probably here that it is found. It is in speech, in contact, that meaning appears. Saying will become a said, which must be unsaid, in order for its meaning to appear. This possibility of the unsaying makes the said infinitely better than the *il y a*. In the concluding remarks of *Otherwise than Being*, after "Skepticism and Reason," Levinas returns to the constant threat of philosophy failing to overcome the *il y a*, the threat of nihilism. This would mean not only a loss of value and human dignity, but also of the very foundations of rational discourse, which would implode upon itself if the possibility of contact—i.e. of a discourse beyond self-interest—would wither away.

---

[19] Eusebius of Caesarea: Praeparatio Evangelica 14.18.

In my understanding, Levinas's philosophy is the discipline of vigilance, of guarding old paths towards the production of meaning and discovering new ones. Nurturing this vigilance means nurturing a certain brand of skepticism, the practice of bracketing what is perceived as truths—be it by sound reason or by the trends of postmodern philosophy—and what is most difficult, that which we intuitively and unquestioningly hold to be true. This is a painful business, yet it seems that Heidegger was wrong to think that the only movement of skepticism would be suicide. The radical critique of reason can be a self-criticism for the sake of something or someone for whom we cannot give account, a criticism of an excluding rationalism in order to open up for something or someone else. This is not an irrationalism—it can be the inspiration for new and other modes of rationalization, making skepticism an ever needed opponent, companion or shadow of philosophy.

Seeing Wonders and the Wonder of Seeing: Religion at the Borders of the Ordinary

Espen Dahl

Wittgenstein and his philosophical heirs have proven to be influential in the philosophy of religion, particularly within analytical philosophy. Much of the debate has revolved around the fruitfulness of the model of language-games and its account of religious rationality: that is, whether such a model leads to fideism or can be released from that charge.[1] I have no intention of entering that debate, but intend rather to focus on another way of inheriting and extending ordinary language philosophy—hopefully more congenial to other, perhaps more "continental" approaches to philosophy. For all the importance of clarifying confusion by referring to the grammar of specific religious games, I want to draw attention to some religiously relevant experiential dimensions of life that seem to bring us to the border of what *any* conventional language game and grammar can account for. To be more concrete, I want to focus on what we might call wonders in the restricted sense of something at once extraordinary and ordinary. I will argue that there are ways to respond to such experiences that do not necessarily lead to irrationalism or madness, if that means being bereft of shareable meaning. And yet, it is equally important to me that the risk of such madness cannot be completely foreclosed. In this chapter I shall follow some lines of thought suggested by Wittgenstein and try to extend these lines according to Cora Diamond's and, most notably, Stanley Cavell's suggestive readings.

This presentation falls into three parts. In the first part, I will sketch out an understanding of intelligibility and reason as conceived within the

---

[1] For Kai Nielsen's classical "Wittgensteinian Fideism" and related accounts by Kai Nielsen along with responses by D. Z. Phillips, see Nielsen and Phillips, *Wittgensteinian Fideism? With critiques by Béla Szabados, Nancy Bauer and Stephen Mulhall* (London: SCM Press, 2005).

framework of the ordinary, and point to how religiously relevant experiences fit into it or, perhaps better, are placed at its border. In the second part, I will propose that Wittgenstein's remarks on a particular dimension of perception, called "seeing aspects", shed further light on those experiences. Finally, I will explore the relation between such perception and its expressions, paying particular attention to how such expressions test our ability to make ourselves intelligible.

The limits of criteria and the difficulty of reality

As the title of Cavell's main work, *The Claim of Reason,* indicates, questions concerning rationality and intelligibility are central to his enterprise. Given the role Wittgenstein plays in that work, it is striking that Cavell places little emphasis on investigating particular language-games or detecting their rules. In place of rules, Cavell attaches unusual significance to the notion of *criteria*; such criteria are internal to our judgments and are the means by which we discriminate and identify phenomena.[2] Put in a way more congenial to ordinary language philosophy: criteria single out the pragmatic circumstances under which something counts as an instance of a concept. The mastery of criteria does not require any special expertise, but is part of what any competent speaker exhibits in his or her application of words.

There are two features of Cavell's criteria that deserve comment. First, even as indispensable as those criteria are for our making sense of both the world and ourselves, they are nevertheless vulnerable and limited; that is, there are things we might feel compelled to know that are not satisfied by the way criteria govern our knowledge. Admittedly, criteria cannot settle a thing's existence, but rather are meant to determine its identity—"not of its *being* so, but of its being *so*"[3]—which means for example that the identification of feigned pain employs the criteria of pain, just as a dreamed world still satisfies the criteria of a world. This means that criteria are vulnerable to doubt and repudiation, but precisely this vulnerability is also its strength. That criteria have limits implies that meaning does not take care of itself; as language is in

[2] Stanley Cavell, *The Claim of Reason: Wittgenstein, Skepticism, Morality and Tragedy* (Oxford: Oxford University Press, 1981), 17.
[3] Ibid, 45.

an emphatic sense *ours*, each of us is responsible for maintaining our mutual intelligibility in the absence of any further foundation.[4]

This leads to the second feature, namely that criteria are not something we have come to agree upon, as we do in contracts or explicit definitions, but are rather the crossroads in the daily traffic of our mutual lives, resting on nothing more and nothing less than our astonishing attunement to the way we see and express the world. This, I take it, is the point that Wittgenstein is making when he writes that "If language is to be a means of communication there must be agreement not only in definitions but also (queer as this may sound) in judgments."[5] In this perspective, criteria are not defined points that fix our agreement. Rather, Wittgenstein is in effect saying that criteria are the expression of an agreement already there; furthermore, such an agreement has no foundation beneath our attunement to what we take interest in saying and doing, that is, beneath a common form of life.[6] Such a common form of life means that we share and know, for example,

> what it is to take turns, or take chances, or know that some things we have lost we cannot look for but can nevertheless sometimes find or recover; share the sense of what is fun and what loss feels like, and take comfort from the same things and take confidence or offense in similar ways. That we do more or less share such forms rests upon nothing deeper; nothing insures that we will, and there is no foundation, logical or philosophical, that explains the fact that we do.[7]

To measure the extent to which we find ourselves attuned to each other, or out of tune with each other, is one of the fundamental tasks of ordinary language philosophy. From this perspective, our intelligibility (or meaningfulness) and rationality (modes of explaining ourselves) are what Cavell calls "claims to community"—implying that such a claim can fail and thus isolate the speaker from that community.[8] It is a conception of rationality that highlights the incredible flexibility and fine-grained precision in speak-

---

[4] Cavell, *In Quest of the Ordinary: Lines of Skepticism and Romanticism* (Chicago: University of Chicago Press, 1988), 5.

[5] Ludwig Wittgenstein, *Philosophical Investigations*, trans. G. E. M. Anscombe (Oxford: Blackwell, 1958), § 142.

[6] Cavell, *The Claim of Reason*, 30. For the best available discussion of criteria, see Steven G. Affeldt, "The Ground of Mutuality: Criteria, Judgment, and Intelligibility in Stephen Mulhall and Stanley Cavell," *European Journal of Philosophy* 6:1 (1998).

[7] Cavell, *Themes out of School* (San Francisco: North Point Press, 1984), 223–224.

[8] Cavell, *The Claim of Reason*, 20.

ing and reasoning that are enabled on the background of such a pervasive, implicit agreement. There are indeed structures and an inner stability, elicited in grammar and criteria, but it is nevertheless a fact that language also allows for plasticity: for examples, we constantly project words into new contexts, immediately reach mutual understanding even as we invent figures of speech, and experience how new shades of meaning are conveyed in art and poetry.[9]

It is against this background that I read Diamond's essay on what she calls "the difficulty of reality." Now, "reality" is a concept that has played a decisive role in her philosophy. In *The Realistic Spirit*, containing central essays on Wittgenstein, literature, and ethics, Diamond defines such a spirit in opposition to empirical and metaphysical realism; her "realistic spirit" is designed to avoid the philosophical tendency to *lay down requirements* in philosophy before consulting what kind of role concepts and attitudes plays in the life we lead with words.[10] We need to come to grips with the embodied, finite perspective that is the only perspective from which our reality makes sense. The realistic spirit invites us to turn around and appreciate the importance of what is in front of us—"don't think, look" is Wittgenstein's advice.[11] What I find particularly intriguing in Diamond's philosophy is how she appreciates not just the elasticity of language, but more specifically the cultivation of an openness toward reality—or better, how we are opened *by* reality, exposed to it, perhaps taken by surprise.[12]

Diamond's more recent essay "The Difficulty of Reality and the Difficulty of Philosophy" takes this openness further. Perhaps we might think of her as taking the realistic spirit to the extreme, putting pressure on those occasions in which we no longer are able to house reality in our form of life. "The difficulty of reality," Diamond writes, concerns "experiences in which we take something in reality to be resistant to our thinking it, or possibly to be painful in its inexplicability, difficult in that way, or perhaps awesome

---

[9] Ibid, 185.

[10] Diamond, *The Realistic Spirit: Wittgenstein, Philosophy, and the Mind* (Cambridge, MA: MIT Press, 1991) 20.

[11] Wittgenstein, *Philosophical Investigations*, § 66.

[12] The openness I have in mind is suggested in the following observation concerning the nature of Anselm's proof of God's existence: Diamond writes that "reality may surprise us, not only by showing us what *is* the case, when we have not suspected it was, but also by showing us something beyond what we have ever taken to be possible, beyond anything we have had thought of at all" (Diamond, *The Realistic Spirit*, 280).

and astonishing in its inexplicability."[13] Cavell coins the corresponding notion "inordinate knowledge"; perhaps from a different angle, it resembles what Derrida would call an aporia, while others again might call it the sublime.[14] One of Diamond's examples is Ted Hughes's poem "Six Young Men", which contemplates the patent liveliness of six men in a photograph who only a few months later were all dead during World War I. As Hughes puts it,

> To regard this photograph might well dement,
> Such contradictory permanent horrors here
> Smile from the single exposure and shoulder out
> One's own body from its instant and heat.

The maddening contradiction that impresses itself from that photograph—the lively presence of those six men, together with their inexorable absence—puts the mind in the presence of something it is not able to encompass.[15] We are "shouldered out"—unhinged, that is—and on the brink of madness. And still, there is a sense in which it remains nothing more than an ordinary photograph. Transposed to Cavell's vocabulary, such a difficulty of reality reaches the limits of criteria but, importantly, it does not necessarily lead to skeptical denial of that reality. It might be "impossible to think, and yet it is there."[16] It exhibits not only our separation from the world owing to the experience of the mind's incapability of encompassing the contradiction, but also the separation from others, those who for some reason fail to be struck or seized in the same way. I want to pick up on two other examples that move us into religious terrain, closer to the notion of wonders. Diamond draws our attention to the Auschwitz survivor Ruth Klüger's memoirs, and her account of how a young woman helped a little girl tell a lie that saved the girl's life. She recounts it in wonder and astonishment, as an act of "incomparable and inexplicable" goodness and grace, and

---

[13] "The Difficulty of Reality and the Difficulty of Philosophy" in Cavell et al., *Philosophy and Animal Life* (New York: Colombia University Press, 2008), 45–46.
[14] Along these lines, I elaborated a notion I have called "the ordinary sublime" in "The Ordinary Sublime after Stanley Cavell and Cora Diamond" in *Transfiguration: Nordic Journal of Religion and the Arts* (2010/2011): 51–68.
[15] Diamond, "The Difficulty of Reality", 44.
[16] Ibid, 63.

yet reports how other people do not find the story astonishing at all: for is it after all surprising that some people are altruistic?[17]

In a parenthetical passage, Diamond finds it helpful to employ some of R. H. Holland's reflections concerning the concept of the miracle in order to shed further light on the sense of astonishment and awe. In his paper, Holland distinguishes between what he calls "the violation concept of miracles" and "the contingency concept of miracles." The former kind of miracles are at once empirically certain and conceptually impossible, such as turning water into wine. Such miracles are extraordinary in the strong sense of breaking up the well-ordered, conceptual grasp of the world, and are those wonders to which Diamond refers. The contingency concept of miracles, on the other hand, refers to the kind of unexpected occurrences that turn out to leave a great impression: for example, that a train manages to stop only inches before a child playing on the tracks. There is no question here of anything conceptually impossible or of laws being violated, even if such incidents are very rare. They are at once ordinary and extraordinary, and can therefore invite different perspectives. To some, these are instances of mere luck; to others, they are seen as the grace of God or miracles, events that call forth thanksgivings and prayers. As Holland dryly reports, "while the reference is the same, the meaning is different."[18] A related duality can be detected in Augustine's conversion, as narrated in his *Confessions*. Sitting weeping in the garden, distressed over his relentless heart, Augustine suddenly hears some children playing in the neighborhood, shouting, "Pick up and read, pick up and read." The children's game becomes absolutely decisive for Augustine's fate: "I interpreted it solely as a divine command to me to open the book and read the first chapter I might find."[19] He picks up the Bible, reads a passage, and experiences the world in a new light. The interesting thing, in my perspective, is how a perfectly ordinary incident can strike one in a religious register—as the vehicle of God's voice, an act of wonder or grace, even enforcing a new orientation of an entire life.

In his "Lecture on Ethics," dating from his early period, Wittgenstein deals with the absolute as it occurs in religion and ethics. Miracles and wonders are explicitly discussed: miraculous and fully unlikely incidents cannot be explained by science, he argues, because scientific logic is tied to

[17] Ibid, 61–62.
[18] R. F. Holland, "The Miraculous," *American Philosophical Quarterly* 2.1 (1965): 44.
[19] Augustine, *Confessions*, trans. H. Chadwick (Oxford: Oxford University Press 1991), VIII, xii.

its relative sense (causal or otherwise), which violently reduces the religious or absolute sense. But there are experiences that invite other attitudes and expressions; for example, there are experiences that Wittgenstein finds most aptly expressed in the phrase "I wonder at the existence of the world."[20] Now, within the confines of his early vision of language, such utterances are deemed to be plain nonsense—they neither depict any possible facts nor trade on a conceivable comparison with facts that could indirectly make sense of them. But if transposed to the register that occupies Diamond, Wittgenstein's final remarks bring us back to the difficulty of reality. He there points out that nonsensicality was "the very essence" of such utterances, and continues:

> For all I wanted to do with them was just to go beyond the world and that is to say beyond significant language. My whole tendency and I believe the tendency of all men who ever tried to write or talk Ethics or Religion was to run against the boundaries of language.[21]

Although language can be said to run up against its boundaries, there are perspectives from Wittgenstein's later thought that still give us clues to why we nevertheless can take this as more than nonsense. I will return to this point, but let me first try to clarify what kind of perception such experiences of wonders entail.

Seeing aspects religiously

All the examples cited above have in common that they can be seen in different ways, and furthermore, that those ways are neither distinguished by different access to information nor are they matters of disagreements concerning criteria and their grammar. Indeed, it is essential that the criteria cannot settle the disagreement between the perspectives. And yet, even if they refer to the same segment of the world, the ways of seeing that

---

[20] Wittgenstein, "A Lecture on Ethics," in *Philosophical Occasions 1912–1951*, ed. J. C. Klagge and A. Nordmann (Indianapolis: Hackett Publishing, 1993), 41, 43. Edward F. Mooney elaborates on the relevant passages in Wittgenstein in a way similar to mine. "Self, Others, Goods, Final Faith: Kirkegaard Past the Continental Divide," *Graduate Faculty Philosophy Journal* 32:1 (2011), 14–15.
[21] Ibid, 44.

segment are oceans apart. In a response to Diamond's paper on the difficulty of reality, Cavell succinctly sums it up thus:

> Diamond's paper takes up certain extremities of conflict associated with phenomena of what she calls the difficulty of reality (call this a difficulty of change, a difficulty that philosophy must incorporate), cases in which our human capacity to respond—she in effect says the bases or limits of our human nature—are, for some, put to the test, threatening to freeze or overwhelm understanding and imagination, while at the same time, for others, the phenomenon, or fact, fails to raise, or perhaps it succeed only in raising, an eyebrow.[22]

What is at stake here?

In that essay, Cavell very helpfully suggests that what is at stake is something Wittgenstein calls "seeing aspects" or "seeing something as something", which is contained in the intricate remarks that make up the major bulk of the second part of *Philosophical Investigations*. The remarks cover a range of related phenomena, tied to perception, expressions of the mind, and experiencing the meaning of words. Wittgenstein begins:

> Two uses of the word "see."
> The one: "What do you see there?"—"I see *this*" (and then a description, a drawing, a copy). The other: "I see a likeness between these two faces"—let the man I tell this to be seeing the faces as clearly as I do myself. [...]
> The one man might make an accurate drawing of the two faces, and the other notice in the drawing the likeness which the former did not see.[23]

This resembles the cases cited above in two respects. First, seeing an aspect is indeed a matter of seeing (or perceiving more generally), which is to be distinguished from what we might call "mere seeing": exhibited in describing a fact, conveying information, or applying a criterion in a perceptual report. Seeing an aspect implies something more, we are told, such as seeing a likeness. Second, it seems to be essential to this way of seeing that it can be missed: even if the other sees the same drawing as I do, he or she might fail to notice this likeness.

Seeing something "more" in aspect perception entails seeing something *as* something, and thus there is obviously a relation to other things implied

---

[22] Cavell, "Companionable Thinking," in *Philosophy and Animal Life*, 92.
[23] Wittgenstein, *Philosophical Investigations*, 193.

in that very seeing. The question is how this relation should be conceived.[24] It can be a likeness to another face, but there is also the case where such likeness is not the relation in question. Children can take a table as a house, a box as a ship, and so on. There is obviously room for a certain amount of imagination, of interpretation, of thinking—but they all merge into the "object of sight" as somehow internally implied in it. However, Wittgenstein dismisses the idea that we confer knowledge or a certain interpretation on top of what is seen, for the unhesitating and immediate character of the expressions suggests that there are no inferences taking place. Nor are they reports of psychological states, since the interest is not directed toward the subject of those expressions, but to the way, perhaps the striking new way, the object occurs.

The second point, the possibility of failing to notice an aspect, brings me to the most famous of Wittgenstein's examples, namely Jastrow's gestalt picture that can be seen as either a duck or a rabbit. We first typically see it as one of the two, and some people might even fail to notice the ambiguity in the simple drawing. But then, occasionally, one is struck by the change, or what Wittgenstein calls "the dawning of an aspect."[25] When we undergo such a dawning, it is as if the very thing in question—either a rabbit or a duck—changes from the one to the other. "I *describe* the alteration like a perception," Wittgenstein says, "quite as if the object had altered before my eyes."[26] And yet we might also "know"—if we look at it as a blueprint or an example in a psychology textbook—that the drawing has not changed. What such a dawning of an aspect captures is the sense of paradox and astonishment that goes with perceiving something new in what others might take as trivially the same. The upshot, as I take it, is that the undergoing of an exposure to the difficulty of reality—in goodness, horror, miracles, or wonders—is an instance of experiencing the sudden dawning of a new aspect.

---

[24] In his instructive account, Stephen Mulhall has made much out of the fact that such "seeing as", or more specifically, "continuously seeing as," is intimately linked to Heidegger's Being-in-the-World, readiness-to-hand, and how equipments, like signs, gain their meaning from reference (seeing *as*) to other entities that make up the world (*Being in the World. Wittgenstein and Heidegger on Seeing Aspects* [London: Routledge, 1990], 106–137). One weakness with this reading is that it seems to suggest that all perception is aspect perception, which is hard to reconcile with Wittgenstein's insistence on some form of distinct "primary" perception or "mere" seeing; cf. "One doesn't '*take*' what one knows as the cutlery at a meal *for* cutlery." (*Philosophical Investigations*, 195).
[25] Ibid, 194.
[26] Ibid, 195.

Seeing a train stop only inches before a playing child can be seen, again, as both incredible luck and a miracle. It is indeed a matter of how the incident strikes one, the way it breaks into a particular perspective. The point is not that seeing it as a miracle requires interpolating an act of God or calling for metaphysical explanation; rather, it is the way in which the surprising event dawns on the perceiver. For some, the extraordinariness of the ordinary is brought to display, while for others it only confirms the well-known contingency of our lives—nothing new really dawns at all. Unlike the duck-rabbit—which, once you realize its ambiguity, can be altered from duck to rabbit at will—the dawning of a miraculous aspect cannot be altered in this way, tending rather to impress itself on us as either luck or a miracle. One might even think of how everyday incidents might trigger a recon-figuration of one's entire perspective of the world, as in the instance of Augustine. And nevertheless, the religious seeing of a miracle might very well coexist with the *knowledge* that it is fully compatible with contingency and luck, even if the two visions can alienate people from one another.

Those who are unable to see the relevant aspect cannot be aided by further information. It is not that such people lack the competence to play some specific language-games: the seeing of aspects depends on nothing more than an ability to extend the primary grammar of seeing. When Wittgenstein writes that "what I see in the dawning of an aspect is not a property of the object, but an internal relation between it and other objects",[27] the implication is that such a dawning of an aspect requires an ability to relate those percep-tions to other perceptions along with their corresponding language-games. Moreover, this ability seems to rely on a deep and intimate familiarity with other practices and games, in a way that goes beyond mastering the grammar of those specific games. Rather, the familiarity makes certain affinities salient and others strange. The familiarity with those related games is immediately awakened in the perception itself, and they present themselves as if they are absorbed into the physiognomy of the current perceptual experience, perhaps analogous to the way Husserl imagines that sedimentation and habitualities flow into our perception.[28]

But why does an incident strike one as a wonder as opposed to mere luck? It certainly relies on what this thing is seen in relation to—that is, on what strikes one as being significantly relevant to the way it appears.

[27] Ibid, 212.
[28] Edmund Husserl, *Erfahrung und Urteil*, ed. L. Landgrebe (Hamburg: Felix Meiner Verlag, 1999), 116–120, 136–139.

Wittgenstein here speaks of our *attitude* in seeing a drawing: "That is what I treat it as; this is my attitude to the figure. This is one meaning in calling it a case of seeing."[29] It is important to note that Wittgenstein's notion of attitude (*Einstellung*) is not an inner state that can be understood apart from what it is an attitude toward. An attitude is an internal, intentional bond that aligns one's orientations and interests toward the object in question.[30] The attitude shows itself in how we treat things, such as what conclusions we draw, which responses we are ready to make, what we find relevantly linked to something else, what is trivial, and what is utterly strange. Think of how two people, entering the same landscape from different angles, will be struck by different features—what appears trivial and familiar seen from one angle might be uncanny or strange seen from the other. Even if the attitude is related internally to the way the world appears, it does not undo our separation from the world; the attitude does not bring about the phenomena in question, but *takes them in* according to different approaches. In this sense, what one encounters as a difficulty with reality is relative to the openness of a certain register for such difficulties, and such openness might be cultivated along a continuum spanning from a distinctly secular to an emphatically religious attitude.

Far from being confined to certain visual experiences, Wittgenstein often speaks of attitude in an overarching sense, concerning our perspective on the world and, correspondingly, the orientation of our life. Unsurprisingly, this also makes attitude central to his understanding of religion. In a late remark, Wittgenstein writes:

> If someone who believes in God looks round and asks "Where does everything I see come from?", "Where does all this come from?", he is *not* craving for a (causal) explanation; and his question gets its point from being the expression of a certain craving. He is namely expressing an attitude to all explanations. – But how is this manifested in his life?

> The attitude that's in question is that of taking a certain matter seriously and then, beyond a certain point, no longer regarding it as serious, but maintaining that something else is even more important. [...]

---

[29] Wittgenstein, *Philosophical Investigations*, 205.
[30] Rush Rhees, *Trying to Make Sense* (Oxford: Blackwell, 1987), 147–148.

> Actually I would like to say that in this case too the *words* you utter or what you think as you utter them are not what matters, so much as the difference they make at various points in your life.[31]

The first part of the passage might be taken as a grammatical remark about what the differences in seeing aspects depend on, namely not new explanation or information but an attitude to whatever information there is.[32] As with seeing aspects generally, the religious attitude tends to make some connections significant while others fade into the background. This is so because there are some cherished values and ideas (Wittgenstein calls them "pictures" in a resolutely non-psychological sense)[33] that make a difference in some people's lives, while for others they play no decisive role at all.

As it seems, one needs to take up a particular attitude in life in order to perceive the difficulty of reality under a religious aspect in the first place— human goodness as an act of God, incidents as miracles, or the existence of the world as a wonder. Hence, one sees according to an attitude that disposes one to seeing the world in a particular manner. It is in this sense, I guess, that Ian Hacking has called reflections of Diamond and Cavell "the born-again version of seeing aspects."[34] But there is certainly also another way in which reality speaks first, and we respond or must change according to its demands. For reality can also *seize us*, turn us around, passively. For Wittgenstein, the sense of being seized and turned around is essential to faith:

> The point is that a sound doctrine need not take hold of you; you can follow it as you would a doctor's prescription. – But here you need something to move you and turn you in a new direction. [...] Wisdom is passionless. But faith by contrast is what Kierkegaard calls a passion.[35]

---

[31] Wittgenstein, *Culture and Value,* ed. H. Wright, trans. P. Winch (Oxford: Blackwell, 1980), 85.
[32] Cavell has in a similar manner commented upon Kierkegaard's treatment of revelation, not as empirical questions but as grammatical ones (*Must We Mean What We Say?* 169).
[33] This use of "picture" is especially prevalent in his lectures on religion in *Lectures and Conversations on Aesthetics, Psychology and Religious Belief,* ed. C. Barrett (Oxford: Blackwell, 1996). I have earlier made an attempt to argue for the interconnection between seeing aspects, attitudes, and religious pictures in "Aspektpersepsjon, instilling og religiøse bilder – en lesning av Wittgensteins religionsfilosofi," *Norsk filosofisk tidsskrift,* 36:1–2 (2001).
[34] Ian Hacking, "Conclusion. Deflection," in *Philosophy and Animal Life,* 145.
[35] Wittgenstein, *Culture and Value,* 53.

Wittgenstein suggests that this passion has a passive sense to it, something like being taken ahold of. The passivity of being seized—say, by the difficulty of reality—results in a turning, perhaps something like a conversion, imposed from beyond the reaches of the self. And as a result, one will now perceive the world from another angle—perhaps in wonder at its sheer existence.[36] It is probably a two-way traffic between being passively moved to see afresh and seeing something according to an attitude: you might be seized by a wonder and then be turned around, but you might also try to hold on to such a conversion, cultivating a certain attitude in order to stay tuned to the possibility of seeing further wonders.

Expressions between isolation and community

Having dwelt on the possible understanding of the religious significance of the perceptual intake of reality, I will now move on to the kind of expressions that typically accompany such an intake. In response to Diamond, Cavell said that for some the exposure to the difficulty of reality means being overwhelmed, while others only raise their eyebrow. Now, if the deepest level of our claim to reason is our claim to community, then this division puts our entire intelligibility and rationality to the test. The question then is how we proceed from there—how do we move on from such individuating experiences toward a common understanding?

Even prior to any such divided visions of the difficulty of reality, the possibility of isolation is inscribed in the open texture of the ordinary. In every word we utter, we have no other authority or ground to go on than our willingness to speak for others, inviting them to accept our words, and conversely, letting others speak for us.[37] The authority of raising one's voice rests on the appeal to our mutual sharing in a communicative "we." The fragility of the appeal to the "we" comes clearly to the fore in aesthetic contexts. It is true that aesthetic judgments do not reach the kind of agreement we expect in mathematics or in logic, but it does not follow that they are inconclusive or irrational. What interests Cavell is the way Kant is willing to call those judgments subjective, while retaining that such subjectivity also entails a claim to a "we", or in Kant's terminology, to uni-

---

[36] Mulhall, "Wittgenstein on Faith, Rationality and the Passions," *Modern Theology* 27:2 (2011), 324.
[37] Cavell, *The Claim of Reason*, 28.

versality. Speaking "in a universal voice" does not "postulate" an agreement the way mathematical proofs explicitly do; but in putting forward our stand—our way of seeing and appreciating, for example, a painting—we voice ourselves exemplarily, and thus invite the community to share in our attitude and appreciations.[38] John Wisdom provides an example that is designed to bring the analogy to religious expressions to the fore: a certain person regards a painting and exclaims, "Divine!" while someone else replies, "I don't see it"—and yet they both see what the other sees. There are ways to proceed and reasons to be given, Wisdom points out, such as emphasizing certain features so that the other might see the painting in a new light. When we reach the limits of our seeing aesthetically or religiously, the first person might feel the other one is blind to what is most important or, conversely, the second person might feel that other person is seeing something that is not there.[39]

Sometimes we feel it is urgent to express something that we have perceived, but have no conventional expressions at hand. We might find ourselves unable to convey it to others; we become isolated, unintelligible, perhaps on the brink of madness. In a passage where he reflects on the particular nature of the claims made in such cases, Cavell writes:

> the right to enter such a claim universally [...] has roughly the logic of a voice in the wilderness, crying out news that may be known (inordinately) to virtually none, but to all virtually. It is a voice invoking a religious, not alone a philosophical, register: it is uninvited, it goes beyond an appeal to experiences we can assume all humans share, or recognize, and it is meant to instill belief and a commentary and community based on belief, yielding a very particular form of passionate utterance, call it prophecy.[40]

Cavell's invocation of prophecy accentuates that the urgency is uninvited, as if it responds to a call from outside, but it also trades on the implied dangers of not being welcomed and understood that go with such prophecy. Cavell specifies those prophetic utterances as "passionate utterances," where the passive sense of passion is explicitly invoked, as something one undergoes or suffers. Expressions of such passions are typically performed in the ab-

---

[38] Cavell, *Must We Mean What We Say?*, 88–94.
[39] John Wisdom, "Gods," *The Proceedings of the Aristotelian Society* 45 (1944–1945): 195–196. Wittgenstein's notion of aspect blindness is linked to the relevant sense of blindness.
[40] Cavell, "Companionable Thinking," 111.

sence of conventions, Cavell argues, and they do not easily generalize, since the speaking subject must express his or her standing in each pertinent situation. Moreover, such utterances invite another's response in kind, a response that is only demanded and assessed by its intimate attunement to the former utterance.[41]

If such considerations highlight the transgression of conventions, they contribute little to understanding what—if anything—makes it possible to find intimate experiences captured and communicated beyond the regular employment of words. But again Wittgenstein's remarks on aspect perception might be of further help, particularly in the regions where he elaborates its relevance for what he calls "experiencing the meaning of a word." What Wittgenstein has in mind is the way we can experience a word's sense in the absence of a particular purpose; we can, for example, experience them as pictures or contemplate them in poetry, or even perceive a kind of physiognomy of a word.[42] Wittgenstein speaks of experiencing Tuesday as lean, Wednesday as fat, the vowel *e* as yellow, and so on. "Here one might speak of a 'primary' and 'secondary' sense of a word," Wittgenstein notes. "It is only if the word has a primary sense for you that you use it in a secondary sense."[43] Just as aspect seeing requires a deep familiarity with the primary sense of seeing, so do words' secondary senses rely on our deep acquaintance with their various applications; it takes, as it were, a second inheritance of language.[44] When Wittgenstein resolutely rejects the notion that secondary sense can be understood in terms of metaphorical and other indirect figures of speech, it is because they suggest that there is another way to express that sense.[45] But when one is struck by the dawning of an aspect, there are simply no other competing alternatives. In his lectures on religion, Wittgenstein discusses the meaning of the utterance: "We might see one another after death." To the objection that this only expresses a feeling or relation that could be accounted for otherwise, Wittgenstein replies: "I would say 'No, it isn't the same as saying "I'm very

[41] Cavell, *Philosophy the Day after Tomorrow* (Cambridge, MA.: The Belknap Press of Harvard University Press, 2005), 155–156, 180–181.
[42] Wittgenstein, *Philosophical Investigations*, 214, 218.
[43] Ibid, 216.
[44] Mulhall, *Inheritance and Originality: Wittgenstein, Heidegger, Kierkegaard* (Oxford: Oxford University Press, 2001), 170.
[45] Wittgenstein, *Philosophical Investigations*, 216.

fond of you'"—and it may not be the same as saying anything else. It says what is says. Why should you be able to substitute anything else?"[46]

My point is that those religiously relevant expressions of miracles or wonders are not translatable to psychological reports or descriptions of facts without reducing the very aspect in discussion. More importantly, such modes of expression depend on our ability to communicate beyond grammars and established language-games. Cavell says that in the region of secondary meaning, we "cannot proceed always by employing language-games and the (a priori) agreement in judgment upon which they depend. Because with figurative meaning there is no such antecedent agreement. You could say that words used in such connections have no grammar—and that would itself be a grammatical remark."[47] So when, for instance, the early Wittgenstein says that to wonder at the existence of the world is nonsense, he is right in pointing out that we run against the boundaries of its primary sense. But as he arguably came to realize, there is another sense in which that utterance is perfectly meaningful, because we have the ability to take such expressions in their secondary sense. In issuing such expressions, I must project words into new contexts in a way that might awaken recognition along the same register in others—or alternatively fail to do so.[48] There is the standing possibility that others do not see things the same way. There are instructions and procedures that might help, but they will soon reach their limits: "Explanations come to an end somewhere."[49] Those utterances might establish an intimate community, but might also bring about isolation.

If there is a threat of madness in religion, I believe such isolation is one of its important faces. Perhaps this is mirrored in the madness that sometimes is found in prophecy: something that urgently needs be expressed and conveyed, yet without any assurance of it being understood—indeed, sometimes it is not likely to be understood at all. To understand one another in this religious register takes more than a shared language: what we have to go on once the conventional grammars and appeals to reasons run out is an attunement to and familiarity with language and the world that goes beyond any fixed agreement. If this is typical for the experience and expressions of wonders, this does not lead to irrationalism, but rather tests the degree to which we share in the same familiarity. If wonders and,

---

[46] Wittgenstein, *Lectures and Conversations*, 70–71.
[47] Cavell, *The Claim of Reason*, 355.
[48] Diamond, *The Realistic Spirit*, 235–240.
[49] Wittgenstein, *Philosophical Investigations*, § 1.

more generally, the difficulty of reality emerge at the borders of our rationality, they also throw us back at ourselves—to the very centre of the ordinary: our ability to extend and move beyond conventional language games depends upon the profundity of our pre-reflective being, at home amidst the ordinary.

Being thus led back to the ordinary, I will round off by asking how the seeing of wonders might be internally related to Wittgenstein's conception of his own philosophical practice. According to Wittgenstein, "Working in philosophy—like work in architecture in many respects—is really more a working on oneself. [...] On one's way of seeing things."[50] For Wittgenstein, such work on oneself comes about when one has become a problem for oneself, and it involves turning around one's attitude in order to see what there is to see—call it conversion. But if we add that it also involves putting one's personal temptations and willingness to correct them on display—not to prove anything, but for others to test their own selves against it—this starts to sound like Augustine's *Confessions*.[51] Indeed, both Wittgenstein and Augustine invite us to take part of the reflective stance, turning back to oneself, by means of remembering something that one cannot fail to know and that is nevertheless forgotten—in Augustine's words, "so old and so new."[52] And perhaps, following Augustine further, turning from the out- ward to the inward, toward the self, one might be led upward—toward the divine.[53] Perhaps what I have said about the dawning of wonders can also invite such a turn. In that case, the upshot is not only the ability to perceive the difficulty of reality at the borders of the ordinary, but to see the wonder that the ordinary bestows on the self with possible meaning and intel- ligibility in the first place: that is, not only seeing wonders in the ordinary, but seeing the ordinary as *itself* a wonder. To me this sheds some light on Wittgenstein's prayer: "God grant the philosopher insight into what lies in front of everyone's eyes."[54]

[50] Wittgenstein, *Culture and Value*, 16.
[51] Cf. Cavell, *Must We Mean What We Say?* 71. Cf. Augustine, *Confessions*, X, iii–iv.
[52] Augustine, *Confessions*, X, xxvii.
[53] Cf. Charles Taylor, *The Sources of the Self* (Cambridge: Cambridge University Press, 1989), 134.
[54] Wittgenstein, *Culture and Value*, 63.

Authors

Jonna Bornemark is Associate Professor of Philosophy and Lecturer at the Center for Studies in Practical Knowledge at Södertörn University. She has been working mainly on phenomenology and philosophy of religion. Recent publications include *Kroppslighetens mystik: Filosofiska läsningar av Mechthild von Magdeburg* (Mysticism of the Body: Philosophical Readings of Mechthild von Magdeburg, 2015), *Monument and Memory* (ed. with Jayne Svenungsson and Mattias Martinson, 2015), and *Ambiguity of the Sacred* (ed. with Hans Ruin, 2012).

John D. Caputo is the Thomas J. Watson Professor of Religion Emeritus (Syracuse University) and the David R. Cook Professor of Philosophy Emeritus (Villanova University). He works in the area of religion and post-modern theory. Among his latest books are *The Insistence of God: A Theology of Perhaps* (2013), which explores the theological implications of Derrida's notion of *"peut-être,"* *Truth: Philosophy in Transit* (2013), part of the Penguin Books series celebrating the 150th anniversary of the London Underground, and *Hoping Against Hope: Confessions of a Postmodern Pilgrim* (2015).

Marcia Sá Cavalcante Schuback is Professor of Philosophy at Södertörn University. She specializes in continental philosophy, with a focus on phenomenology, hermeneutics, German Idealism, and contemporary existential philosophy. She is the author of several monographs in Swedish, Portuguese and English. Recent publications include *Att tänka i skisser* (Thinking in and on Sketches, 2011), *Being with the Without: A Conversation with Jean-Luc Nancy* (2013), and *Dis-orientations: Philosophy, Literature and the Lost Grounds of Modernity* (ed. with Tora Lane, 2015).

Carl Cederberg is Senior Lecturer in the Theory of Practical Knowledge at Södertörn University. His research draws on the resources of classical and continental philosophy, focusing on the crossings of political philosophy and metaphysics. Cederberg is also interested in the practical application of philosophy to contemporary professional life. His publications include *Att läsa Platon* (ed. 2007), and *Resaying the Human. Levinas Beyond Humanism and Antihumanism* (2010), as well as translations of Heidegger, Gadamer, and Derrida.

Espen Dahl is Professor of Systematic Theology at The Arctic University of Norway. He has published numerous articles on religion, phenomenology, and ordinary language philosophy, and is the author of *Stanley Cavell, Religion, and Continental* Philosophy (2014,) *In Between: The Holy Beyond Modern Dichotomies* (2011), and *Phenomenology and the Holy: Religious Experience after Husserl* (2010).

Monique David-Menard is Director of Research the University Paris-Diderot. Her research interests include the philosophy of biology and psychopathology, psychoanalysis, and gender studies Among here recent books are *Eloge des hasards dans la vie sexuelle* (2011), *Deleuze et la psychanalyse: L'Altercation* (2005), and *Tout le plaisir est pour moi* (2000).

Anders Lindström is a Ph.D. student in comparative literature at Stockholm University and co-editor of *Aiolos*. His research is focused on early Greek thinking, with a particular emphasis on tragedy. His publications include a series of articles on the impact of ancient thought on Swedish modernity, most recently "Resenären vid historiens veck," in *Omvägar till sanningen: Nya perspektiv på Eyvind Johnsons författarskap* (ed. with Christer Johansson, 2015).

Hans Ruin is Professor of Philosophy at Södertörn University. He is President of the Nordic Society for Phenomenology, co-editor for Nietzsche's Collected Works in Swedish, and member of the Board of *Nietzsche Studien* and *Jahrbuch für Hermeneutische Philosophie*. He is currently responsible for the six-year research program Time, Memory and Representation (www.histcon.se). Recent publications include *Rethinking Time: Essays on History, Memory, and Representation* (ed. with Andrus Ers, 2011), *Fenomenologi, teknik och medialitet* (ed. with Leif Dahlberg, 2012), and *Frihet, ändlighet, historicitet: Essäer om Heideggers filosofi* (2013).

Gustav Strandberg is a PhD-student in Philosophy at Södertörn University. He is working on a dissertation on the philosophy of the Czech phenomenologist Jan Patočka, entitled *Abyssal Politics*. His areas of interest include phenomenology, political philosophy, the philosophy of history and aesthetics. He has also published translations of works by, among others, Slavoj Žižek, Jean-Luc Nancy, and Jan Patočka. Recent publications include "A Place in Movement," in Tora Lane and Marcia Sá Cavalcante Schuback (eds.), *Dis-orientations* (2015) and "Förfrämligandet som utopi," in Tora Lane (ed.), *Andrej Platonov: Revolution och existens* (2015).

Sven-Olov Wallenstein is Professor of Philosophy at Södertörn University and editor-in-chief of Site. He is the translator of works by Baumgarten, Winckelmann, Lessing, Kant, Hegel, Frege, Husserl, Heidegger, Levinas, Derrida, Deleuze, Foucault, Rancière and Agamben, as well as the author of numerous books on philosophy, contemporary art, and architecture. Recent publications include *Translating Hegel: The Phenomenology of Spirit and Modern Philosophy* (ed. with Brian Manning Delaney, 2012), *Foucault, Biopolitics, and Governmentality* (ed. with Jakob Nilsson, 2013), and *Heidegger, språket och poesin* (ed. with Ola Nilsson, 2013).

Södertörn Academic Studies

14. Mikael Lönnborg et al. (eds.), *Money and Finance in Transition: Research in Contemporary and Historical Finance*, 2003.

15. Kerstin Shands et al. (eds.), *Notions of America: Swedish Perspectives*, 2004.

16. Karl-Olov Arnstberg & Thomas Borén (eds.), *Everyday Economy in Russia, Poland and Latvia*, 2003.

17. Johan Rönnby (ed.), *By the Water. Archeological Perspectives on Human Strategies around the Baltic Sea*, 2003.

18. Baiba Metuzale-Kangere (ed.), *The Ethnic Dimension in Politics and Culture in the Baltic Countries 1920–1945*, 2004.

19. Ulla Birgegård & Irina Sandomirskaja (eds.), *In Search of an Order: Mutual Representations in Sweden and Russia during the Early Age of Reason*, 2004.

20. Ebba Witt-Brattström (ed.), *The New Woman and the Aesthetic Opening: Unlocking Gender in Twentieth-Century Texts*, 2004.

21. Michael Karlsson, *Transnational Relations in the Baltic Sea Region*, 2004.

22. Ali Hajighasemi, *The Transformation of the Swedish Welfare System: Fact or Fiction? Globalisation, Institutions and Welfare State Change in a Social Democratic Regime*, 2004.

23. Erik A. Borg (ed.), *Globalization, Nations and Markets: Challenging Issues in Current Research on Globalization*, 2005.

24. Stina Bengtsson & Lars Lundgren, *The Don Quixote of Youth Culture: Media Use and Cultural Preferences Among Students in Estonia and Sweden*, 2005.

25. Hans Ruin, *Kommentar till Heideggers Varat och tiden*, 2005.

26. Ludmila Ferm, *Variativnoe bespredložnoe glagol'noe upravlenie v russkom jazyke XVIII veka* [Variation in non-prepositional verbal government in eighteenth-century Russian], 2005.

27. Christine Frisch, *Modernes Aschenputtel und Anti-James-Bond: Gender-Konzepte in deutschsprachigen Rezeptionstexten zu Liza Marklund und Henning Mankell*, 2005.

28. Ursula Naeve-Bucher, *Die Neue Frau tanzt: Die Rolle der tanzenden Frau in deutschen und schwedischen literarischen Texten aus der ersten Hälfte des 20. Jahrhunderts*, 2005.

29. Göran Bolin et al. (eds.), *The Challenge of the Baltic Sea Region: Culture, Ecosystems, Democracy*, 2005.

30. Marcia Sá Cavalcante Schuback & Hans Ruin (eds.), *The Past's Presence: Essays on the Historicity of Philosophical Thought*, 2006.

31. María Borgström & Katrin Goldstein-Kyaga (ed.), *Gränsöverskridande identiteter i globaliseringens tid: Ungdomar, migration och kampen för fred*, 2006.

32. Janusz Korek (ed.), *From Sovietology to Postcoloniality: Poland and Ukraine from a Postcolonial Perspective*, 2007.

33. Jonna Bornemark (ed.), *Det främmande i det egna: filosofiska essäer om bildning och person*, 2007.

34. Sofia Johansson, *Reading Tabloids: Tabloid Newspapers and Their Readers*, 2007.

35. Patrik Åker, *Symboliska platser i kunskapssamhället: Internet, högre lärosäten och den gynnade geografin*, 2008.

36. Kerstin W. Shands (ed.), *Neither East Nor West: Postcolonial Essays on Literature, Culture and Religion*, 2008.

37. Rebecka Lettevall & My Klockar Linder (eds.), *The Idea of Kosmopolis: History, philosophy and politics of world citizenship*, 2008.

38. Karl Gratzer & Dieter Stiefel (eds.), *History of Insolvency and Bankruptcy from an International Perspective*, 2008.

39. Katrin Goldstein-Kyaga & María Borgström, *Den tredje identiteten: Ungdomar och deras familjer i det mångkulturella, globala rummet*, 2009.

40. Christine Farhan, *Frühling für Mütter in der Literatur?: Mutterschaftskonzepte in deutschsprachiger und schwedischer Gegenwartsliteratur*, 2009.

41. Marcia Sá Cavalcante Schuback (ed.), *Att tänka smärtan*, 2009.

42. Heiko Droste (ed.), *Connecting the Baltic Area: The Swedish Postal System in the Seventeenth Century*, 2011.

43. Aleksandr Nemtsov, *A Contemporary History of Alcohol in Russia*, 2011.

44. Cecilia von Feilitzen & Peter Petrov (eds.), *Use and Views of Media in Russia and Sweden: A Comparative Study of Media in St Petersburg and Stockholm*, 2011.

45. Sven Lilja (ed.), *Fiske, jordbruk och klimat i Östersjöregionen under förmodern tid*, 2012.

46. Leif Dahlberg & Hans Ruin (eds.), *Fenomenologi, teknik och medialitet*, 2012.

47. Samuel Edquist, *I Ruriks fotspår: Om forntida svenska österledsfärder i modern historieskrivning*, 2012.

48. Jonna Bornemark (ed.), *Phenomenology of Eros*, 2012.

49. Jonna Bornemark & Hans Ruin (eds.), *Ambiguity of the Sacred: Phenomenology, Politics, Aesthetics*, 2012.

50. Håkan Nilsson, *Placing Art in the Public Realm*, 2012.

51. Per Bolin, *Between National and Academic Agendas: Ethnic Policies and 'National Disciplines' at Latvia's University, 1919–1940*, 2012.

52. Lars Kleberg & Aleksei Semenenko (eds.), *Aksenov and the Environs/Aksenov iokrestnosti*, 2012.

53. Sven-Olov Wallenstein & Brian Manning Delaney (eds.), *Translating Hegel: The Phenomenology of Spirit and Modern Philosophy*, 2012.

54. Sven-Olov Wallenstein and Jakob Nilsson (eds.), *Foucault, Biopolitics, and Governmentality*, 2013.

55. Jan Patočka, *Inledning till fenomenologisk filosofi*, 2013.

56. Jonathan Adams & Johan Rönnby (eds.), *Interpreting Shipwrecks: Maritime Archaeological Approaches*, 2013.

57. Charlotte Bydler, *Mondiality/Regionality: Perspectives on Art, Aesthetics and Globalization*, 2014.

58. Andrej Kotljarchuk, *In the Forge of Stalin: Swedish Colonists of Ukraine in Totalitarian Experiments of the Twentieth Century*, 2014.

59. Samuel Edquist & Janne Holmén, *Islands of Identity*, 2014.

60. Norbert Götz (ed.), *The Sea of Identities: A Century of Baltic and East European Experiences with Nationality, Class, and Gender*, 2015.

61. Klaus Misgeld, Karl Molin & Jaworski *Solidaritet och diplomati: Svenskt fackligt och diplomatiskt stöd till Polens demokratisering under 1980-talet*, 2015.

62. Jonna Bornemark & Sven-Olov Wallenstein (eds.), *Madness, Religion, and the Limits of Reason*, 2015.

SÖDERTÖRN PHILOSOPHICAL STUDIES

Södertörn Philosophical Studies is a book series published under the direction of the Department of Philosophy at Södertörn University. The series consists of monographs and anthologies in philosophy, with a special focus on the Continental-European tradition. It seeks to provide a platform for innovative contemporary philosophical research. The volumes are published mainly in English and Swedish. The series is edited by Marcia Sá Cavalcante Schuback and Hans Ruin.

PREVIOUSLY PUBLISHED TITLES

The Past's Presence: Essays on the Historicity of Philosophical Thought
Marcia Sá Cavalcante Schuback & Hans Ruin (eds.), (2006)

En annan humaniora, en annan tid/Another humanities, another time
Carl Cederberg & Hans Ruin (eds.), (2009)

Phenomenology and Religion: New Frontiers
Jonna Bornemark & Hans Ruin (eds.), (2010)

Rethinking Time: Essays on History, Memory, and Representation
Hans Ruin & Andrus Ers (eds.), (2011)

Phenomenology of Eros
Jonna Bornemark & Marcia Sá Cavalcante Schuback (eds.), (2012)

Ambiguity of the Sacred
Jonna Bornemark & Hans Ruin (eds.), (2012)

Translating Hegel
Brian Manning Delaney & Sven-Olov Wallentein (eds.), (2012)

Foucault, Biopolitics, and Governmentality
Sven-Olov Wallenstein & Jakob Nilsson (eds.), (2013)

www.ingramcontent.com/pod-product-compliance
Lightning Source LLC
Chambersburg PA
CBHW020155090426
42734CB00008B/824